ROSSETTI AND THE FAIR LADY

Dante Gabriel Rossetti (1828–1882)
Photographic portrait by W. & D. Downey, 1862
Courtesy of Radio Times Hulton Picture Library, London

Rossetti and the Fair Lady

By

DAVID SONSTROEM

Wesleyan University Press

MIDDLETOWN, CONNECTICUT

ISBN: 0 – 8195 – 4019 – 6

Library of Congress catalog card number: 70-105506

Manufactured in the United States of America

FIRST EDITION

To my parents
Arthur M. Sonstroem
Lillian Meyer Sonstroem

Contents

List of Illustrations

Acknowledgements

I am very pleased to thank those who helped me with this study. In an earlier form it served as my doctoral thesis at Harvard University, and I am much obliged to two men for their pains and helpfulness. I am grateful to Professor Jerome H. Buckley for the fund of information, criticism, and encouragement that he generously provided. I am also indebted to Professor Reuben A. Brower, whose sharp literary eye and great good sense came to my rescue more than once.

More recently I have received invaluable assistance from Mrs. Virginia Surtees, who brought wit, charm, and goodness to her labors in my behalf, and I thank her especially for these gratuities. In the midst of seeing her catalogue raisonné of Rossetti's artistic works through press, Mrs. Surtees took the time to write informative, prompt, and delightful replies to a stranger importuning her with long lists of Rossetti's paintings to be located. She has made it possible for me to double the number of works reproduced here.

In addition I thank Professor G. H. Fleming for supplementing my defective knowledge of London; Professor Stephen Kaplowitt, my defective knowledge of German; and Professor Marcia Lieberman, my defective knowledge of French. I thank the staffs of the Widener and Houghton Libraries and Fogg Art Museum of Harvard University, and the staff of the Wilbur Cross Library of the University of Connecticut. I thank the University of Connecticut Research Foundation Typing Pool, and

Mrs. Selma Wollman especially, for the typing of my manuscript. I also thank the Research Foundation for a grant toward the expenses connected with recent research and the publication of this work. Finally I thank my wife for a multitude of labors— from the most menial proofreading and collating to the creation of a household conducive to and tolerant of my bookish behavior.

DAVID SONSTROEM

Storrs, Connecticut

ROSSETTI AND THE FAIR LADY

Preface

THE beautiful lady is Rossetti's principal motif, ruling all others. Some ninety-five percent of his poems and ninety-eight percent of his paintings and drawings treat of love or feminine beauty[1]— altogether, almost six hundred original works. And his Italian translations, a corpus almost as large as his original poetry, are just as dedicated to the theme.

In Rossetti's works, as in life itself, behind every beautiful woman there is almost always a story. The stories tend to be borrowed or adapted rather than created, and their heroines, familiar literary or historical figures. Taken together, Rossetti's works include hundreds of diverse plots, but there is a sense in which they all tell but one tale. It is not hard to assign all but a handful of Rossetti's imaginative works concerning fair ladies to one or more of four categories—four fantasies—each a variation on the theme of salvation (the term subsumes its opposite, damnation):

(1) The Blessed Damozel, Rossetti's many Beatrices, and his Virgin Marys help to define the largest group, composed of heavenly Madonnas instrumental in saving men.

(2) The second largest category is made up of femmes fatales, ladies instrumental in destroying men. A few typical heroines are Lilith, Helen of Troy, Ligeia Siren, and Circe.

(3) A third category is formed of Rossetti's sinful women in need of help—usually prostitutes. Almost without exception the fallen fair lady is saved or helped in some way by a man. Thus

this category may be seen as a humbler version of the first, with a reversal of sexes. Jenny, Mary Magdalene, and the lost lady of *Found* are a few of its members.

(4)   The fourth and smallest category may be seen as the second with a reversal of sexes; a fair lady, victimized by a man, is rendered beyond help. It includes Ophelia, and the beloved in *Michael Scott's Wooing*.[2]

Within each group there are chronological clusters, indicating that at different times in his career Rossetti emphasized different fantasies. For example, the Madonna predominates at first; in 1853 and for a while thereafter, the sinful woman; about 1860, the victimized woman; in the mid-1860's, the femme fatale; and later, something of a combination of Madonna and femme fatale. Moreover, the category of the moment seems repeatedly to be an extension of Rossetti's own life, as it was or as he imagined it. The tales that he borrowed were seldom taken over whole, but were refashioned, apparently, in such a way that he could more easily see himself in them. Changes in his own life were answered by removals from one fantasy to another.

The study that follows is intended as a history of a motif—that of the fair lady—in the works of Rossetti. As such it serves as a basic definition of "the Pre-Raphaelite woman." It is also intended as a biography of a fantasy. As such it presents the fair lady, in her various aspects with respect to salvation, as a central preoccupation or governing principle of Rossetti—a principle that makes comprehensive sense when applied to him at any point in his life, and when applied to almost all of his works, paintings as well as poems. It displays the close relationship between Rossetti's life and works, and indicates the consequences of that closeness. I hope no one will be disappointed to find neither thoroughgoing biography nor strict aesthetic criticism here, for I examine what lies quite exactly between—the intercourse between the life and the works.

Before proceeding, however, I wish to address myself to a few matters concerning my approach, about which the reader deserves some explanation and reassurance. First, paradigms are not things of beauty in themselves, but shine only in use.

Mine is important only because the facts apply. It is useful only because it reveals a pervasive preoccupation of the man and a unity in his works, and because it facilitates meaningful discriminations within that preoccupation. The unlikelihood that Rossetti ever saw himself in quite these terms only emphasizes the fact that the terms, however applicable, can serve only as the beginning of inquiry.

Second, I do not pretend to present Rossetti in the round. The nature of the study—I presume to explore fantasy—limits it to those facets of the man that are revealed in and relevant to the imaginative works. Consequently, traits that never found poetic or artistic expression are largely ignored. There is a split between the "poetic" Rossetti and the joshing, jolly, public, "prosaic" Rossetti, which I have remarked upon elsewhere.[3] But the "poetic" Rossetti presented here is nonetheless valid for what is excluded.

Third, there are pitfalls inherent in relating a man's creative works and his life, naiveté in easily extrapolating from one to the other.[4] Art and biography do not mix well; so each deserves protection from the other. In fact, in the case of Rossetti, the critic or biographer must be especially careful to maintain a clean demarcation, because, paradoxically, Rossetti himself did not do so.

Indeed, the frequent recourse to Rossetti's life for a key to his works, and vice versa, is less a commentary upon his explicators than it is upon Rossetti himself, who (I would argue) often let art and life complete and answer for each other—who insisted upon the personal application. Almost everyone who has ever written about him, those who knew him and those who studied him, from Christina and Watts-Dunton to Doughty and Grylls, has remarked on his habitual way of seeing events and people (in Miss Grylls' phrase) *sub specie litterarum*. He seems to have looked for the reappearance of literary figures in real life, and also to have translated his own experiences into literature (his good friend Theodore Watts-Dunton observed that "there is not one love-sonnet in his book which is a merely literary production"[5]). Rossetti also seems to have defined himself in the terms of the great literary, historical, or mythological characters that he portrayed, wrapping himself in the cloak of the heroes, and playing opposite the heroines. Seconding Professor Baum's judgment that "in Rossetti's case we can apply the biographic test with some security; for other poets we are often left to surmise merely,"[6] I proceed to explore the extent to which it is possible to relate Rossetti's imaginative works and his life—one might say, the extent to which he, as artist, disregarded the critical strictures upon keeping them separate and self-contained.

If, then, Rossetti's life and work are dependent and supplementary, a critical approach that commits itself categorically to a separation between them is going to miss the mark. Nevertheless, the strictures, rightly observed, still hold. Studying the relationship between art and life does not release one from distinguishing between them. For example, I grant that the only contribution I can legitimately make to Rossetti's biography is a full account of that very relationship between life and works. Anything further would be either dependent upon circular reasoning or incidental. With respect to aesthetic criticism, I can show the relevance of some biographical material—to be used in the supplemental, "dictionary" way to which Lees (quoted in footnote 4) would limit it. Furthermore, I can describe a framework of Rossetti's intentions, by which to gloss his work, and yet observe the dictum that a poem must stand, irrespective of authorial intentions, on its own prosodic feet. For recognition of intentions often brings about the appreciation of aspects truly present in a work of art that have gone unnoticed. And even when one quickens, via biography, an otherwise incomplete work of art, obviously one is the gainer—as long as the boundary between art and life is acknowledged as one crosses it. In the world of criticism, awareness makes the difference between smuggling and legitimate commerce.

Finally, let me be the first to point out that, although I hope to be persuasive, I cannot truly prove anything about Rossetti, because the area of exploration—fantasy life—obviously does not admit of objective, conclusive demonstration. The study is founded upon the beforementioned observation that Rossetti's imaginative works are intimately related to personal fantasies, and this observation, in the absence of Rossetti's explicit admission, must remain only speculation, however many coincidences between life and works are adduced to support its likelihood. But the fact that the study is necessarily speculative in nature does not mean that it is irresponsible. Conjecture is answerable to Rossetti's works, to the facts of his life, and to the scholarly opinions of others.

Uncertainty is compounded when I turn for the support of my speculation to areas of Rossetti's life for which we possess only conjectural accounts. Naturally I present all that I honestly can in the promotion of my argument, including much conjecture. But truth takes precedence over preconceptions; I offer only those conjectures that seem probable to my most objective cast of mind. My feelings in writing this study have repeatedly been those of surprise and discovery, not of straining to fit intractable matter to a Procrustean bed. Also, let it be noted that the study does not rest on a concatenation or tissue of hypotheses. There is but one basic conjecture, that concerning the relationship between imaginative works and personal fantasies. If occasionally other conjectures do not persuade, they may be discounted as incidental, because the evidence for my views is aggregate and accumulative rather than mutually dependent.

CHAPTER ONE

The Cloak of Fantasy

AT twenty-seven Rossetti described his approach to literature in a letter to William Allingham:

> . . . one can only speak of one's own needs and cravings: and I must confess to a need, in narrative-dramatic poetry . . . of something rather "exciting", and indeed I believe something of the ~~"schoolgirl"~~ [*sic* in MS] "romantic" element, to rouse my mind to anything like the moods produced by personal emotion in my own life. . . . Keats' narratives would be of the kind I mean.

Later in the same letter he refers to literature capable of ". . . rousing one like a part of one's own life, and leaving one to walk it off as one might live it off."[1] The mention of Keats is appropriate. Both Keats and Rossetti easily saw themselves as the heroes of the stories they read, relating themselves to the fictive situation. But Keats' empathic, Protean "negative capability" was a forgetting of the self in the story, whereas Rossetti's habit of the imagination was, so to speak, egocentripetal, an assumption of the story by the self. Imagination served Keats as wings, to carry him beyond himself; it served Rossetti as a cloak, to adorn himself. Although his imagination furnished a fabulous ambience, it never transported him beyond his own skin.[2]

Rossetti began wrapping himself in literary situations very early in childhood. At five he wrote *The Slave*, a short play of violent chivalry inspired by Sir Walter Scott's verse romances and perhaps by *Hamlet*. By this time he could read, of course, and he did so with sustained eagerness. From William's detailed account of his brother's early reading and literary interests we can easily see that Gabriel read for the usual boyish end of vicarious adventure. The list is heavy with books of chivalric derring-do and mystery; after *Hamlet* and other Shakespearian tragedies and histories come Sir Walter Scott's verse romances, *The Arabian Nights*, Scott's novels, with *Ivanhoe* the favorite, a series entitled *Brigand Tales*, the *Iliad*, Scottish and English ballads, Allan Cunningham's *Legends of Terror*, Bürger's *Lenore*, the poems of Byron (especially the ones with more plot than reflection: "*Childe Harold* he read, but without special zest; in fact, throughout his life, the poetry of sentimental or reflective description had a very minor attraction for him"[3]), the novels of Maturin, Monk Lewis's *Tales of Wonder*, and Meinhold's *Sidonia the Sorceress*. William once remarked that Gabriel's "intellectual life was nurtured upon fancy and sympathy, not upon knowledge or information."[4]

The extent to which Rossetti applied his reading to himself can be appreciated from William's account of Gabriel at twelve or thirteen; by way of punctuating an impromptu recital of Othello's death-speech, he stabbed himself in the chest with a chisel, inflicting a considerable wound.[5] Such was the price of heroic identification, and the gesture serves nicely as an omen of his imaginative career. Throughout his life he outstripped his critical faculty in the enthusiasm of his reading, proclaiming each new writer to pass under his eyes, from Shakespeare, Keats, Coleridge, or Chatterton to William Bell Scott, Charles Wells,[6] or Ebenezer Jones, a *nonpareil*. His willingness to pay in worshipful idolatry the price for total envelopment in his reading was an inclination established as soon as he knew how to read.

In addition to affording him amusement, the cloak of fantasy about the boy could also serve to protect him from the disagreeable in everyday life. For example, the young Rossetti seems to have been something of a physical coward: "He often described himself as being destitute of personal courage when at school, as shrinking from the amusements of schoolfellows, and fearful of their quarrel . . . in the main . . . reclusive in habit of life."[7] His earliest aesthetic productions show that any mortification suffered on this account was discharged in bellicose fantasies. The afore-mentioned *Slave* was marked more by swordplay than by plot.[8] Then, at nine or ten, he drew a scene of schoolboy violence involving the Master of the Lower First, whose nickname was "Bantam." William entitles it, "*Bantam Battering* (i.e., pummel-ling a boy); *Lower Division-Upper Division*," and says of it that " . . . these two Divisions of the schoolboys are represented as indulging in a free fight."[9] Gabriel's self-inflicted wound reveals that he lived by the sword at least until he was twelve. In that year he also drew a pen-and-ink illustration for every book of the *Iliad*. Most of the drawings were battle scenes, and great attention was given to the armor and weapons of the combatants. A year later he illustrated a military anecdote: " 'As you are not of my parish,' said a gentleman to a begging sailor, 'I cannot think of relieving you.' 'Sir,' replied the tar with an air of heroism, 'I lost my leg fighting for *all* parishes.' "[10] As late as 1845 we find him writing *The End of It*, a poem on Napoleon. Again the subject was military, but the concept of battle had matured along with the poet, a fact that heralds Rossetti's relinquishment of the colors:

> There was a great shouting about him
> And the weight of a great din:
> But what was the battle he had around
> To the battle he had within?[11]

As Rossetti grew older, life presented other battles to be escaped: "As soon as a thing is imposed upon me as an obliga-tion, my aptitude for doing it is gone; what I ought to do is what I *can't* do." We have William's word that "this went close to the essence of his character, and was true of him through life."[12] One does not have to look far for evidence of obligations neglected, for his life was full of them: familial (he loved his mother dearly, yet almost invariably forgot her birthday), social, financial, marital, and artistic. When he attended art school, even his drawing became an obligation; so he spent his time translating and writing poetry to avoid it, excusing his behavior to his teachers as a "fit of idleness."[13] In later life his commissioned paintings were always in arrears. He avoided not only physical violence (even exercise), not only obligation, but also such arenas of life as science (he did not even concern himself with the question of whether the sun revolved around the earth, or vice versa), geography, theology,[14] politics, philosophy,[15] and history, in all of which he seems to have had less than a layman's knowledge. What he tried to escape throughout his life may be summarized in Robert Browning's expression, "a world of men."[16] The term includes not only battle, but all vigorous, ordered, public, daylight pursuits.

To meet these newer challenges Rossetti did not again create a compensatory "world of men" in his imagination; instead of an imaginative replica of those qualities of everyday life that did not suit him, he formulated a contrasting alternative. The worlds of the imagination in which he involved himself now were languorous, dark, intimate, and disorderly. The new area for fantasy is easily discerned in his own mature work. Most of his paintings show enclosed spaces with oppressive atmospheres that confine the figures. Colors are diffused and gradated, preventing severity, clarity, definiteness. In the poetry we find the same dark disorder celebrated:

> In painting her I shrined her face
>   'Mid mystic trees, where light falls in
> Hardly at all; a covert place
>   Where you might think to find a din
> Of doubtful talk, and a live flame
> Wandering, and many a shape whose name
>   Not itself knoweth, and old dew,
>   And your old footsteps meeting you,
> And all things going as they came.
>
>   *The Portrait*
>
> A land without any order—
>   Day even as night
>
>   *The Card-Dealer*

The state is an achieved confusion, a self-induced disorder, a kind of willful blurring of the eyes.[17]

At its best the tendency led Rossetti to the creation of romantic paintings and poems that revelled in the remote and mysterious—works like *How They Met Themselves* and *The Card-Dealer*, in which boyish delight is scarcely suppressed and decidedly infectious. Seldom has the romantic impulse been expressed with such verve. At its worst the escapism took over Rossetti's life, producing acute reclusiveness and lethargy.[18] A natural inclination toward sleepy, fugitive indolence was only encouraged and exaggerated by the success of his active imagination in producing attractive trances from the books he read, or the poems and paintings he produced: "the pursuit of art is a bore, except when followed in the dozing style."[19] At worst his own life was as dark and disorderly as the subjects of his works, but without their beauty. An effective symbol for his life when it was dominated by his rejection of the "world of men" is his bedroom at Cheyne Walk. The following is a description of it by Henry Treffry Dunn, Rossetti's housemate for several years (Hall Caine has given a similar description of it with a similar revulsion):

> I thought it a most unhealthy place to sleep in. Thick curtains, heavy with crewel work in 17th century designs of fruit and flowers (which he had bought out of an old furnishing shop somewhere in the slums of Lambeth), hung closely drawn round an antiquated four-post bedstead. . . . The only modern thing I could see anywhere in the room was a Bryant and May's matchbox! . . . The deeply recessed windows, which ought to have been thrown open as much as possible to the fresh air and cheerful garden outlook, were shrouded with curtains of heavy and sumptuously patterned Genoese velvet. On this fine summer's day light was almost excluded from the room. . . . Even the little avenue of lime-trees, outside the windows helped to reduce the light, and threw a sickly green over everything in the apartment.[20]

It is a ludicrous accident, but true, that the bed was the very one on which Rossetti was born. Psychologists may make of that what they will.

Counteracting Rossetti's reclusiveness was his growing interest in women, for they gave him reason to keep his imagination in touch with everyday life. One can trace the establishment of the fair lady in his adolescent works, as ideas brought forth by developing sexual feelings supplanted the military motif of his childhood.

It is somewhat of a relief to see that there was no "female interest" in *The Slave*, written at the age of five. "At this age," reports William, " . . . the 'gushing or ecstatic female' was, to all of us infants, a personage less provocative of sentiment than of mirth. . . . Often and fatuously did we laugh over Coleridge's poem of *Love* (*Genevieve*)—the very poem which . . . my brother, in one of his latest years, marked with the word 'Perfection'."[21] In Gabriel's twelfth year each of the four Rossetti children set out to write a romantic novel. Only Gabriel's *Roderick and Rosalba* was ever finished. The lady, Rosalba, is captured by a "marauder," who tries to force her to marry him, but she is rescued by her affianced knight, Sir Roderick. Although the rudimentary love-interest marks the first appearance of a heroine in Rossetti's work, either literary or artistic, she is decidedly subordinate to the swordplay, serving merely as the occasion for it. For all four of the proposed novels Gabriel made a circular drawing of the hero, each in a similar stance, but carefully differentiated by the design of shield and armor, and by the plume of the helmet.[22] In addition he illustrated a leading incident of each story, which meant a battle scene. In the illustration for *Roderick and Rosalba* the "marauder" and Sir Roderick are opposing swords, while the fainting Rosalba is held as a shield by the villain. The heroine is on stage, but the young artist has lavished most of his attention on the costume of Sir Roderick; even the columns of the hall within which the fight occurs are drawn with more care and detail than she. Rossetti's attitude toward womankind at this age was the properly heroic one: as in the *Iliad*, she was but the cause and rightful spoils of battle, and the external manifestation of glory.

At thirteen Rossetti began *Sir Hugh the Heron*, which he left unfinished for two years. The plot is very similar to that of *Roderick and Rosalba*: Sir Hugh leaves his betrothed in the care of his cousin, who betrays the trust and (in William's words) is "offering violence to the lady."[23] The knight hastens home, slays the aggressor, and recovers his bride. But although the plots are

Illustrations for *Roderick and Rosalba &c.*
Courtesy of Owner, Private Collection, England

similar, there is some difference between offering marriage and offering violence; in the latter case all socioeconomic factors are weeded out, leaving the matter a purely sexual one:

> In vain she pleads; his brawny arm her waist encircled
> round;
> The lady raised, in dire alarm, her voice with fearful
> sound.

Rossetti, with the added knowledge of the extra year, apparently realized potentialities in his earlier plot that, in his innocence, he had overlooked, and hence rewrote it accordingly. It should be added, however, that the major interest is still in the battle-scenes.

His next work, *Sorrentino*, a prose romance written in the year he completed *Sir Hugh*, followed up his new discovery. In it Mephistopheles "interfered in a very exasperating way between the lover and his fair one."[24] William (our only source of evidence, since Gabriel destroyed the only manuscript) hesitantly buries amidst less imaginative possibilities the suggestion that the exasperating interference consisted of Mephistopheles's creating an illusion in which he engaged in sexual intercourse with the lady before the deluded eyes of the lover. Whatever the incident, the Rossetti family bombarded it with charges of indecency and brought about a chaster revision. A surviving illustration drawn for the work (see Marillier, p. 214) has as its principal figure a pretty young lady most distinguished, perhaps, by large breasts. Clearly Rossetti's interests had shifted from the military toward the sexual. In this year, 1843, he wrote to his mother of a prospective drawing, "The next subject is to be the Parting of two Lovers, unspecified and indefinite, which I intend to treat in several different manners, and to get up in prime style."[25] A year later he wrote to William from Boulogne, "The window of what Mrs. Wood would call our 'salon' looks out upon the market . . . whose pretty groups of pretty girls are at this moment regaling my eye."[26] While at Boulogne he made an intentionally amusing drawing of a pretty chambermaid (see Marillier, p. 216). Thus, by the age of eighteen he had put away his childish interests in battle and models of male virtue to explore the more intriguing romantic notions of fair ladies.

At this stage a problem is presented to Rossetti. The beautiful woman is easily assimilated by his imagination. All he need do is dream on and elaborate. But his sexual nature will not be satisfied with mere fantasies of fair ladies. The dilemma may be put as follows: if he spends his time lethargically in fantasy, how can he satisfy his very real sexual desires; if, on the other hand, they *are* satisfied in the here and now, how can the actual experiences live up to his ideal ones? His desires demand palpable gratification, but the intended object of his desires, because of his escapist fantasies, exists first and indelibly in his mind, with an entourage of associations that must travel with her if she is to make her appearance in his actual experience. In short, he is faced with a conflict of ideal and real in sexual terms.

As we shall see, the conflict makes Rossetti's life and creative work more attractive and interesting than it would have been if he were merely a sensualist or merely a reclusive dreamer. His "leopardine" acts[27] are thrown into a better light because of the ideal of womanhood that he held in his mind and hoped to discover in the objects of his pursuit; and his "soul images"[28] that found expression in his poems and designs are more varied, meaningful, and vital than they would have been if his dreams had not been troubled by longing for their realization in flesh and blood. Rossetti's dilemma subjected his creative work to a double demand. This consideration shows Robert Buchanan's condemnation of Gabriel's work as merely "fleshly," and (to name but one name) Arthur Symons's praise of it as "that house of dreams in which the only real things were the things of the imagination,"[29] to be, both of them, oversimplifications. Rossetti attempted and achieved more than either critic seems to have realized, although the dilemma caused him great pain and difficulty.

CHAPTER TWO

The Heavenly Lady:

Literature

AT the time that fair ladies began to make their place in Gabriel Rossetti's imagination he spent the hours spared from art school translating Italian poets of courtly love: Dante, of course, but also Guido Cavalcanti, Cino da Pistoia, Lapo Gianni, Dino Frescobaldi, Guido Guinicelli, Jacopo da Lentino, and Fazio degli Uberti, among others. The translations, forming a corpus of respectable size, were made in the years 1845–1849, the bulk of them in 1846 and 1847.

Rossetti's new enthusiasm follows easily from the development I have noted. His growing interest in the opposite sex could enjoy full play among these poets of courtly love, who chose beautiful women as the subject for almost all their verse. Courtly love combined sexual and poetic instincts; Rossetti, possessing both in full measure, could indulge them both at once by pursuing his new literary interest. Cultism appealed to him—it was his idea to make the Pre-Raphaelites a "Brotherhood" with all the boyish paraphernalia of secrecy—and courtly love was, broadly speaking, a cult. Dante's "school," the *stilnovisti*, may be seen as a cult within the larger cult, professedly the gentlest of hearts within the cult of the gentle heart. One assumption of courtly love, the gentle heart's superiority to all others, the rather spoiled and self-willed boy would certainly take to his own heart. Further, the *stilnovisti* strove to create a dreamy poetic world apart from the mundane. They offered particularly great and obvious opportunities for fantasy, and Rossetti was an habitual dreamer.

The translations had at least three effects upon Rossetti's development. First they helped him to establish his distinctive poetic style, which gives the impression of being archaic.[1] A practice that contributes to the impression was his use of many words that are rather dusty, perhaps, but hardly unknown to the reader of popular romance: *doth, saith, ween, puissance, behest, compleasaunce, hie, servitor, misaventure, dule, guerdon.* He went out of his way especially to use conjunctions, prepositions, and ad-verbial expressions—the humbler parts of the sentence—that are long, unfamiliar, and a little awkward: *erst, wherewith, of likeness unto, whereof, in sooth, thereon, therewithal, on this wise, oft-times, thereby, of very surety, I wis, suchwise, betwixen, forasmuch.* By virtue of his translating the large corpus of Italian courtly poems he developed his own literary style, carrying over these devices into his original poetry.

A second result of the translations was their fixing the ideal type of feminine beauty for Rossetti. Although there are surpris-ingly few physical descriptions in the poems, the few give a decided effect because they are all, without exception, in com-plete agreement.[2] As Rossetti translated, the names of the poet and of the beloved changed, but the description of the ladies remained the same: " . . . the beautiful bright hair / That shed reflected gold / O'er the green growths on either side the way"; " . . . and the green leaves did yield / The golden hair their shadow"; " . . . whom I then called my love, / Fair-haired, with silver brows"; "She who has the bright face and the bright hair"; "I look at the crisp golden-threaded hair / Whereof, to thrall my heart, Love twists a net: / Using at times a string of pearls for bait"; " . . . that smile of hers / Where whiteness as of snow was visible / Among the roses at all seasons red!" "The spacious forehead which her locks enclose, / The small white teeth, the shapely nose"; "And almost pale her face for delicacy"; "I look at her white easy neck, so well / From shoulders and from bosom lifted out"; "Even as she walks she hath a sober grace"; " . . . the calm, erect, dignified walk"; "Soft as a peacock steps she, or as a stork / Straight on herself, taller and statelier."[3] In 1850 Rossetti wrote *Hand and Soul*, a short story generally conceded to have elements that are (to use his own word) greatly autopsychological.[4] In it there appears to the hero a beautiful woman who tells him that she is "an image . . . of thine own soul within thee." She is, as we might expect, an object of reverence, gentle and stately, with long golden hair. By the time Rossetti was twenty-two, the conventional medieval beauty had become his own ideal.

Third, the Italian translations made Rossetti think of fair ladies as heavenly creatures. Today "heavenly" is an overworked, colorless adjective of approbation; the Italian poets certainly abused its literal meaning, but at least they knew what it meant, and that they were playing with holy things when they wrote as follows (the translations and titles are Rossetti's):

> An angel of the spheres
> She seems, and I am hers;
> > Anon., *One Speaks of his Feigned and Real Love*

> . . . my heart before her faints and dies,
> And into Heaven seems to be spirited;
> So that I count me blest a certain while.
> > Jacopo da Lentino, *Of his Lady's Face*

> Ne'er was the mind of man so nobly led,
> Nor yet was such redemption granted us
> That we should ever know her perfectly.
> > Guido Cavalcanti, *A Rapture Concerning his Lady*

> Thy lovely lady who is in Heaven crown'd,
> > Who is herself thy hope in Heaven.
> > Cino da Pistoia, *To Dante on the Death of Beatrice*

In these expressions the poets, with various degrees of belief in Christianity, commandeer the superlatives of Christianity to express the peculiar excellences of their ladies. The greatest praise would thus be the greatest effrontery to Christianity; the lady is taken as the standard or prototype, and heaven itself as a mere imitation of her:

> For only thus our intellect could know
> That heavenly beauty which resembles her.
>   Guido Cavalcanti, *In Praise of Guido Orlandi's Lady*

As might be predicted, Rossetti began to describe beautiful women in religious terms. More specifically, in *The Blessed Damozel* and other poems, he began to think of the beautiful woman as a savior, who strove to bring him to the heaven that he associated with her.

In the years of the Italian translations, Gabriel, as his father had done before him,[5] increasingly identified himself with Dante, even promoting "Dante" to the head of the list of his given names. As a nineteen-year-old in 1847, while engaged in translating the *Vita Nuova*, he began four poems (*The Blessed Damozel, The Portrait, Ave,* and *For an Annunciation: Early German*) that treat of woman as savior of man, and three of them employ the situation of the *Vita Nuova:* that of the woman in heaven and the man yet on earth. Although he was turning away from belief in the Anglican faith in which he had been raised—indeed, all formal religion—throughout his late teens and early twenties he posed in his works as a devout Christian, even calling his poems, "Songs of the Art Catholic." One reason seems to have been his interest in the Virgin Mary, whom he depicted repeatedly in both poetry and art. No one can say certainly why Rossetti was so attracted to the fair lady as savior, but I might suggest that the young man, in rejecting the comforts of Christianity, turned, as he often did, to his imagination to supply the lack; and in his fantasies he found a Beatrice or Virgin Mary offering a compensatory salvation accordant with his own notions. Dante's beloved suggested his own ideal, and Dante's conception of a woman as heavenly savior, when applied to himself, appealed to important imaginative and religious needs of his own in addition to his more general sexual needs.

In some very important matters, however, Rossetti differed from Dante even as he imitated him. The difference can be seen best by comparing Rossetti's *The Blessed Damozel* with the *Vita Nuova.*[6] Rossetti wrote the one while he translated the other, and they are similar in several respects: setting (heaven and earth), characters (beloved and lover), dramatic situation (bereavement through death), and incidental techniques (use of symbolic numbers).[7] But the disparity between the Damozel and Beatrice is even more impressive. The Damozel, though in heaven, has lost none of her humanity in translation, and in fact is a more recognizable human being than Beatrice ever was on earth. She addresses herself to the reader's senses more than Beatrice does, for her physical description (if the term may be used of spirits) is more detailed: we know the color (in the first, 1850, version of the poem) and the appearance of her eyes, the way she wears her hair, and her hair's color. We hear her speak, whereas Beatrice says nothing throughout the *Vita Nuova.* We even know the warmth of her bosom, and we cannot imagine Beatrice's breast making any bars warm. What is true of the Damozel's appearance is true also of her personality. Even in heaven she possesses the emotions of any sweet and sensitive girl. She feels innocent wonder at heavenly things, and is somewhat "abashed and weak" in spite of her wishes to be otherwise. She broods in love-sick longing for her earth-bound lover, and has fearful qualms that God may not answer their prayers for reunion. The attitude has little in common with Beatrice's gracious condescension, her "unspeakable courtesy," towards Dante. The poem ends with the Damozel weeping; yet one would have thought heavenly tears forbidden, if not impossible. If she is perfect she is so only in weakness.

Like Dante, Rossetti uses numbers that are manifestly symbolic of hidden significances:

> She had three lilies in her hand,
>> And the stars in her hair were seven.

When, however, we attempt to discern the submerged meanings we are frustrated. The three lilies might indicate the Damozel's purity in body, mind, and soul, but the interpretation is necessarily arbitrary; since we lack context, the number comes to us like a word from a language foreign to us. "Three" suggests the Trinity, of course, but we can say little more. Similarly, the number of stars in her hair is reminiscent of the Seven Sorrows and Seven Joys of Mary, but the application to the Damozel remains in mystery. Unlike Dante, with his symbols that open into light, Rossetti wraps his Damozel in murky mysteries that are, like her eyes, "deeper than the depth / Of waters stilled at even."[8] Rossetti uses the hocus-pocus to let us know that she is immersed in a mystical ambience, but this is all we are meant to know.[9]

Readers of Dante's *Paradiso* know that after Beatrice guides Dante to the Empyrean, she ascends, her mission done, to her place in the Celestial Rose:

> e quella, sì lontana
> come parea, sorrise e riguardommi;
> poi si tornò all 'etterna fontana.[10]

Dante is thus left free to explore and admire God's heavenly wonders, of which Beatrice is but a small part. The heaven of the Blessed Damozel is not at all like that. Though the setting of heaven is supernatural and mysterious, the activities and joys of heaven are not. What the blessed are enjoying, and what the Damozel is desiring, is nothing but a good earthly time:

> To have more blessing than on earth
>   In nowise: but to be
> As then we were,—being as then
>   At peace. Yea, verily.
>
>   (1850 version)

The earthly passion of lovers does not, as in Dante, merely lead to heaven, but rather *is* a veritable heavenly state. The only differences between earthly and heavenly bliss are, first, a difference in duration:

> —only to be,
> As then awhile, for ever now
>   Together, I and he.
>
>   (1856 version)

And, second, a difference due to the shedding of any prudish restraint:

> And we will step down as to a stream
>   And bathe there in God's sight.
>
>   Then will I lay my cheek
> To his, and tell about our love,
>   Not once abashed or weak:
> And the dear Mother will approve . . .

In the original version Rossetti described the other spirits of heaven as "playing at holy games." In 1870 he changed the phrase to "loving games." In the last revision the earthly activities of heaven are even more apparent:

> Around her, lovers, newly met
>   'Mid deathless love's acclaims,
> Spoke evermore among themselves
>   Their heart-remembered names . . .

In the Fogg Museum is the first version of Rossetti's oil painting *The Blessed Damozel* (1876–1877), which illustrates the poem; in it we see graphically expressed what Rossetti is saying in the poem. Heaven is composed of lovers' souls standing two-by-two, completely absorbed in one another. God is without function— only barely suggested in an inconspicuous dove overlooking the oblivious lovers.[11]

That Rossetti's heaven is not Dante's ought not to be cause for disparagement. I compare the two because Rossetti himself invites the comparison, only to discourage it; because his readers have often been troubled by his differences from Dante; and finally because the comparison helps to focus upon what is truly characteristic of him. Rossetti's worth is his own, and to see him (as he sometimes saw himself) as a second Dante is only to becloud him in the aura of another. Rossetti's difference from Dante is marked both by his unconcern for what lies behind apparent mystery, and by his heaven of human appearances, feelings, and activities.[12] His heaven is less perspicuous than Dante's and heretical besides, although his conceptions are like-

First sketch for background of *The Blessed Damozel*
Courtesy of Fogg Art Museum, Harvard University (Bequest of
Grenville L. Winthrop)

wise bold and unique. But final evaluation can wait until he has had the run of his vision.

It is worth noting, however, that the characteristics in question were intentional; errors or no errors, at least they were no blunders. First, it will be remembered from Chapter One that one of the characteristics of Rossetti's imagination was a kind of self-induced, intentional disordering—what I have called a blurring of the eyes. Rossetti fled from life's ordered pursuits to enjoy, in his imagination, "a land without any order." When the heavenly woman found her place in his imagination, one of the things from which she saved him was order, and among the pleasing sensations that she induced in him was a devil-may-care giddiness:

> Love on: who cares?
> Who cares? Love on.
>> Trans. of song from Victor Hugo's *Burgraves*

> My mouth to thy mouth as the world melts away.
>> *The Song of the Bower*

> Lady, I fain would tell how evermore
> Thy soul I know not from thy body, nor
> Thee from myself, neither our love from God.
>> "Heart's Hope," *House of Life* V

> Ah! let not hope be still distraught,
> But find in her its gracious goal,
> Whose speech Truth knows not from her thought,
> Nor love her body from her soul.
>> *Love-Lily*

Conversely, when the lady is absent, the poet's vision does not blur, and he sees adventitious objects with memorable clarity:

> One thing then learned remains to me—
> The woodspurge has a cup of three.
>> *The Woodspurge*

Since, then, Rossetti saw heavenly bliss as earthly, human love,

and since he found the love passion to be a great "melting
mood," a state of pleasurable confusion, it follows that he would
diverge from Dante in depicting a shadowy heaven that included,
as one of its joys, a vague, mysterious atmosphere.

Rossetti also seems to have been perfectly aware of what he
was doing in filling heaven with earthly beings, feelings, and
activities. Heaven and earthly love were frequently associated
for him:

> Some sweet caress or some sweet name
> Low-breathed shall let me know her thought the same;
> Making me rich with every tone
> And touch of the dear heaven so long unknown . . .
>
> *The Stream's Secret*[13]

And in *The Portrait* (begun in 1847) again we find the situation of
The Blessed Damozel, an earthly lover yearning for heavenly
reunion with his beloved. As in *The Blessed Damozel* the projected
heavenly state is nothing other than that reunion: at death the
lover's soul " . . . enters in her soul at once / And knows the
silence there for God!" The beloved's eyes are spoken of as "the
spirit's Palestine." Heaven is pictured as holding its breath to
hear "the beating heart of Love's own breast," which beats, in
its yearning, with the strength of "the iron-bosomed sea." Again
the strength and sound of heaven come from the love of all the
paired souls for their partners.

There is also evidence of Rossetti's awareness and consistency outside of his own poems. Shortly after *The Blessed Damozel*
was written he rightfully objected when Leigh Hunt referred to
the "Dantesque heavens" of Rossetti's poetry.[14] Years later, in
1874, he was to say of Beatrice that she was "sacred to the
young; to each of whom the figure of Beatrice, less lifelike than
lovelike, will seem the friend of his own heart."[15] Here he puts
his finger very plainly on his objection to Dante's Beatrice—
"less lifelike than lovelike"—at the same time implying her
great influence over him. In his life he took every opportunity
to stress Beatrice's earthly, actual qualities, calling attention
to ". . . what I believe to lie at the heart of all true Dantesque
commentary; that is, the existence always of the actual events

even where the allegorical superstructure has been raised by Dante himself."[16] When faced with the theory—far less common, but held by his father—that Beatrice was a "merely symbolic personage," he "was entirely for the real woman, scouting and ignoring any arguments to the contrary."[17] Thus he consciously did what he could to make the remote Beatrice as palpable as his own Blessed Damozel.

Heaven was meant to be composed of earthly dalliances because he envisioned a terrestrial heaven, a heavenly state achievable on earth, a natural supernaturalism. He confounded heaven with earth, adopting heavenly concepts and vocabulary to earthly personalities and feelings because, as he saw it, the path to salvation led into the senses, not away from them. Therefore he rejected Dante's salvation, with love of an angelic personage as the means, in favor of a salvation with love of a very real girl as the end. In 1869 he planned to write a poem, *The Harrowing of Hell*, which, according to William, he meant " . . . to treat from the point of view of love-passion—as if the redemption wrought by Christ were to be viewed as an elevation of the conception of love from pleasure into passion, hence entailing the redemption from Hell of Adam and Eve, David and Bathsheba, etc., etc."[18] The dubious William adds, "I very much question whether the ideas involved are not self-conflicting." I hope to show, in due time, just how conflicting they were. But the assertion of a fusion of heaven and earth, spirit and flesh, *eros* and *agape*, was entirely characteristic and implicit in all of Rossetti's imaginative works of salvation throughout his career.

Perhaps Rossetti's conceptions may be explained, first, by his youth. When he immersed himself in courtly love he was just coming to sexual consciousness; he would hardly have been willing to relinquish his newly won sensuality upon its first possession. He could not imagine a more perfect bliss; to him all experiences rooted in sexuality would have a freshness and projected importance that might well lead him to equate them with the joys of heaven. When Dante wrote his *Vita Nuova* he was in his late twenties, and hence was better prepared psychologically to place sexual passion properly among the natural wonders of the world, and to raise his hopes accordingly to other, higher things.

Second, Rossetti did not consider himself a Christian, and Dante did. Rossetti's rejection of the Anglican religion in which his mother had assiduously raised him seems to have been visceral and spontaneous rather than considered; perhaps the Church became just another "obligation" to flee. Because of his truancy he had reason to feel that Dante's substantially orthodox heaven was too remote and unsure for him to hope for its attainment. He might well appreciate its attractions ruefully, and look for them closer at hand. Yet he was rather *alter*-Christian than *anti*-Christian. Although he rejected the institution of Christianity, many of its forms and promises still appealed to him. So, like the courtly poets of an earlier day, he stole from Christianity what he considered of value—its beauties of language, attitude, and situation, and its rewards—and left the toils behind.

Third, there was Rossetti's childish, spoiled quality that made him insist on having his own way, even when that way was choosing both sides of a mutually exclusive alternative. He wished to be a great painter but he did not wish to labor over developing technique; he wanted to be good to his wife but he wanted other women too. It is likely that Rossetti was exhibiting this strain in expecting to find all the appointments of heaven in an earthly passion for an earthly girl.

Finally we may turn to that Sargasso Sea, the temper of the time. The nineteenth century had inherited and cultivated the conception that what was spiritual in the world, and hence what was important, lay in man's thoughts, will, and emotions. The application of the conception to Rossetti is obvious: thought, will, emotion meant one thing to him—human love, and especially sexual desire. If the spiritual resides in human emotion, then sexual desire is eminently spiritual. A mutual sexual desire would result in a blended, mutual spirituality, a condition that is really what Rossetti meant by salvation, as his heavens reveal. It is in this way that we might explain his divergences from Dante—his refusal to distinguish between human love and heavenly love, between the body and the spirit, and his insistence upon a palpable heroine.

I should add that it is wholly unlikely that Rossetti ever reasoned thus in self-justification. His aversion to all hard, dry cogitation has been indicated in the first chapter. He was interested in neither the roots nor the ramifications of his own fantasy, but merely in its simple expression.

Like Beatrice, the Virgin Mary could lead man to heavenly salvation; so it is not surprising to find Rossetti concerning himself with the Virgin as well. In *Ave*, written in the same year as *The Blessed Damozel*, he again dwelt on the ordinary humanity of the heroine rather than her intangible qualities:

> Oh when our need is uttermost,
> Think that to such as death may strike
> Thou once wert sister sisterlike!

He preferred her a little fearful, and overly delicate:

> Work and play,
> Things common to the course of day,
> Awed thee with meanings unfulfilled;
> And all through girlhood, something stilled
> Thy senses like the birth of light . . .

Thus he tried to put Mary, customarily as remote as Dante's Beatrice, into the mold of his Damozel. But although she could be made human, the outlines of her story left little room for love-passion. He made the most of Mary's Assumption, using the language of love to describe Christ's taking her into His arms:

> When thy Beloved at length renew'd
> The sweet communion severèd,—
> His left hand underneath thy head
> And his right hand embracing thee?—
> Lo! He was thine, and this is He!

He envisioned Mary's blessing him as the comforting nearness of a beloved one:

> Hear us at last, O Mary Queen!
> Into our shadow bend thy face,
> Bowing thee from the secret place . . .

But finally he found Mary difficult to adapt to his idea of salvation through the senses. Opportunities for demonstrating sensibility were few, and the relationship between savior and saved was not so intimate and exclusive as could be desired. Nevertheless she continued to find a place in his poetry; he wrote *For an Annunciation: Early German* in the same year, 1847, and proceeded with *For "Our Lady of the Rocks"* (1848), *Mary's Girlhood* (1849), and *For a Virgin and Child* (1849).

CHAPTER THREE

The Heavenly Lady:
Art and Life

I

ROSSETTI met with more success in expressing the fantasy of the heavenly woman when he turned to another medium. Although painting had been his chosen vocation from earliest childhood, and although he had been schooled in art since he was fourteen, it was the literary enthusiasm just described that really launched his artistic career. Previously, at art school, he had been lazy, wayward, rebellious, and undistinguished,[1] probably because of his instinctive aversion to "obligation." In fact it is probably because painting was "obligation," and opposed to poetry, which was delightful "idleness,"[2] that he did not think to take his fantasy to the drawing-board sooner. But in March 1848 his artistic career suddenly became an important concern to him; impatient with the formal exercises in technique that he was obliged to perform, and disdainful of his teachers' paucity of inspiration, he quit the Academy School and persuaded Ford Madox Brown, a sturdy young painter of twenty-seven, to take him as a pupil.

A suggestive little incident is helpful in determining the motivation behind Rossetti's decision. Brown, too, put Rossetti to work on solving the primary problems of technique rather than the ultimate problems of existence; he set him to painting some pickle-jars.[3] Rossetti completed the distasteful canvas, but within two months he left Brown for William Holman Hunt—first, however, making sure that his new tutor would require no more bottles, and would permit him to work on a subject of his own choice.[4] Rossetti, it seems, had something to say, and was impatient with the prospect of waiting until he was proficient in technique to express it. Some years later he came upon his old canvas of pickle-jars, which was still in his friend Madox Brown's possession, and he daubed into the background a large, voluptuous, reclining woman. One might say that the lady was in truth there all the time, and that she was the reason for his eagerness to paint his own subjects. His brother affirms that at the time Gabriel "had plenty of ideas."[5]

Painting his fantasy of salvation had advantages over inscribing it. Chiefly, it permitted an easy insistence upon the material, human aspects of his Beatrices and Virgin Marys without his having to build these qualities into the incident or assert them in the narration. All he had to do was depict the heroine as a girl of feeling and flesh, and nothing more needed to be done about it. Also, Rossetti seems to have entered frequently into the imaginative experience of a much closer, and almost supernatural, connection between a graphic or plastic representation and its original. In *Sister Helen*, for example, the melting of a wax image of the lover brings about his death; in *How They Met Themselves* a couple encounter their visual doubles, whose sight (according to the assumed superstition) brings death; in *The Portrait* Rossetti gives an eerie sense to the relationship between portrait and subject:

> This is her picture as she was:
> > It seems a thing to wonder on,
> As though mine image in the glass
> > Should tarry when myself am gone.

A similar sense of an uncannily close connection is given in *St. Agnes of Intercession* (1850): in the prose tale the narrator discovers, to his horror, four-hundred-year-old portraits that are exact likenesses of his beloved and himself. There are likenesses in crystal balls in *Sir Hugh the Heron* and *Rose Mary*. To Rossetti's imagination, a graphic representation could be so successful in portraying actual, palpable qualities that it seemed supernaturally related to its original.

Holman Hunt was an especially happy choice of instructor. Not only did he permit Rossetti free choice of subject, but his own particular artistic message, "paint from Nature," "follow Nature," was exactly the encouragement that Rossetti needed to hear, and the method that he desired to follow.[6] Hunt's method, which was soon taken over as gospel by the Pre-Raphaelites, was really quite simple, emphasizing the closeness of the artistic work to its subject: " . . . nothing is done until the model and the painted figure are so much alike that one might almost take the one for the other in a momentary glance."[7] Using this procedure, Rossetti could express the lifelike qualities of the fantasies he harbored by painting them, with Hunt's help, from life itself. Soon Rossetti was at work on *The Girlhood of Mary Virgin*.

In the painting, as we might expect, the Virgin appears as a real girl of flesh and blood. Except for a distracting halo there is nothing about her person that suggests superhumanity. Rather than bow down and worship we feel more inclined to sympathize or reassure, for she seems very lonely as she faces the symbols of her future task. Her parents, St. Joachim and St. Anna, are aware only of the present; from their dull preoccupation we know that they do not see the symbolic significance of the fruitful vine and embroidered lily that they are regarding. The angel has eyes only for the symbol of Mary's future—of her flowering—and is inattentive to the Virgin herself. The Dove remains outside the room, and does not appear as a comforting protector. So the Virgin is left to the contemplation of her divine mission. She looks like any girl of delicate sensibilities, possessing all the human weaknesses; yet she will act with almost impossible grandeur. We admire her silence, her rigid control, as she continues to copy the lily, working out her own innocence in preparation for "the fulness of the time." Our final attitude is one of admiration—not for the Virgin's exalted position, but for

The Girlhood of Mary Virgin
Courtesy of The Tate Gallery, London

her strength in controlling her own human fears and weaknesses.

The Girlhood is and is not an example of Hunt's precept to follow Nature. First, even though all the objects of the painting are natural ones, the scene is quaintly unnatural in that many of the objects are "not really there." We do not condemn St. Anna as an untidy housekeeper for leaving thorns lying about the floor, but see them as symbols only. Second, the painting is a careful reproduction of natural objects in only some of its details, whereas Hunt and Millais at this time were uniformly and indiscriminately meticulous.[8] The Virgin herself is one such detail, her face, especially, being finely painted. In general it is the supernatural or symbolic objects that receive realistic treatment, while the natural objects are only broadly indicated. For example, the fruitful vine, especially, and also the cross, the lily, the angel, and the seven-thorned briar are all vivid and closely articulated, but the floor, the tapestry, St. Anna (excepting her face), and the landscape in the background are rather vaguely indicated. The disparity suggests a fluctuation of interest rather than a failure of technique, and reveals where Rossetti's interest lay. He was not very considerate of nature itself, as was Hunt, but rather of the Virgin and her story. His true occupation is seen also in a flat contradiction of Pre-Raphaelite practice: he made the Virgin's hair gold instead of the brown of the model, his sister Christina. This was following his fantasy, and not nature, for in this way he brought the Virgin closer to the ideal medieval beauty, and made her somewhat less his sister, avoiding an association that would have complicated his worship of the Virgin unduly.

What has been said of *The Girlhood* is likewise true of his next oil painting, *Ecce Ancilla Domini* (1849–1850; later called *The Annunciation*). Rossetti's Virgin, just awakened by the angel, is entirely girlish and human—not impassive, splendid, and enthroned as she has often been depicted elsewhere. Here she crouches silently upon her pallet, her smallness emphasized by foreshortening and the masculine physique of the angel. Again she is fearful, but again she is self-controlled, and steadfast in her gaze. The symbolic lilies—the same lilies of the previous painting—again stand out and are carefully drawn, but in this

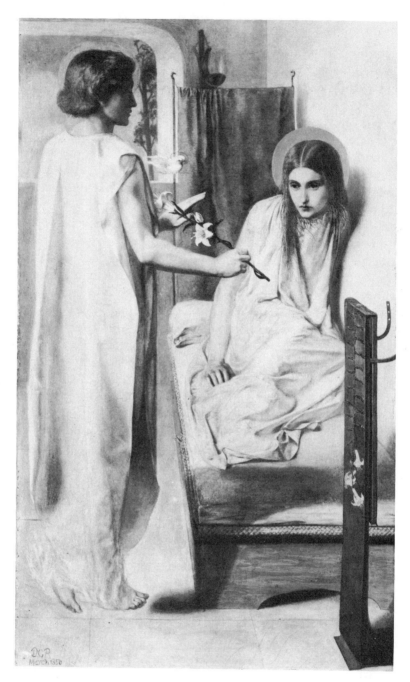

Ecce Ancilla Domini (*The Annunciation*)
Courtesy of The Tate Gallery, London

austere painting Hunt's "Nature" is almost eliminated. As in the first lines of the two sonnets written for these pictures, "This is that blessed Mary," and "These are the symbols"—and that is all. Again the model was Christina, hardly an object of worship for the older brother, but comely and available.

In 1849, the year that Rossetti finished *The Girlhood* and began *Ecce Ancilla Domini*, he also made two pen-and-ink drawings from Dante: a diptych, *Il saluto di Beatrice* (Marillier, p. 24), and *The First Anniversary of the Death of Beatrice* (*Dante Drawing the Angel;* Marillier, opp. p. 36.). I need say only that the drawings are evidence that Rossetti was making his first efforts to transport this form of his fantasy to the drawing board. Beatrice, in the diptych, is predictably beautiful and substantially "lifelike," but she gives the unfortunate impression of being uninteresting and ordinary; she has no aura about her. Rossetti seems to have gone *too* far in making her true to nature. *Dante Drawing the Angel* continues the old theme of longing lovers separated by death.

Holman Hunt's precept was helpful to Rossetti in his efforts to express the realistic qualities of his imaginary heroines, but, as I have suggested, Rossetti was not in basic agreement with Hunt. Like his own hero in *Hand and Soul* he recognized a visionary woman, "an image . . . of thine own soul within thee," who commanded him to paint her. The command conflicted somewhat with Hunt's to paint Nature. Rossetti's conciliatory attempts were painful struggles:

> Rossetti's tendency then in sketching a face was to convert the features of his sitter to his favorite ideal type, and if he finished on these lines, the drawing was extremely charming, but you had to make believe a good deal to see the likeness, while if the sitter's features would not lend themselves to the preordained form, he, when time allowed, went through a stage of reluctant twisting of lines and quantities to make the drawing satisfactory.[9]

These are Hunt's words. Limited in imagination and blinded by his own professions, he could not recognize the drama being performed before him, and he blamed on faulty technique or naughtiness what was largely a conflict of loyalties.

Rossetti was now in exactly that predicament which was forecast at the end of the first chapter. How was he to square the woman of his imagination, including all her medieval and metaphysical characteristics, with some counterpart from nature? True, his ideal woman was "lifelike," but was the reverse true, did any living woman embody the perfection required by Rossetti's ideal? His early Pre-Raphaelite associates and his brother William, who were all good stolid creatures deaf to exacting visionary demands, must have made matters worse by assuming easily that ideal personages did have their counterparts who could be found by searching London:

> A leading doctrine with the Praeraphaelites (and I think a very sound one) was that it is highly inexpedient for a painter, occupied with an ideal or poetic subject, to portray his personages from the ordinary hired models; and that on the contrary he ought to look out for living people who, by refinement of character and aspect, may be supposed to have some affinity with those personages— and, when he has found such people to paint from, he ought . . . to represent them as they are. . . . In other words, the artist had to furnish the conception; nature had to furnish the model. . . . [10]

This practice of Rossetti's friends, reinforced by his own habitual tendency to confuse literature and life, sent him out-of-doors to find the Beatrice or Virgin of his dreams. William records on March 3, 1850 that Gabriel "is now looking for a woman with red hair for the Virgin."[11] Christina, it seems, was being made to do only until the real thing was found. And that veritable Madonna would be known by her effect upon him; she must, like Chiaro's Soul in *Hand and Soul*, give him back his own dreams: "It seemed that the first thoughts he had ever known were given him as at first from her eyes, and he knew her hair to be the golden veil through which he beheld his dreams." That is, tangible hair, an actual situation, and an old, clearly defined dream.

Rossetti's poems written in 1850 express longing and indecision:

> Here dawn today unveiled her magic glass;
>   .   .   .   .

And here the lost hours the lost hours renew
While I still lead my shadow o'er the grass,
Nor know, for longing, that which I should do.
                    "Autumn Idleness," *House of Life* LXIX

Other works of this time are likewise dominated by symbols of
counterparts such as the verbal echoes, magic mirrors, and
shadows of "Autumn Idleness." In *The Mirror* there is a mistaken
identification of object and image:

As who, of forms that crowd unknown
Within a distant mirror's shade,
Deems such an one himself, and makes
Some sign; but when the image shakes
No whit, he finds his thought betray'd,
And must seek elsewhere for his own.

In a pen-and-ink drawing of about this time, *A Parable of Love*,
a lover is guiding the hand of his lady as she paints her own
portrait; like the lady in *Hand and Soul* she is giving him back
the image of his own dreams. I have already mentioned the
unfinished prose tale of this year, *St. Agnes of Intercession*, in
which the hero discovers four-hundred-year-old portraits that
are perfect likenesses of his love and himself. Rossetti's preoccupation with counterparts at this time is surely indicative of his own
concern, that of matching Dante with himself, and the Beatrice
of his fantasies with her living double.

II

During 1850 he met Elizabeth Siddal. Evidently he found in
her his living model of Beatrice, and found the encounter to be
a *déjà vu*, an eerie and frightening experience. *How They Met
Themselves* expresses the shock of self-encounter, just as *St. Agnes
of Intercession* had presaged it. "Rossetti once told me," reports
Brown, "that when he first saw her, he felt his destiny was
defined."[12] Rossetti's expression means more than that he recognized the encounter to be a turning point of his life; it means
that he recognized, at the moment, that his own destiny was to

How They Met Themselves
Permission of the Syndics of The Fitzwilliam Museum,
Cambridge University

be the same as Dante's. Even after ten years of acquaintance with Lizzie Siddal he could write, addressing his dead father,

> And didst thou know indeed, when at the font
> Together with thy name thou gav'st me his,
> That also on thy son must Beatrice
> Decline her eyes according to her wont . . . ?
>
> *Dantis Tenebrae* (1861)

His vivid imagination told him that history was repeating itself.

Miss Siddal's appearance might well make him think so, for it was strikingly similar to the stylized beauty treated in his own Italian translations. Although little has been made of this fact by recent commentators, it was generally remarked upon by her acquaintances. John Ruskin said that "she has more the look of a Florentine fifteenth-century lady than anything I ever saw out of a fresco."[13] Lady Burne-Jones found her beauty to be that of a painting.[14] William Rossetti remarked that "she had a face and demeanour very suitable indeed for a youthful Madonna."[15] She was graceful, long-necked, tall, and slender, with the paleness and aloofness of Dante's Beatrice. Her heavy-lidded eyes were gray-green, and her abundant hair, a striking red-gold.[16] Frederic Stephens, another pupil of Hunt's and a Pre-Raphaelite, unchivalrously claimed that she had some freckles,[17] but surely these maculations went unnoticed in a face that seemed stiff, flat, and deathlike, almost a caricature of characterless medieval simplicity—an effect heightened by her speaking hardly more than Beatrice in the *Vita Nuova*. Hers was an esoteric beauty, reserved for the eye habituated to frescoes, illuminated manuscripts, and medieval poetry of courtly love. Without such preparation the beholder saw only an unbecoming plainness of feature. Even John Ruskin (who later admired her appearance), seeing her likeness for the first time, found her face an "unfortunate type," and objected to her "commonness of feature."[18] The average Victorian disapproved with even greater vigor. A buyer of Brown's wrote to him as follows:

> Our pictures seem to come out badly in the Reviews this year, and it is owing to nothing but the ugly female faces in the bulk of

Drawing of Elizabeth Siddal
Courtesy of Victoria & Albert Museum, London

the Pre-Raphaelite works. Rossetti has much to answer for this, for he has constantly *red hair and the same type of face* in his models. I feel sure that this is the great obstacle to the popularity of the Pre-Raphaelite works. I consider *you* are *not* liable to this charge, but those who follow Rossetti are. . . . I am sure you will get two or three pretty models for the young ladies in my picture, and don't have red hair, please!![19]

But whatever the world might think of Miss Siddal, Rossetti thought her the answer to his dream of salvation. He painted her repeatedly throughout her life and even thereafter as Beatrice and Mary, and as a few other Madonnas.[20] He refashioned his earlier designs from Dante, perhaps because now he knew how Beatrice had looked. He made drawing after drawing of her, filling his rooms with sketches. He forbade his friends to use her for a model, as they had done at first.[21] He spent almost all of his time with her, weakening old friendships through disregard. Within a year or so of meeting they were engaged to be married.

But all did not go well. As long as Elizabeth Siddal sat like a picture, graceful and silent, meeting Rossetti's fantasy half-way, his imagination would do the rest; but when she acted and spoke her mind she betrayed a personality that must have troubled his dreams. Although Rossetti was as blind to her signs of mere humanity as he was to her freckles, it was obvious to the matter-of-fact that Miss Siddal was no Beatrice or Mary. Sometimes his love must have resembled, not Dante's, but Cecco Angiolieri's—an Italian poet whom Rossetti called the "scamp" of Dante's circle, a ridiculous fellow who made a burlesque of courtly love by holding (in Rossetti's words) "an infatuated love for the daughter of a shoemaker."[22] Miss Siddal was far from being gently born and raised; her father was a Sheffield cutler, and she, after a meager education, had been put to work as a milliner's assistant in Cranborne Alley. Certainly she was decent enough, nervously sensitive, and admirable in making as much of herself as she did, but she did not possess the refined, aristocratic manners of a medieval lady-fair. Although Rossetti was hardly sensitive to social distinctions, even he might have felt the difference between Beatrice's gracious elevation and Lizzie's uneasy reserve. Also, Lizzie was poor, phthisical, neurotic, and lonely. Far from proffering salvation, she was in great need of help herself.

Furthermore, Lizzie's long silences were occasionally broken by shrieking, hysterical rages. Professor Doughty sees her as engaging in

> . . . violent and noisy demonstrations of disapproval, deeply tinted with the local colors of her native Kennington Oval. For amidst the stress of battle, the higher mental and social qualities . . . gave place to the more primitive culture of the Old Kent Road.[23]

The following verses of hers are a more dignified example of her fury than Doughty leads us to expect:

Ope not thy lips, thou foolish one,
    Nor turn to me thy face:
The blasts of heaven shall strike me down
    Ere I will give thee grace.
.   .   .   .
And turn away thy false dark eyes,
    Nor gaze into my face:
Great love I bore thee; now great hate
    Sits grimly in its place.

Love and Hate[24]

Poor Lizzie soon learned that she could best control her independent fiancé by varying these rages with bouts of illness. The origins of her fitful malady were ever mysterious, but its effect was predictable: the wayward Gabriel grew meek and contrite. His eventual attitude toward her found expression in his letters at the time of their marriage: "The constantly failing state of her health is a terrible anxiety indeed."[25] " . . . poor dear Lizzy's health has been in such a broken and failing state for the last few days as to render me more miserable than I can possibly say."[26] "I need not say what an anxious and disturbed life mine is while she remains in this state. . . . in fact her health sometimes demands my constant care."[27] This was far from being the first or the last time that Lizzie was ill. As a meeting-place for souls, the sickroom was a poor substitute for Paradise.

Even when things were going well for them there was a disconcerting disparity between Gabriel's feelings toward Lizzie and Dante's toward Beatrice. At the beginning Rossetti was properly worshipful, as we see in this letter of August 1852 to Christina: "I have had sent me, among my things from Highgate, a lock of hair shorn from the beloved head of that dear, and radiant as the tresses of Aurora, a sight of which may perhaps dazzle you on your return."[28] Except for a touch of ebullient self-mockery, Rossetti's attitude here is perfectly consonant with the lover's in *The Blessed Damozel*:

> But shall God lift
> To endless unity
> The soul whose likeness with thy soul
> Was but its love for thee?

Soon, however, Rossetti descended to diminutives of endearment—"Lizzie," "the Sid," "Gug," "Guggums," "Dove"—irreverent little bill-and-cooisms. Imagine Dante speaking thus:

> Come back, dear Liz, and looking wise
> In that arm-chair which suits your size
>   Through some fresh drawing scrape a hole.
>   Your Valentine and Orson's soul
> Is sad for those two friendly eyes.
>
>   *Valentine—To Lizzie Siddal*

This is pleasant verse; but it does reveal that in the expression of his love for Lizzie, Rossetti had lost the expression of his ideal. Instead of worship and dependence we find increasing concern and pity, and belittling fondness for her—attitudes inimical to the concept of her as savior.

So Lizzie, guilty of nothing but her mere humanity, failed Rossetti's imaginative requirements. She also seems to have failed him in a second way, a failing of which he was far more aware. The indications are that, although in love with Gabriel, she did not give herself to him—at least not in the early years of their courtship, and possibly not till their marriage. William Rossetti informs his reader that "this continual association of an engaged

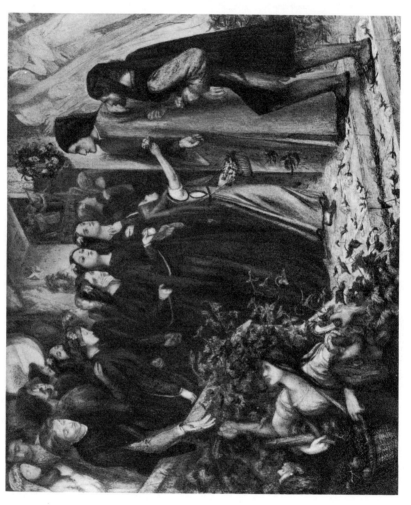

Beatrice Denying Her Salutation to Dante, replica
Courtesy of Ashmolean Museum, Oxford University

couple, while it may have gone beyond the conventional fence-line, had nothing in it suspicious or ambiguous, or conjectured by anyone to be so."[29] Rossetti's own works suggest that William speaks the truth, but also that the virtuous unwillingness to consummate their love sexually was entirely Lizzie's disposition. Significantly, one of Rossetti's first drawings of her was entitled *Beatrice Denying her Salutation to Dante* (1851). A year later he painted her in *Giotto Painting the Portrait of Dante* as a member of a virginal company passing in religious procession by Dante, as he sits to Giotto and carves a pomegranate, "the fruit of Adonis and symbol of passion."[30] The work establishes a priority of influences: Beatrice refuses to be distracted by Dante from her ceremony even as he is distracted by her from his artistic preoccupation. His love-passion takes precedence over his art, but her religious purity will not be influenced by his love-passion.

In Rossetti's poetry we find sexual frustration expressed without recourse to Dante for analogy. In "Broken Music" (*House of Life* XLVII, 1852) the speaker blames his "bitterly beloved" for "the pang of unpermitted prayer." This last expression is paraphrased by William, "prayer for a boon not to be granted."[31] A year later, in a poem entitled, aptly enough, "Known in Vain" (*House of Life* LXV), Rossetti speaks of

> . . . two whose love, first foolish, widening scope,
> Knows suddenly, to music high and soft,
> The Holy of holies; who because they scoff'd
> Are now amazed with shame, nor dare to cope
> With the whole truth aloud, lest heaven should ope;
> Yet, at their meetings, laugh not as they laughed
> In speech; nor speak, at length; but sitting oft
> Together, within hopeless sight of hope
> For hours are silent . . .

William described "Known in Vain" as "more or less autobiographical."[32] Finally I give an omitted stanza from *Love's Nocturne* (1854) that presents an important analogy:

> As, since man waxed deathly wise,
> Secret somewhere on this earth

Unpermitted Eden lies—
Thus within the world's wide girth
Hides she from my spirit's dearth,
    Paradise
Of a love that cries for death.[33]

The passage says plainly what the previously mentioned works have also been implying: the "dearth" was spiritual as well as physical. In denying Gabriel "passion of the naked kind"[34] Lizzie was also denying him Paradise. Rossetti's strong sexual desires and his equation of earthly and heavenly love make it easy to see why he would see sexual consummation as the salvation of his spirit. But his doing so, coupled with Lizzie's strong-willed, though loving, denial of herself, meant that Lizzie was failing his fantasy of salvation in yet another way.

The disparities, which Rossetti was unwilling to recognize as such, between Lizzie and his ideal Madonna threw him into great vagaries of behavior and uncertainty of purpose. No longer did he know quite what he wanted or how to obtain it. He vacillated between enthusiastic acceptance of Lizzie and flight from her. In his flights he took two avenues, the sensual and the imaginative. He soon turned for his physical satisfaction to other women. And his tendency to dream increased; he fell more and more into his sleepy, lethargic dozes, returning to the comforts of his imagination and shutting out the problems of a disparate world.[35] He retained his old fantasy of salvation, but he also evolved a new fantasy—one that coincided with, and in a measure justified, his new practice of pursuing women more ready than Lizzie to satisfy his desires.

CHAPTER FOUR

The Sinful Woman

THE year 1853 brought about a change in Rossetti's works; he set aside his interest in religious topics and temporarily chose the prostitute as his dominant theme.

In his poetry of this year we find a literal departure from church. Gabriel, as if in church, addresses Christina, bidding her to

> Rise up out of thy seat,
> Though peradventure 'tis an irksome thing
> To cross again the threshold of our King
> Where His doors stand against the evil street,
> And let each step increase upon our feet
> The dust we shook from them at entering.
> *The Church Porches*, Sonnet II

Although it is "clear and cool" in the church, the two must endure the dust and misty heat of the secular world because "it is so bidden." The poem was anticipated somewhat by *Pax Vobis* in 1849.[1] In the earlier poem Father Hilary climbs to the belfry, from which he regards the world. His vision is whirling and chaotic:

> 'Twas a sick sway of air
> That autumn noon within the stair,
> As dizzy as a turning cup.

> His brain benumbed him, void and thin;
> He shut his eyes and felt it spin;
>
> .   .   .   .
>
> Close to his feet the sky did shake
> With wind in pools that the rains make . . .

By now we are accustomed to expect Rossetti to treat such a giddy sensation as desirable. In spite of the turbulence Father Hilary can say paradoxically, "the air is calm outside"; "calm hath its peace outside"; "there is the world outside." The cloistered Father Hilary recognizes and longs for what the speaker in *The Church Porches* has considerately willed to explore.

A conscious decision on the part of Rossetti to change his course from heaven to earth may be reflected also in "The Hill Summit" (*House of Life* LXX, 1853). In this sonnet the poet describes himself as a "belated worshipper" of the sun, who, arriving at the Hill's summit at sunset, can see only "the gold air and the silver fade, / And the last bird fly into the last light." The sun is treated in religious terms ("his altar," "vespersong," "a belated worshipper"), and the poet regards himself as a Moses, for he has had glimpses of the godly sun like "A fiery bush with coruscating hair." The poet has had his vision, however intermittent and belated,

> And now that I have climbed and won this height
> I must tread downward through the sloping shade
> And travel the bewildered tracks till night.

Disappointed with the diminished vision, and reluctant to descend, he is, nevertheless, resigned to the downward, deathly journey. The attitude is similar to that of *The Church Porches*, even to the consideration of the withdrawal from the holy place as a religious "calling"; like Moses he must leave the presence of God to promote the will of God, just as, in *The Church Porches*, departure was "so bidden."

Rossetti's artistic works for the year 1853 express the same sentiments that are found in the poetry. He produced only one painting dealing with his old fantasy of salvation (the water-color version of *Dante Drawing the Angel*), and in the following year there were none.[2] His stated reason for abandoning his religious themes was that they did not sell well enough.[3] This is hardly a sufficient explanation, for his poems, written with no eye to "the market," changed in accordance with the paintings. William Bell Scott, whom Rossetti visited in 1853, found that " . . . the spirit that had made him choose 'Songs of the Art-Catholic' as a general title died out. The only sign of it among the MSS. he had brought with him was to be found in two sonnets called *The Church Porches.* . . . "[4] And we have seen that the second of these was hardly an exception to Scott's observation, for it was a valedictory to that departing spirit.

So Rossetti, half prophet and half backslider, turned away from his pursuit of Paradise to enter the *selva oscura*, the Cities of the Plain. To some extent he also turned from Elizabeth Siddal, for to him she was associated with holiness (there is even a suggestion of Lizzie's crowning glory in the line, "A fiery bush with coruscating hair"). William Bell Scott says of this time, "Perhaps Rossetti was already beginning to revise his intention of marriage."[5] At least Rossetti felt free enough to take long journeys without her. And there must have been long journeys without her in fantasy too. His creative work of the year is dominated by sinful women rather than saints: we find a pen-and-ink drawing, *Hesterna Rosa*; a sketch for *Mary Magdalene*; a sketch on the subject of sirens, *Lo Marinaio Oblia che Passa per Tal Via*; and four studies for *Found*. Miss Siddal as the Blessed Damozel may have filled Paradise for Rossetti, but "the evil street" had its own queen to hold his interest—the fallen woman.

Rossetti's expressed attitude toward harlotry and illicit love was strongly moral: he abhorred it because of its degrading effect upon the lady. While visiting Scott at Newcastle he engaged in long arguments with this exponent of free love. Scott says that " . . . one of the subjects of our evening talks had been *self-culture*. The egotistic side of this popular English Goetheism of the day was the only one he could see."[6] After leaving Scott Rossetti continued the argument by letter in his most urbane and convincing manner:

> The *Life Drama* [of Alexander Smith] has nothing particular to say except that it seems to bear vaguely towards the favourite doctrine

that scoundrelism is a sacred probation of the soul. But I find this everywhere. I am reading *Wilhelm Meister*, where the hero's self-culture is a great process, amusing and amazing one. On one page he is in despair about some girl he has been the death of; in the next you are delighted with his enlarged views of Hamlet. Nothing, plainly, is so fatal to the duty of self-culture as self-sacrifice, even to the measure of a grain of mustard seed. The only other book I have read for more than a year is St. Augustine's *Confessions*, and here you have it again. As soon as the saint is struck by the fact that he has been wallowing, and inducing others to wallow, it is all horrible together, but involves no duty, except the comfortable self-appeasement of getting out of it himself. As for the women, no doubt they are nascent for hell. . . . I should like to hunt up as many instances of this noble theory as possible, and form them into an encyclopaedia for the benefit of self-cultivators.[7]

In *Hesterna Rosa* and *Borgia* (1851) lust is depicted as a monkey scratching itself. In *Jenny* he had called it a "toad." The worst was that the foulness was contagious; Rossetti saw man's promiscuous sexuality as destroying women. Although *The Honeysuckle* finally discourages narrow interpretation, it does figure forth the possession and eventual discarding of a once pure girl. In *Hesterna Rosa*, the monkey on one side is contrasted with an innocent little girl playing the lute on the other; in *Found* the calf being taken to town for sale and slaughter is symbolic of the harlot. Two years earlier, in *Borgia*, he depicted Lucretia Borgia teaching a girl to move her little body in rhythm with her own in a sensuous and degrading dance.

Rossetti's attitude toward illicit love is certainly surprising in the light of his fantasy of the heavenly lady, in which strong love-passion is generally celebrated; but his attitude here admits of at least two explanations. One involves a very understandable inconsistency with respect to sexual fulfillment. Although sexual relations with a Blessed Damozel would have been considered sacred, the road to the seduction of a defenseless, ordinary girl was a dirty thing, a "wallow," a befouling "quag-water."[8] But the Blessed Damozel, too, was noteworthy for her ordinariness of character. The difference lay, then, not in the girl, but in the fantasy applied to her. The fantasy of the heavenly lady expresses desire; that of the sinful woman, guilt. That sexual fulfillment can indicate both purity and pollution to Rossetti would seem to be an expression of conflict between feelings of desire and guilt.

The second explanation of the difference between the two fantasies involves no inconsistency: "pure" sexual fulfillment, as expressed in the first fantasy, is marked by strong mutual affections (what I have called "soul"); sexual fulfillment in the second fantasy will be seen to be simple lust, with no "higher" feelings to sanctify it. The two fantasies permit Rossetti to discriminate between the two kinds of passion.

Rossetti's moral crusade is also somewhat surprising in the light of his turning away from religious considerations, his imminent sexual behavior, and his own heedless "self-cultivation." Professor Doughty calls his attitude at this time "sex disguised as moral idealism."[9] The phrase calls attention to the fact that the two elements were closely related. But Professor Doughty's implication that Rossetti's "moral idealism" was a mere veneer, a cover for his true, sexual motivations, does not do his "moral idealism" justice; for his attitude was well-founded.

First, Rossetti's moral stand with respect to irresponsible sexuality grew out of genuine fear for lost feminine purity. It was only natural that a boy who thought of fair ladies as holy things should have been disturbed by encountering beautiful women of degraded personality and behavior. By protecting and protesting their purity he was also protecting the Madonna of his fantasies. *A Last Confession* (1849) expresses perfectly Rossetti's fears for his heavenly fantasies, for in it the laugh of a heavenly lady gone bad wakens the hero from his dream of blessedness: in his dream a company of celestial ladies

> . . . all laughed up at once
> For the strong heavenly joy they had in them
> To hear God bless the world. Wherewith I woke:
> And looking round, I saw as usual
> That she was standing there with her long locks
> Pressed to her side; and her laugh ended theirs.

In the poem the hero adopts a little girl who seems a child of heaven:

She might have served a painter to pourtray
The heavenly child which in the latter days
Shall walk between the lion and the lamb.

He adopts her to protect her from evil, sexual evil; to obtain
money for food, "women that I knew / For wives and mothers
walked the public street," and therefore he determines to take
the child with him. Under his protection she grows in appearance into Rossetti's usual Madonna; as she kneels by "an image
of Our Lady," "they seemed two kindred forms." The hero's
feelings develop in keeping with her growth:

... the father's, brother's love—was changed,
I think, in somewise; like a holy thought
Which is a prayer before one knows of it.

But she turns from his pure love to the evil love of other men.
He remembers a time when

A woman laughed above me. I looked up
And saw where a brown-shouldered harlot leaned
Half through a tavern window thick with vine.
Some man had come behind her in the room
And caught her by the arms, and she had turned
With that coarse empty laugh on him, as now
He munched her hair with kisses, while the vine
Crawled in her back.

Then, when his ward laughs scornfully in rejecting him, he is
reminded of the harlot's laugh, and he kills the young girl in his
frenzy. For the protagonist as for Rossetti himself, the spiritual
fall of the lady meant the fall of heaven itself:

Your Heaven? Conceive it spread
For one first year of all eternity
All round you with all joys and gifts of God;
And then when most your soul is blent with it
And all yields song together,—then it stands
O' the sudden like a pool that once gave back
Your image, but now drowns it and is clear
Again,—or like a sun bewitched, that burns
Your shadow from you, and still shines in sight.

The mirroring pool and the shadow are terms which Rossetti was using in 1849 and 1850 to describe his search for his own Madonna. In the purity of the woman lay the integrity of his own fantasy; so there is little wonder that he was revolted by her degradation.

His concern for feminine purity is seen in other works prior to 1853. In *Retro Me, Sathana*, attempted unsuccessfully in oil in 1847, and executed in pen-and-ink in 1848, a priest is protecting a slender, praying girl from a somewhat puzzled devil. Evil triumphs over a pure young lady in two designs of *Gretchen and Mephistopheles in the Chapel* (1848)—works that anticipate Rossetti's objections to Bell Scott's "Goetheism of the day." I have already mentioned *Borgia* (1851), and shall discuss *Jenny* shortly.

A second trait of Rossetti's that indicates the strength and genuineness of his "moral idealism" is his chivalrous helpfulness. In *A Prayer* (1846) the poet addresses his lady with great courtly deference, characterizing her as proud, distant, and somewhat bored with him as an inferior. Yet he does have the temerity, at the end, to offer himself as *her* savior, thus upsetting the traditional courtly order of things:

> Lady, has not my thought
>   Dared much? For I would be
> The ending of darkness and the dawn
>   Of a new day to thee,
> And thine oasis, and thy place of rest,
>   And thy time of peace, lady.

In his lady's distant air he sees loneliness rather than self-sufficiency. What he is suggesting here is really a mutual reciprocity, a pact between equals, each incomplete and lonely without the other. In the light of the courtly tradition of male subservience behind the poem, it is a presumptuous proposal, but because of this unusual mixture of elements the poem is fresh and original. The notion of man as the salvation of his own heavenly lady is also found in *The Blessed Damozel*, where the damozel can no more be blessed without her lover than he without her. The two sonnets, *For "Ruggiero and Angelica" by Ingres* (1849), describe the lover's rescuing his beloved in a

Found
Courtesy of The Wilmington Society of the Fine Arts, Delaware Art
Center (Samuel and Mary R. Bancroft Collection)

more traditional manner that recalls the bellicose daydreams of Rossetti's youth: Ruggiero is slaying the monster that threatens his naked and bound Angelica. Similarly, in *The Staff and Scrip* (1851–1852), the pilgrim saves the lands of Queen Blanchelys in battle.

Rossetti's fears for the purity of his Madonna and his somewhat presumptuous helpfulness go together very nicely. The lover could rescue his lady most appropriately when she was in need of help, and no woman was more in need of help than the fallen woman. The situation occurs often enough in Rossetti's works to be described as a separate fantasy. The combination of the two impulses is perfectly illustrated in Rossetti's most important depiction of the fantasy, his *Found,* begun in his year of change, 1853. In the painting the drover stands above his old sweetheart, who has fallen in both senses of the word. Grasping her wrists, he endeavors to lift her from the street.

Although Rossetti's fantasy of the sinful woman did not find frequent expression until 1853, we can find glimpses of it as early as 1848. Contests of *bouts-rimés* were one of the pastimes of the Rossetti children, in which one would create a sonnet as quickly as possible, using the rhyming words supplied by another. Gabriel, who performed the most quickly under these conditions, produced the following sonnet, *The Sin of Detection:*

> She bowed her face among them all, as one
> By one they rose and went. A little scorn
> They showed—a very little. More forlorn
> She seemed because of that: she might have grown
> Proud else in her turn, and have so made known
> What she well knew—that the free-hearted corn,
> Kissed by the hot air freely all the morn,
> Is better than the weed which has its own
> Foul glut in secret. Both her white breasts heaved
> Like heaving water with their weight of lace;
> And her long tresses, full of musk and myrrh,
> Were shaken from the braids her fingers weaved,
> So that they hid the shame in her pale face.
> Then I stept forth, and bowed addressing her.

There is nothing in the rhyming words to provoke Rossetti's

choice of dramatic situation. We may be surprised to find the poet condoning the lady's sin, but the courtly courtesy as he comes to her rescue in the last line is in character.

Rossetti's long poem, *Jenny*, begun in the same year, also expresses sympathy for a sinful woman. A young student spends an innocent night with a pretty young prostitute, Jenny, asleep in his lap. As she sleeps he philosophizes upon her double nature: "so pure,—so fall'n!" The paradox would be appropriate to any of Rossetti's works expressing this fantasy. Throughout the poem there is a constant insistence upon Jenny's basic purity, as the similes in the following passage reveal:

> Whose eyes are as blue skies, whose hair
> Is countless gold incomparable:
> Fresh flower, scarce touched with signs that tell
> Of Love's exuberant hotbed:—Nay,
> Poor flower left torn since yesterday . . .
> Poor handful of bright spring-water
> Flung in the whirlpool's shrieking face;
> Poor shameful Jenny, full of grace . . .

There are really two attitudes expressed, separated by the break in the fourth line quoted. When the student looks on her, he sees nothing but innocence and purity; but when he remembers that she is a prostitute, he has melodramatic visions of helpless purity corrupted. He vacillates between praise and pity throughout the poem.

In *Jenny* we may see Rossetti exercising his own chivalric generosity. The student helps Jenny in a small way. He lets her sleep peacefully, for "sometimes, were the truth confess'd, / You're thankful for a little rest." He treats her like a fellow human being, and gives her a brotherly love rather than the lust that is usually her lot. And he gives her gold coins, putting them in her hair as she sleeps. Jenny, like Rossetti himself, augments her earthly experience with dreams—dreams of a harlot's heaven, where men are kind and lavish. This time, when she awakes, she will "shake / My gold, in rising, from [her] hair, / A Danaë for a moment there." The student makes possible a momentary elevation, a momentary achievement of her dreams.

We may also see in *Jenny* Rossetti appeasing his own fears for the loss of feminine purity. He alternates between excusing the sinner—blaming instead man's lust or God's will—and insisting nevertheless upon a basic purity because Jenny *looks* so pure. He is careful, however, to consider her as no higher than human; the student's feeling toward Jenny is condescending throughout, an attitude that bothers him a little: "And must I mock you to the last?" The condescension could well be for Rossetti's own protection, to keep him from the painful considerations of *A Last Confession*—thoughts of *heavenly* innocence corrupted.

Jenny may be seen as an inverted version of *The Blessed Damozel;* it is the old theme of salvation with the lover rather than the lady cast in the role of savior. The theme is an octave lower, for, first, instead of trying to rise from earth to heaven, the student tries to raise a degraded woman from hell to earth, and, second, the feelings expressed are in a correspondingly lower pitch. In *Jenny* as in *The Blessed Damozel* the saving force comes from a very human love, albeit not a very strong one.

In *The Sin of Detection* and *Jenny*, Rossetti first expressed his interest in the theme of the sinful woman. Related stories and paintings that soon came to his attention were Sir Henry Taylor's *Philip van Artevelde* (1834), Bell Scott's *Rosabell* (ca. 1837), G. F. Watt's *Found Drowned* (1850), Spenser Stanhope's *Thoughts of the Past (1852)*, Millais' *Virtue and Vice* (1853), and Holman Hunt's *The Awakening Conscience* (or *The Awakened Conscience;* early 1854). For the first and last time Rossetti, rather by accident, found himself in the midst of a social movement.[10] The Pre-Raphaelites were especially fond of the theme,[11] and even engaged in ungracious spats over precedence of ideas. But the theme belonged to Rossetti as much as to anyone. It remained from 1848 to 1853 a fantasy secondary to his primary one. When it came into dominance in 1853 it was not an entirely new conception, nor, as we have seen, was it unrelated to his fantasy of Beatrice.

Why Rossetti decided in 1853 to turn most of his attentions from paradise to the evil street, changing his subject accordingly from the heavenly lady to the degraded lady, we cannot say certainly, although it is easy to construct a probable reason.

Perhaps he was first beginning to suspect the disparities between Miss Siddal and the Blessed Damozel, and in his frustration turned away from the fantasy itself as well as its unsuccessful embodiment. The theme of the sinful woman would be a reduced fantasy, closer to realization than the first. Also, sexual considerations, which Lizzie as his Madonna was discouraging, were inescapable in the contemplation of the sinful woman. Again, sexuality was not divorced from sanctity, for his love for the lady was inseparable from his charitable thoughts for her salvation.

Lizzie was not entirely excluded from the new thoughts, and in fact may have been partly responsible for bringing them on. Although neither prostitute nor, apparently, his mistress, she exercised Rossetti's charitable inclinations by calling upon him for help. In her frequent sicknesses she demanded his ministrations, and she became financially beholden to him. Following the practice of his student in *Jenny*, Rossetti "used to find funds for Miss Siddal whenever required."[12] In this way Lizzie served as a link between the heavenly lady and the sinful woman, although the latter fantasy is basically in reaction to her.

What was lost or missing from the new interest was the supramundane. Rossetti toiled for years over *Found*, his most important work on this theme, but died with it unfinished. Significantly, while the harlot, the innocent lover of her youth, the calf, and the brick wall were all carefully painted, the heavens above remained a blank. The other paintings on the theme have interior settings, for there was nothing in the fantasy that led Rossetti to look up.[13] There was no paradise, no protection, no salvation for himself, no one for him to worship. Therefore Beatrice remained and Lizzie remained, for the old fantasy, though somewhat eclipsed, was still needed.

In the next four years after 1853 his two themes, two "separate hopes which in a soul had wooed / The one same Peace" ("Lost on Both Sides," *House of Life* XCI, 1854), now "roam together." He continued to work extensively on *Found;* composed the ballad, *Stratton Water* (1854), in which Lord Sands does right by his pregnant sweetheart; drew in pen-and-ink a new study from Goethe, *Faust and Margaret in the Prison* (ca. 1856);

and did a subject probably taken from Bell Scott's *Rosabell*, a water-color called *The Gate of Memory* (1857), in which a prostitute sadly observes the innocent play of young children. Works including a heavenly lady are even more extensive, partly because of the requirements of his new patron, Ruskin. A few of the more important designs are a water-color, *The Annunciation* (1855); another entitled *Dante's Vision of Rachel and Leah* (1855); another, *The Passover in the Holy Family* (1855); a wood-cut of *St. Cecelia* (1856–1857); and a water-color, *The Damsel of the Sanc Grael* (1857?). There was also sketch after sketch of Lizzie.

The ballad, *Stratton Water*, marks an important change in Rossetti's treatment of the sinful woman. Previously, illicit sexual relations had been forbidden to sympathetic characters; the way to help the lady was to abstain and to be kind to her. Now, according to *Stratton Water*, it was enough to be kind. The sin was not in the sexual act, but in the callous casting aside. In *Jenny* Rossetti had objected to loving and leaving, condemning the man

> Who, having used you at his will,
> Thrusts you aside, as when I dine
> I serve the dishes and the wine.

In *Jenny* this condemnation was buried amidst the general excoriations of lust, but by *Stratton Water* Rossetti was capable of a more convenient discrimination. The latter poem, dealing with saving face and making amends, prepares the way for Rossetti's own yielding to sexual temptation. The spring of 1854 brought Annie Miller, a beautiful, uncultivated girl whom Holman Hunt painted in *The Awakening Conscience* as a prostitute undergoing (in the phrase of our day) an identity crisis on the lap of her lover, and to whom Hunt became engaged. The trusting Hunt left his fiancée in the care of his friend, allowing her to sit to Rossetti during his two-year absence in the Holy Land. Eventually "the voice of scandal was raised."[14] Bell Scott said of Rossetti at this time, "His curious materialistic piety now disappeared, burst like a soap bubble, and the superficial prismatic colours vanished into air. The early views of self-culture and self-sacrifice

Fanny Cornforth, a study for *Fair Rosamund*
Courtesy of The Cecil Higgins Art Gallery, Bedford, England

we have noticed, underwent a similar bouleversement."[15] In the light of Rossetti's behavior in subsequent years, *Stratton Water* could well indicate a retrenchment of his original ideals.

It was probably in 1856 that Rossetti first met Fanny Cornforth.[16] According to Fanny the first meeting was in this year, at a display of fireworks at the Old Surrey Gardens. Rossetti, along with three other artists, disturbed her hair as if by accident, so that it came tumbling down. In the ensuing apologies Rossetti persuaded her to come the next day to his studio, where "he put my head against the wall and drew it for the head in the calf picture."[17] So began an association that lasted until Rossetti's death.

William Rossetti describes Fanny as "a pre-eminently fine woman, with regular and sweet features, and a mass of the most lovely blonde hair—light-golden or 'harvest yellow.' "[18] Rossetti's pictures show her to be a large, plump woman (he called her "Elephant"), with a beauty that owes much to physical health. In Rossetti's paintings we see her as an object rather than a personality; we spend little time wondering what her thoughts or feelings are (as we do with Rossetti's paintings of Madonnas, such as *The Girlhood* and *The Blessed Damozel*), but rather concentrate upon her appearance, admiring the easy curves of her figure, her carnation, and her softness. Rossetti's first major work painted from her, *Bocca Baciata* ("The Kissed Mouth"), as the title indicates, puts the emphasis where it belongs. William says that "she had no charm of breeding, education, or intellect,"[19] and there were few to contradict him. Swinburne simply called her a "bitch."[20] The anecdotes of her throwing blue china at guests, or cracking nuts with her teeth, while they may be actually untrue, can hardly be entirely false to her character. Her grammar and accent were vulgar, and she must have been quite simple-minded, if we are to judge by Rossetti's letters to her. The following is representative:

> The first letter I got from you must have cost the Elephant an effort. It was the most beautiful specimen of handwriting you ever accomplished. I was most sincerely glad to hear that you thought Margate had benefited you. It was very nice of Mrs. Villiers to

take so much care of you, and I am pleased above all things to learn that your hearing is somewhat better.[21]

She seems to have been a prostitute before Rossetti knew her. In view of Rossetti's way of combining literature with life, and the Pre-Raphaelites' practice of finding the appropriate model in Nature, it is significant that Rossetti painted her first and often as a prostitute, and that Spenser Stanhope also painted her as such.[22] An acquaintance of Rossetti believed her to be the inspiration for *Jenny*, which Rossetti did indeed revise and enlarge upon meeting her. Her address before Rossetti knew her was a notorious one. The fact that Gabriel's friend George P. Boyce encountered her one evening alone in the Argyll Rooms, a place "of unsavory reputation," also speaks to her notoriety.[23]

This is the woman who became Rossetti's mistress,[24] and who remained "a kind of punctum indifferens . . . the one stable element"[25] relative to the other women of his life. Her staying power has always been a perplexing question, to Rossetti's friends as well as to later students of his life and work. Her obvious sexual attractions are only a partial answer, for the friendship lasted for twenty-five years, till both were over fifty years of age, and Rossetti was quite sickly.

Another reason is that she presented no problems. She was no Madonna, but then no one would be tempted to imagine her as such, as Rossetti was with Lizzie. Fanny's perpetual vulgarity served as a constant insurance against any inclinations of his to think her so. She effected no tension between heaven and earth, no frustration when the two would not become one. A sign that their relationship was completely terrestrial was his associating her constantly with animals rather than angels; I have already noted that his pet-name for her was "Elephant," and so he drew her in the little sketches that he sent in his letters to her.[26] In the mid-sixties, when he saw Fanny most frequently, he also had a small zoo in his back yard at 16 Cheyne Walk, where he kept wombats (his favorite animal), deer, a raccoon, a peacock, a zebu, armadillos, and kangaroos.[27] Much the same spirit may account for his acquisition of Fanny—another such animal, another pet.

Furthermore, Fanny lived up to Rossetti's fantasy of the sinful woman. There was no problem of counterparts, of fitting the human being to the fantasy, for it seems Fanny was indeed the fallen woman that she represented to him. The quality that set her apart from other prostitutes was her ready acceptance of moderate salvation; she allowed Rossetti to love her and not leave her, to rescue her in his own fashion. In 1858–1859, when their friendship first seemed really to take hold,[28] she moved from Dean Street to the more respectable Tennyson Street, Battersea; Doughty says that Rossetti "probably" covered the cost of the removal. And then, year after year, Gabriel put golden coins in her golden hair as his letters to her amply reveal:

" . . . you are the only person whom it is my duty to provide for, and you may be sure I should do my utmost as long as there was a breath in my body or a penny in my purse." "I am sure you must be needing a change, so I send you a cheque for travelling expenses." "Here is a little cheque to put in a little hole. I will send another little one soon." "I now send £20, and am sorry I cannot send more at present, but am beginning to get rather low. I shall be having more tin before long, however. How much have you put away altogether in the Elephant's hole now? I must try to send you some more for that purpose as soon as I can." "I am glad to hear you have such a pretty penny laid by." "Here is a little cheque for the Elephant to take up with its trunk for present necessities. I cannot as yet send more for the elephant's hole, but shall do so as soon as possible." "It strikes me that you may be in want of a small cheque for the poor Elephant's trunk, so I enclose a tiddy one."[29]

Things had a way of disappearing at 16 Cheyne Walk. Rossetti's friends and relatives suspected Fanny, but he, who was often quick to charge others with abusing him, almost never accused her. Perhaps he treated her thefts as just another way of contributing to her, for the quotations above expose his willingness and desire to do so. Giving to Fanny was a need, not a mere duty, for it was thus that his fantasy was satisfied.

Finally, Fanny presented no sexual problems. It is important to realize that both of Rossetti's fantasies were charged with sex, but, it seems, only the flesh-and-blood representative of the humbler one would permit him complete sexual expression. As a consequence of Fanny's compliance, Rossetti concentrated his sexual attentions on her rather than Lizzie. The works of this time drawn from Fanny emphasize the sensual, almost to the exclusion of all else, and those depicting heavenly women are purified of sex. Often when he painted Fanny it was as a prostitute, but he also depicted her with no ambient story, quite simply as an object of physical beauty. These works include *Bocca Baciata* (1859), a portrait (1862), *The Blue Bower* (1865), and *The Lady with a Fan* (1870). All of them (to which the adjective "sumptuous" is often applied) point directly to "the marvellous fleshliness of the flesh."[30] They do not *lead* anywhere—into consideration of dramatic situation or the thoughts and feelings of the lady. She is neither symbolic nor profound, without a past or a future. She is no more than what we can see—beautiful. All the paintings are heavy with an abundance of rich cloth and flowers, suggestive of Fanny's own natural splendors. Even the fantasy of the prostitute is left behind in these works, for the lust of the flesh, the lust of the eyes, and the pride of life are all that matter. A crusty critic from Liverpool called Rossetti "the greatest *animal* painter alive."[31] He was not wrong if these appealing canvases were the only ones he had in mind.

In *The Song of the Bower* (1860), which has Fanny as its subject (Swinburne said, "In fact, I may almost say I know it, from Gabriel's own admission."[32]), we find the same gusto, the same direct pleasure in sensuality:

> What were my prize, could I enter thy bower,
> This day, tomorrow, at eve or at morn?
> Large lovely arms and a neck like a tower,
> Bosom then heaving that now lies forlorn,
> Kindled with love-breath, (the sun's kiss is colder!)
> Thy sweetness all near me, so distant today;
> My hand round thy neck and thy hand on my shoulder,
> My mouth to thy mouth as the world melts away.

The absent lover's longing is drowned in the impassioned catalogue and in the exuberance of the uncharacteristic anapestic
meter. The poem's sheer joy in a woman recalls Fazio degli
Uberti's *Portrait of his Lady*, which Rossetti's portrait of Fanny,
Fazio's Mistress, illustrates. Rossetti translated the Italian poem,
which was one of his favorites. "Never," he said, "was beauty
better described."[33] Here is one stanza:

> I look at her white easy neck, so well
> From shoulders and from bosom lifted out;
> And at her round cleft chin, which beyond doubt
> No fancy in the world could have design'd.
> And then, with longing grown more voluble,
> "Were it not pleasant now," pursues my thought,
> "To have that neck within thy two arms caught
> And kiss it till the mark were left behind?"
> Then, urgently: "The eyelids of thy mind
> Open thou: if such loveliness be given
> To sight here,—what of that which she doth hide?
> Only the wondrous ride
> Of sun and planets through the visible heaven
> Tells us that there beyond is Paradise.
> Thus, if thou fix thine eyes,
> Of a truth certainly thou must infer
> That every earthly joy abides in her."

It is only "earthly joy," only the lady's body, that really matters;
the irreverent comparison of her hidden parts to Paradise is a
calculated impertinence born of high spirits. But when Rossetti
in *The Song of the Bower* speaks of "thy soul" and "my spirit"[34]
the result is less satisfactory, for there seems to be no awareness
of the disparity between the animal passion described and the
elevated conceptions suddenly thrust upon it. We appreciated
Rossetti's earlier attempts to equate heavenly joy with earthly
passion because that passion included consideration of the "spiritual" (that is, the inner life of the other party, "the holiness of
the heart's affections"); but now, when a love is described that
is concerned almost completely with bodies, we find the metaphysical vocabulary most out of place. The poem is a sign of
Rossetti's conceptual confusion. Yet it, as well as his translation

of Fazio and his "animal paintings" of Fanny, is admirable as a successful expression of erotic magnificence, of delight in the five senses.

In fine, Rossetti satisfied his sexual desires by turning to Fanny and other sinful women. His behavior was directed and controlled somewhat by his imagination, to which he was always greatly subject: he had produced a second fantasy of salvation in which the male lover was the savior, and the woman was raised from the evil street to happiness and respectability. The fantasy reflected his own great concern for feminine purity (it was necessary if his first fantasy were to be maintained), and his own generous nature. The prostitute Fanny satisfied both the sexual and the imaginative demands. But Fanny, obviously no more than mere woman at best, had nothing spiritual, soulful, or heavenly about her; so the Madonna remained in his imagination and works to supply his desires for the supramundane. Fanny's taking over the delights of the five senses as her own province caused his early union of body and soul, heavenly love and earthly love, to collapse. Although Rossetti himself did not realize it, body and soul were now divided.

CHAPTER FIVE

Dreamland Diversion

THESE celebrations of the body may be contrasted with contemporary works of Rossetti that celebrate soul. In the years when Fanny was first appearing in his work he was painting Lizzie too. Drawn from her are the faces of all the weeping queens tending King Arthur in the Vale of Avalon, in the woodcut for the Moxon edition of Tennyson (1856–1857); *The Damsel of the Sanc Grael* (1857); and *A Christmas Carol* (1857–1858). These works are reminiscent of the heavenly ladies described in Chapter Three, but there is a decided difference. Instead of the down-to-earth qualities that Rossetti insisted upon in his early poems and paintings of Beatrice and Mary, we find a mysteriousness, an ethereality, a sense of long ago and far away. The women are beautiful, but their distance renders any sexually motivated response to them inappropriate. In *A Christmas Carol*, where two ladies-in-waiting dress the hair of a damsel as she plays upon an ornate keyed instrument, the ladies direct our reaction to the painting through their own example. They have begun by attending to the beautiful hair, but under the influence of the music they fall to musing till each is completely lost in a world of her own making, and the hair, the coronet, and the keyboard are forgotten. Likewise, we, as we look at the painting, are to leave behind the beauty of the scene and the ladies to listen for the music or imagine the ladies' private thoughts. The movement of the painting is away from the here-and-now, away from the five senses. In this respect the work and those similar

A Christmas Carol
Courtesy of Fogg Art Museum, Harvard University (Bequest of
Grenville L. Winthrop)

to it are exactly opposite to the "animal paintings" of Fanny.

The three paintings of Lizzie form but a small part of a group of works that mark Rossetti's "romantic" period. This was the time (1856–1859) of his first and closest association with Edward Burne-Jones and William Morris, and it is the more surprising that the association, characterized by innocence, idealism, boyish pranks, and high spirits, shared his attentions with Annie Miller and Fanny Cornforth. The two undergraduate Oxonians admired Rossetti before they ever met him; in fact they pleased him mightily with a highly favorable review in the *Oxford and Cambridge Magazine*, an organ founded by them in imitation of the *Germ*. Burne-Jones, on a trip to London, met Rossetti towards the final week of 1855 and was thoroughly awed by him. The flattered Rossetti took him as a pupil, and "Ned," having lost his earlier desire for the Protestant priesthood, left Oxford for London. Morris joined them on weekends, and, when the architect for whom he was working moved to London in the fall of 1856, Morris did too. The two younger men occupied the quarters at Red Lion Square that Gabriel had shared with Walter Deverell five years earlier. The three, with Gabriel the dominant member of the group, now worked and played together daily with joyous enthusiasm. Burne-Jones spoke for all when he described 1856 as "a year in which I think it never rained, nor clouded, but was blue summer from Christmas to Christmas, and London streets glittered, and it was always morning, and the air sweet and full of bells."[1]

Rossetti offered the younger men artistic encouragement, and served their genuflective inclinations as an object for worship. He could cast a spell, and must have infected Burne-Jones and Morris greatly with his own enthusiasms. In turn there were things that they could offer him—flattery and unquestioning obedience, of course, but more important, youth and purity. Professor Doughty believes that their "enthusiasm of imaginative, idealistic adolescence revived [Rossetti's] own fading adolescent dream," and notes Rossetti's "breaking out into irresponsible gaiety [in their presence] as if, belatedly enough at twenty-nine, he were enjoying that undergraduate life which . . . he had never known."[2] Along with their youth he now shared, in their presence, a very rarefied attitude toward women and love. The shy, slender Burne-Jones, while at Oxford, had contemplated the foundation there of a celibate, almost monastic brotherhood of refined souls. He eventually married happily, but we learn in his wife's *Memorials* to him that she found a discreet pursuit necessary before he would wed. Burne-Jones described his design, *Love's Wayfaring*, as "Love and his overdriven steeds," and the gentle Georgiana confirms his view: "The figure of Love is exactly as he saw it first, expressing might only, and no pity."[3] William Rossetti says of him, "Burne-Jones was more truly morbid; in this sense—that he, in various instances, diffused an air of languor and quietism over subjects which, to an ordinary mind, are more suggestive of vivacity and ardour."[4] The more robust Morris was more interested in love and beautiful women, but shyness and chivalry combined to make him hold his distance, a worshipful beholder:

> I charge you straightly in this rime,
> What, and wherever you may be,
>
> . . . .
>
> To kneel before her; as for me,
> I choke and grow quite faint to see
> My lady moving graciously.
>
> *Praise of My Lady* (1857)

The story is told of a friend's repeatedly flushing him, late at night during his quiet courtship of Jane Burden, and always discovering only a somewhat bored Janey listening to Morris reading *Barnaby Rudge.*[5] Whether the presiding genius was that of Dante or Dickens, the respectful distance from the lady remained the same. The timid desire to remain aloof from physical encounter was hardly characteristic of Rossetti, but now he played the celibate along with his two younger friends.

Burne-Jones and Morris kept their distance, not only from sex, but from the here-and-now in general. At least Rossetti saw them as doing so. A few months after meeting Burne-Jones he described him to Allingham as "one of the nicest young fellows in—*Dreamland*. For there most of the writers in that miraculous piece of literature [i.e., *The Oxford and Cambridge Magazine*] seem to be."[6] Later he described him to Boyce as "an angel on earth and too good for this world."[7] Of his other friend Rossetti remarked, "The dreamy romantic really hardly needs more than one vast Morris in a literature—at any rate in a century."[8] Morris himself wrote, "My work is the embodiment of dreams in one form or another."[9]

Rossetti rejoiced in his friends' remoteness from life, but, as the quotations reveal, he correctly differentiated their attitudes from his own. I have observed that, before meeting them, he had been most anxious to have his dreams come to life; a vision of Beatrice or Jenny was frustrating until the counterpart from Nature was discovered. But Burne-Jones and Morris would rather dreamland had no openings onto actuality, for to them the dream was enough. Rossetti gleefully joined them in their escape to a medieval dreamland, but for him the attitude was an assumed and a temporary one. He wrote to Professor Norton in July 1858, "These chivalric Froissartian themes are quite a passion of mine,"[10] but four years later, in another letter to Professor Norton concerning the same painting, *Before the Battle*, he looked back on his "passion" condescendingly as an indulgence: "on mature consideration of the drawing, I myself think it rather ultra-medieval,—it having been produced during a solitary stay in the country of some length, at a time when I was peculiarly nourishing myself with such impressions."[11] The condescension is seen also in the remark of his friend William Sharp that Rossetti "always had an affection, based on the poetic sentiment, for what he termed his romantic in opposition to his later imaginative period."[12]

In spite of the difference between Rossetti and his two disciples in their uses of the imagination, he is commonly lumped with them in this respect, even by his best critics.[13] Rossetti joined the two Oxonians in their lotos-eating, but, as his comments reveal, it was they who taught him the practice. For him it was something of a lark, and soon he was back trying to fit real women to his fantasies. The attitudes attributed to Rossetti in the passages quoted in the notes were his, but only for a year or so, and even then only occasionally.

The paintings of this, his self-styled "romantic" period, are clearly different from his earlier works. A few of the more important titles are *The Palace of Art* (1856), *The Blue Closet* (1857; not to be confused with *The Blue Bower*), *The Tune of the Seven Towers* (1857), *The Wedding of St. George* (1857), *A Christmas Carol* (1857–1858), and *Before the Battle* (1858). The setting is always medieval, but not Dantesque. The importance of the distinction is that Dante and Beatrice were real people to Rossetti, whereas all the knights and the slender maidens of these paintings were completely and unquestionably imaginary. We can see from the way in which the ladies are painted that Rossetti had no intention of bringing them to life. They are all beautiful, but no care has been taken to give them individuality or personality. So indeterminately are they depicted that it would be hard to identify the models that posed for them. The features are drawn—eyes, nose, mouth—but no attention is paid to what is between them or behind them; there are no peculiarities or irregularities of skin, nor are the features composed to anything that could be called an expression. The effect is of feminine beauty rather than of a beautiful woman. For once Rossetti's women were as similar and as vague as those in the Italian poems of courtly love that he had translated.

While the ladies' features were indicated as simply as possible, the pictures themselves were not done in haste, for the canvases are crowded and elaborate. Great care is lavished on the costumes, furniture, and decorations. In *The Tune of the Seven Towers* (Marillier, opp. p. 80) a woman, for no obvious reason, leans into the chamber through a small, sliding window to place a branch of oranges upon a bed, and a pole holding a banner cuts diagonally across the foreground of the picture, somewhat obstructing our view. What is gained is a sense of crowding richness. In the woodcut, *The Palace of Art* (Marillier, p. 76), the background is composed of an entire siege: cannon and medieval instruments of war, castles, ships in the harbor, and pennants flying. In the left foreground a brutish spearsman gnaws an apple. In *The Wedding of St. George* the lovers' trance has for a background two angels playing on bells, and, in the foreground, a ludicrous, grotesque dragon's-head lying in a crude box that looks like an orange-crate. The grotesqueries of the last

The Wedding of St. George and Princess Sabra
Courtesy of The Tate Gallery, London

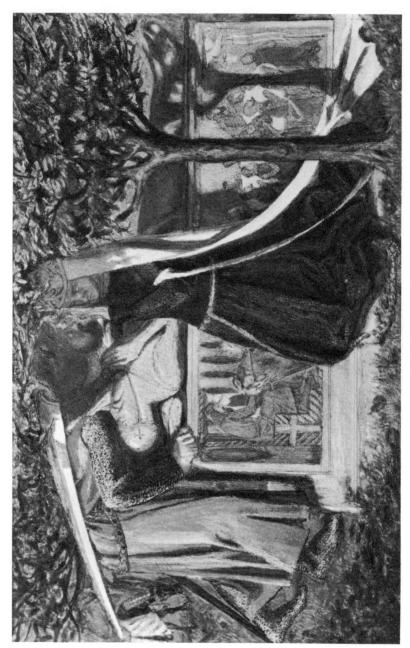

Arthur's Tomb, replica
Courtesy of The Tate Gallery, London

two paintings contrast with the ethereal ladies and refined emotions at the center of the works, but also, and quite simply, they contribute to the sense that anything can happen here, the sense of dreamlike unreality. So Rossetti prolonged the dream as he crowded the canvas, keeping always the fair lady at the center of the painting as nebulous as she had become in his own fantasies.

The music of *A Christmas Carol* pervades all the works. In *The Palace of Art* the Soul rests her fingers upon the keyboard of a small organ; the four ladies in *The Blue Closet* are singing and playing instruments; the lady in *The Tune of the Seven Towers* plucks strings of a sounding-board that is fitted to her chair. A bell-rope hangs by her side. In *The Wedding of St. George*, "angels creep in through sliding panel doors, and stand behind rows of flowers, drumming on golden bells."[14] The works carry their own musical background, which helps to cast the magical spell that pervades them. Like those in *A Christmas Carol*, the principal figures in all the works are motionless, entranced by the music or by their own thoughts.[15] I have already indicated Rossetti's association of inner feeling with the soul. For him the word, "soulful," meant just that, for a person of strong desires and deep thoughts did indeed possess this quality. Since music is the accompaniment to trances of deep thought in the principals of his paintings, we may consider music to be the sound of the soul, and its presence in a work of Rossetti to be indicative of soul.

Usually there is no concomitant story. Instead, the viewer is invited, in his musing over the work, to make up his own. In some of Rossetti's "romantic" works, however, there is enough of a plot implied to indicate a continued interest in the heavenly woman. Now she is revealed through Malory's tales of King Arthur, for Malory was the meeting-place for Rossetti, Burne-Jones, and Morris. Gabriel and the two undergraduates had come upon Malory independently,[16] and their common enthusiasm for him had helped to decide the friendship. Rossetti's concern with the heavenly woman is seen in *The Death of Arthur* (1856) where the king is surrounded by attentive queens; in *The Damsel of the Sanc Grael* (1857); *Sir Galahad Receiving the Sanc Grael;* and *Sir Galahad at the Shrine* (1857).

The love of Launcelot and Guenevere was the story from

Water-color version of *Launcelot at the Shrine of the Sanc Grael*
Courtesy of Ashmolean Museum, Oxford University

Malory that meant most to Rossetti, if one is to judge from the number and importance of his productions. As early as 1854 he had painted *Arthur's Tomb*, in which Launcelot, his shield awry, leans gracelessly across the effigy of Arthur as the kneeling Guenevere soberly resists him. The features and effect of the two figures resemble those of Lizzie and Gabriel himself in his humorous sketch, *Rossetti Sitting to Miss Siddal* (Marillier, p. 59), dated Sept. 1853. The likeness to Rossetti is especially noticeable, for there is the same hairy, humorous fury in both figures. Rossetti, identifying himself with Launcelot, may have been alluding in this work to Lizzie's refusing to let him carry out his illicit sexual desires. Like Launcelot he cut an awkward figure, being caught between his desires and his scruples, as Launcelot here is caught between the branches of the living, fruitful tree and the cold marble of the tomb.

During his association with Burne-Jones and Morris, Rossetti made a woodcut for Moxon's Tennyson, *The Lady of Shallot* (1856–1857), in which Launcelot is gazing into the face of the dead Lady; a pen-and-ink design for the Oxford Union, *Launcelot Escaping from Guenevere's Chamber* (1857); and *Launcelot at the Shrine of the Sanc Grael* (1857). The last is the most important of the works about Launcelot, and the only other one I shall discuss. It, too, was designed for the walls of the Oxford Union, which Rossetti, Burne-Jones, Morris, and several other young artists and would-be artists had undertaken to decorate in tempera with Arthurian motifs. Because of their ignorance of the proper preparation of brick surfaces for paint, their works soon faded and crumbled from the walls.[17] Rossetti described his design to Professor Norton as

> Sir Launcelot prevented by his sin from entering the chapel of the Sanc Grail. He has fallen asleep before the shrine full of angels, and, between him and it, rises in his dream the image of Queen Guenevere, the cause of all. She stands gazing at him with her arms extended in the branches of an apple-tree.[18]

The snake and Eve are confounded in Guenevere, for the sin that stands in the way of salvation is sexual temptation. Again body and soul are divided; Guenevere with the apple is opposed to the Ancilla Sanc Grail crowned in light and accompanied by a choir of singing angels.

We must relate the work to Rossetti's own situation with care. Professor Baum believes that "it takes no great power of imagination to see Fanny in the role of Guenevere standing 'in the branches of the Tree of Temptation, with the apple in her hand' (so Lady Burne-Jones phrases it), coming between Gabriel and Lizzie."[19] But it does take imagination, even more than Rossetti had, to see Fanny as a queen. The first model for Guenevere was not Fanny, but Lizzie, and Lizzie had already served for Guenevere in *Arthur's Tomb*. Since models meant something to Rossetti, a better interpretation might be that the physical presence of Lizzie in his life, and his attraction to her, stood in the way of his search for his true Madonna.[20] For the first time Lizzie and the heavenly lady were differentiated and opposed.

He soon left Oxford to go to the side of his sick fiancée, and even before he left he had found another model for Guenevere, a "soulful," dark-haired girl named Jane Burden. There is more of her later. It suffices for now to speculate that Rossetti had come to suspect that Lizzie was not his Beatrice, and contrasted her human qualities with the rarefied, angelic qualities of the Madonna of his dreams. In drawing Lizzie as a sensuous temptress he certainly falsified her, a fact that may account for his substituting a new model. Sins of the flesh pertained more to Fanny, whom, however, he did not use as model for Guenevere, perhaps because of her unqueenliness, because he was careful to keep her and her fantasy out of his dreams of salvation, or because the perpetually frustrating Lizzie was the more satisfying scapegoat for his failure to achieve his desires.

Rossetti's association with Burne-Jones and Morris served as a counterbalance to his affairs of the flesh, affairs undertaken in part, it would seem, to escape the problem of trying to see Lizzie as the living counterpart to his ideal Beatrice. Association with Burne-Jones and Morris was also an escape from the same problem, for their medieval "dreamland" was a simple flight from actuality, with no backward glances after counterparts in everyday life. Using their practices for his own purposes, he withdrew from Nature his fantasy of heavenly salvation to where it was born, deep in his imagination. His paintings in this, his "romantic" period were of rarefied, remote medieval maidens in musical trances, signifying soul. They were directly opposite to his "animal paintings" of Fanny, which emphasized the "marvelous fleshliness of the flesh." The contrast, dramatized in *Launcelot Before the Shrine*, indicates the division for him of "body" and "soul" as components of feminine beauty, for in his earlier works he had insisted upon the unity of the two qualities.

Like the paintings of Fanny's physical beauty, some of the escapist, "romantic" paintings do not assume a story as background. When they do, however, they bring Rossetti back to his old problem of finding his heavenly lady. His paintings of Launcelot and Guenevere suggest impatience with Lizzie and guilty self-accusations for his sins of the flesh. His changing models for Guenevere and his omitting of Fanny may indicate his own confusion, as may his misapplying the words "spirit" and "soul" in *The Song of the Bower*. Self-pity and irritation at his own inability to set things straight is evident in a letter of July 1858 to Professor Norton. Referring to Professor Norton's home, he observed that

> Your "Shady Hill" is a tempting address, where one would wish to be. It reminds one somehow of the *Pilgrim's Progress* where the pleasant names of Heavenly places really make you feel as if you could get there if the journey could only be made in that very way,—the pitfalls plain to the eye and all the wicked people with wicked names. I find no shady hill or vale, though, in these places and pursuits which I have to do with. It seems all glare and change, and nothing well done.[21]

No longer was Gabriel clearly a Dante at the beginning of his journey through hell to heaven, facing

> il dilettoso monte
> ch'è principio e cagion di tutta gioia
>
> *Inferno*, I, 77–78

No longer was he clearly Moses upon "the hill summit" preparing for a descent to the evil street. What had started so simply as a search for Beatrice was bogged down in a morass of names and faces, and one could hardly tell virtue from vice.

CHAPTER SIX

The Victimized Woman

I

THE two fantasies that I have described—that of Beatrice and that of Jenny—are the two optimistic fantasies of elevation, which Rossetti tried to seek out and realize in his life. But pessimistic versions of the two fantasies would impose themselves upon his imagination and life without his asking. These two retrograde fantasies may be called the theme of Ophelia or the victimized woman, and the theme of Lilith or the femme fatale. In the first the lover destroys the beloved, and in the second the beloved destroys the lover.

It is altogether probable that Rossetti would have developed some form of the two fantasies of degradation even if his own experiences had not encouraged them. In fact he did depict victimized ladies and femmes fatales long before his life gave him reason to do so. And many of the sentiments characteristic of the fantasies—namely, guilt, self-accusation, sexual desire, and regrets for the past—occur as well in the poetry of Christina, who, one may reasonably assume, had no comparable experiences. It seems that Gabriel, like Christina, had an innate tendency to express these feelings. But I hope to show in the course of this chapter and the next that his tendency was emphasized, directed, and qualified by actual events.

The facts of Rossetti's later life come close to the two fantasies of degradation. First, he helped to drive Lizzie to her death, or so he feared. Their dismal story is familiar: he finally married her in the spring of 1860 at a time when she seemed very ill. Conscious of his wrongdoing toward her, and expecting her death, he guiltily rushed her to the altar before she could fall into the grave[1]—an act reminiscent of his ballad, *Stratton Water*. Lizzie rallied somewhat, and, after a honeymoon in France, they returned to Gabriel's old unhealthy quarters at Chatham Place. His fears for her temporarily subsided. Meanwhile Fanny Cornforth was suffering over Rossetti's marriage. Boyce wrote of Fanny on June 5, "It appears she frets constantly about R., who is with his wife in Paris, the latter very ill and in a deep decline. Altogether a most melancholy state of things. F. was seeing a doctor and was in a very nervous, critical state."[2] She was not inconsolable, however, for soon after his return Gabriel was painting her again, this time as *Fair Rosamund*, the mistress of Henry II, and the bitterly hated rival of his wife, Queen Eleanor. With Lizzie's pregnancy there was hope for a while of a greater happiness, but when she was delivered of a dead daughter matters worsened. The shock encouraged her morbid and hysterical tendencies to the point of mental breakdown.[3] There are stories of her rocking an empty cradle, silencing others lest they waken her child; and her wandering abruptly away from homes where she was visiting without a departing word to her hosts. She found drugs necessary to obtain sleep, and drank laudanum in large quantities. On February 10, 1862 she died from an overdose of the drug, taken while Gabriel was away from home, possibly even while he was with Fanny.[4] Her act was probably intentional.[5] There is food to nourish scandal here, but it is sufficient to quote Hall Caine's very general account of the whole marriage. Caine claims that Rossetti confessed the following to him: Rossetti's story was that of

> . . . a man who, after engaging himself to one woman in all honour and good faith, had fallen in love with another, and then gone on to marry the first out of a mistaken sense of loyalty and a fear of giving pain instead of stopping, as he must have done if his will had been stronger and his heart sterner, at the door of the church itself. It would be the figure of a man who realised that the good woman he had married was reading his secret in spite of his

Fair Rosamund (Fanny Cornforth)
Permission of The National Museum of Wales, Cardiff

efforts to conceal it, and thereby losing all joy and interest in life. It would be the figure of a man who, coming home late at night to find his wife dying, probably by her own hand, was overwhelmed with remorse, not perhaps for any unkindness, any want of attention, still less for any act of infidelity on his part, but the far deeper wrong of failure of affection for the one being to whom affection was most due.[6]

The account probably flatters Rossetti more than he deserves ("*still less* any act of infidelity" is suspect), but it does report Rossetti's uneasy suspicion that Lizzie had killed herself largely because of his misdeeds.

Rossetti's subsequent life is no more cheerful a story. His feelings of guilt made him miserable, and their consequences led him to degradation and probably hastened his death. The first few years after Lizzie's suicide were spent in frenetic activity[7]— painting, travelling, drinking, dining out, and collecting animals and objects d'art (including the blue china soon to become the rage). The conviviality is easily seen as an attempt to escape from troubles. Georgiana Burne-Jones, whose observations are trustworthy, said that "he seemed to wear a surcoat of jesting,"[8] a superficial covering for a predominantly unhappy nature. Eventually his guilty conscience caught up with him, taking the form, in 1867, of a terrible chronic insomnia, of which his brother William said, "I consider that painful thoughts, partly but not wholly connected with his wife and her death, were at the root of it. . . . His active imagination gave him no respite. . . ."[9] The worst was not the sleeplessness but the accompanying self-accusations that found him when he ceased from distracting activity and lay defenseless. In acknowledging a complimentary copy of *Fifty Modern Poems* by his friend William Allingham, he reported that "they fared well with me, for I read them one evening right through when I felt much in want of other voices than some plaguey ones from inside and outside. . . ."[10] The "plaguey voices" seem to have been a nightly experience. In his feelings of guilt he lost some command of his imagination, as is indicated by the versicle written in 1871,

I shut myself in with my soul,
And the shapes come eddying forth.

The "voices" and "shapes," in the extreme, became definite hallucinations. On at least two occasions, for example, he believed that birds spoke to him accusingly, once with the voice of Lizzie.[11]

To escape from the "voices" and "shapes" into sleep, he took to drink and the drug chloral, to which he became addicted. When the drug became ineffective for bringing sleep, he increased the dosage. Both chloral and insomnia were his companions for the remaining twenty years of his life. Twice he came near to suicide. In 1869, according to Scott, Rossetti almost leapt from a ledge into the "Devil's Punchbowl," a black whirlpool at the base of a ravine.[12] In June 1872 he unsuccessfully attempted suicide from an overdose of laudanum, the very drug by which his wife had brought about her end.[13] At both times Lizzie was much on his mind.[14] Thus the dead Lizzie, a posthumous femme fatale, was driving Gabriel close to his own death. The facts may sound melodramatic, but they are indeed the facts of Rossetti's life.

As usual there appears to be interplay between fact and appropriate fantasies. In comparatively few works Rossetti effected a combination of the two fantasies of degradation, where lover and lady share a mutual destruction. William Rossetti recorded in the *P. R. B. Journal* for November 18, 1849, "Gabriel began at his design for Paolo and Francesca."[15] We see, then, that Gabriel took an interest in a story of double damnation even before he met Elizabeth Siddal. The attraction probably lay in the plain fact that the story was Dante's. No further work was done on the theme until 1854, when an unfinished study in pencil was made, and then in 1855, when, to earn some quick money for a trip to Paris, he made a triptych[16] in water-colors within a week (see Marillier, opp. p. 66 for 1862 replica). It shows in one compartment the first kiss of the two lovers, and in the last their two embracing souls adrift in hell. The vigorous love in the one is more evident than the suffering in the other. Rossetti himself must have recognized the greater success of the first, for in 1861 he painted a more elaborate version of the first compartment only. This, the most successful version, places greater emphasis upon the heedlessness of their love (the Book

Paolo and Francesca
Courtesy of The National Gallery of Victoria, Melbourne, Australia

of Launcelot is falling from Paolo's lap onto the floor, and the flowers have fallen from Francesca's hands). Their blind and helpless passion is to be contrasted with the strict, formal order of the rest of the scene. The painting loses none of its meaning in the absence of a second compartment, for the whole story is alluded to in the title, and implied in the symbolism. Still another painting of the story followed in 1862, this a replica of the first water-color.

I have already had occasion to mention *How They Met Themselves*, in which a couple meet their ghostly doubles in an encounter portentous of death. Rossetti drew the subject twice, shortly after meeting Lizzie in 1851, and again on their honeymoon in 1860. According to William, the female figures were done from her.[17] In 1864 there were two replicas in water-color.

A third story that Rossetti undertook to paint was that of *Sir Tristram and La Belle Yseult drinking the Love Potion*, done in ink in 1862. A replica was made in water-color in 1867. Finally there was *Paetus and Arria*, a design in pencil made in 1872 for an unexecuted picture.

All of the works except the first ones of *Paolo and Francesca* can be directly applied to Gabriel and Lizzie. Four of the pictures were executed in the two years of their marriage, or within a few months of it. Four more belong to the guilty years that follow. Thus, perhaps, did Rossetti express his premonitions and beliefs that their love was a maleficent one, that they were destined to destroy themselves or each other. In a way the works are Rossetti's self-exoneration, for the love of Dante's lovers is beautiful and powerful, and the destruction of Tristram and Yseult and the pair in *How They Met Themselves* is beyond their control. There is no accusation, just pity. The epigraph for all might be the simple "O Lasso!" that Rossetti puts in the mouth of Dante in the triptych.

The latest of these works, the *Paetus and Arria* (Marillier, p. 169), is somewhat different, and it is especially notable for its clear relationship to Rossetti's life. The story is that of the noble Roman wife who, when her husband hesitates to kill himself when sentenced to death, mortally stabs herself and hands him the dagger, saying, "Paetus, it does not hurt me." The year of the drawing is the year of Rossetti's attempted suicide, and the drawing takes on even more significance in the light of his wife's successful suicide, his own earlier hesitation upon its brink, and his attempt to kill himself by using his wife's very "weapon." Perhaps Rossetti was expressing his admiration for Lizzie, and acceptance of suicide. Perhaps there was an admission of his own greater weakness, and a suggestion that if he were to end his life, all would be made right, and his wife's spirit would approve. In the absence of the completed work, or similar works at the time, it is difficult to say exactly what facet of the old story caught his eye, but the coincidences with his own life reveal that he made the personal application.

II

In the fantasy of the victimized woman, each of the two characters—the lady and the lover—figures forth a peculiar concern. The lady tries to reconcile feminine purity with all-too-human behavior, and the lover expresses guilt, either for seducing the lady, or for playing her false—for tormenting her through neglect, discourtesy, or unfaithfulness. One or the other of these related concerns, and sometimes both, are met with in each of the poems and paintings to be discussed.

The Bride's Prelude was begun in 1847 and added to sporadically, but left unfinished. In it the delicate, soulful Aloÿse, within an hour of her wedding, opens her heart to her sister, Amelotte. She has surrendered to the illicit desires of Urscelyn, a squire in her father's service, having borne a child by him after his flight from her and her father in a time of need. Now, with his return in fair weather, her family is about to force her to marry her faithless and loathed lover. Here the narrative breaks off, in large part because Rossetti did not know how to continue the plot.[18] Another reason for not continuing was that the basic concern of the poem, that of reconciling an apparent innocence with sinful sexual behavior, had already been fully treated in the terms of the poem. The concern, more interesting than the rather commonplace plot, is almost exactly the same as that of *A Last Confession*, which was begun at approximately the same time.[19]

The paradox of sinful purity is indicated in the situation of the poem. Aloÿse is a bride, but she is also an unwed mother. Like Jenny she is simultaneously "so pure,—so fall'n!" Her innocence is maintained despite her behavior by giving her an extremely weak and passive nature. As she awaits her wedding, "the whole day's weight / Lay back on her like lead." She indicates her physical weakness by fainting, and by complaining to her sister,

> the sun
> Sheds judgment-fire from the fierce south:
> It does not let me breathe: the drouth
> Is like sand spread within my mouth.
>
> I am not blithe and strong like thee.

And her weakness at the time of her seduction was even greater:

> The last bird's cry upon mine ear
> Left my brain weak, it was so clear.
>
> i' the autumn noon
> My feeble brain whirled like a swoon.

The seduction was foreshadowed and prepared for by an incident with sexual implications: Aloÿse was made to ride to the hunt, but was thrown from her horse and injured. In her weakened condition she was even less able to defend herself from Urscelyn's advances:

> He craved my pardon first,—all else
> Wild tumult.
>
> what grace his lips did crave
> I know not, but I know I gave.

Thus Rossetti presents her as physically and emotionally powerless to resist the sin, with her knowledge of her own act obfuscated by her emotional "tumult."[20]

We see that Rossetti's earliest work portraying a victimized woman grew from the same impulses that produced his Jennys: the attempt to reconcile the pure appearance of a soulful, beautiful woman with her bad behavior ("Oh Hill, you could never hang a stunner!" exclaimed Rossetti in 1857[21]). The treatment of the problem in *The Bride's Prelude* is probably his most primitive, for here Rossetti refused even to admit the sin, although admitting the act. Here there is really no pollution from which to save Aloÿse. Although she is being destroyed she has never been degraded; she has never really "fallen," in the most important sense of the word.

With time Rossetti's interest shifted from the seeming guilt of the lady to the guilt of the lover in deserting her. The story that gave form to his concerns was that of Hamlet and Ophelia, a favorite of Rossetti's artistic friends. In 1850 Walter Deverell had made a design for *The Converse of Laertes and Ophelia*.[22] Two years later Millais executed his famous *Ophelia*, with Lizzie the model; and Arthur Hughes did an *Ophelia*, exhibited in the same year.[23] Rossetti probably took the association of Lizzie with Ophelia from Millais,[24] beginning his pen-and-ink *Hamlet and Ophelia* in 1854, and returning to complete it in 1858. The drawing was considered by Rossetti to be one of his most intricate intellectual conceptions; "deeply symbolic and far-sighted, of course,"[25] he described it, in August 1854, with tongue falsely in cheek, and almost exactly twenty-five years later he said, "the Hamlet subject has a lot of accessory meanings."[26] In fact the drawing is a remarkable adaptation of the story to his own situation.

The setting for the drawing is Act III Scene 1 (quoted text Kittredge ed.), in which the spurned Ophelia is returning her gifts to Hamlet. The scene interested him with good reason, for it contains several remarks dealing with his concern expressed in *The Bride's Prelude*, the relationship of beauty to purity. The Queen makes the connection when she tells Ophelia,

> . . . your good beauties be the happy cause
> Of Hamlet's wildness. So shall I hope your virtues
> Will bring him to his wonted way again.

Some lines later Hamlet tells Ophelia that the two qualities do not go together easily:

Hamlet and Ophelia (1854–1858)
Courtesy of the Trustees of The British Museum, London

the power of beauty will sooner transform honesty from what it is to a bawd than the force of honesty can translate beauty into his likeness.

Included in Hamlet's feigned criticism of her is genuine self-accusation:

I am myself indifferent honest; but yet I could accuse me of such things that it were better my mother had not borne me. . . . What should such fellows as I do, crawling between earth and heaven?

And not only these passages from *Hamlet* but the dramatic situation in general is reflective of Rossetti's position, for he, like Hamlet, was encouraging his beloved against his own will to madness and suicide.

The drawing suggests that it is Ophelia who is spurning Hamlet rather than vice versa. She sits with her head thrown back and away in an offish pose characteristic of Lizzie. Hamlet is all tenderness and suffering, his left hand describing a gesture of futility. He, more than Ophelia, is expressive of grief, and he dominates the composition, embracing our attention in his open arms.

The work contains much symbolism not found in the play, symbolism more indicative of Hamlet's than of Ophelia's situation and mind, and even more of Rossetti's. The stalls of the oratory, upon which Hamlet leans, are decorated with carvings in wood. One panel is of the fatal tree of Eden, entwined by the snake. Adjoined to the panel are the words, *Eritis sicut deus scientes bonum et malum.* Another panel is of Uzzah, "the man who touched the ark and died."[27] Rossetti meant the scenes on these panels to be "symbols of rash introspection."[28] The forbidden knowledge upon which Rossetti's Hamlet cogitates is sexual knowledge in particular. The Tree of the Knowledge of Good and Evil, it will be remembered, appears also in *Launcelot at the Shrine*, a design on which Rossetti was still working when he finished *Hamlet and Ophelia*. In the design for the Oxford Union, Guenevere, the sexual temptress, stands in the tree, proffering an apple. Her stance is remarkably like that of Hamlet here:

Hamlet and Ophelia (1866)
Courtesy of Mr. Kerrison Preston

her arms are likewise extended, and her hands are similar in attitude.

Furthermore, Hamlet, like her, grasps a tree in his right hand: here, a rose-bush. The rose was used consistently by Rossetti as a symbol for sexual passion: for example, the roses in the hair of the harlots in *Hesterna Rosa;* the title of the painting of Fanny, *Fair Rosamond;* the lines from *Jenny,*

> But must your roses die, and those
> Their purfled buds that must unclose?
> Even so; the leaves are curled apart,
> Still red as from the broken heart,
> And here's the naked stem of thorns . . .

Finally there are the following lines from the sonnet written to reflect *Mary Magdalene at the Door of Simon,* a painting executed in the same year as *Hamlet and Ophelia.* The Magdalene's sinful lover speaks:

> Why wilt thou cast the roses from thine hair?
> Nay, be thou all a rose . . .

Both the tree of temptation and the rose-bush meant sexuality to Rossetti, and he took the liberty with Shakespeare's text to load it upon his own Hamlet. Love-passion is only one aspect among many in Shakespeare's play, and even in this scene, yet it dominates Rossetti's drawing.

As a result of the modifications of Shakespeare's portrayal of Hamlet, the story was brought closer to Rossetti's own situation, that of a self-conscious, sexually guilty lover unhappily rejecting an innocent beloved whom he was indirectly but unquestionably destroying. On the one hand (in the picture, quite literally so) there was sexual knowledge, destructive and self-destructive; on the other, separated from Hamlet by the sword of chastity, was the pure lady, only a bud as the design on her dress indicates, who was likewise a cause for grief, for she was being destroyed along with the guilty. If Hamlet were to touch her he could only destroy her as he does the rose-bush; yet she, in turning away from her baneful lover, is destroyed in part by the severance. Their predicament may be symbolized by the two oscillating staircases in the background, touching and drawing apart, yet never becoming one. Lizzie's ensuing madness and suicide show how uncannily successful Rossetti was in adapting a literary analogy to reflect their predicament.

In 1866, four years after Lizzie had proved him prophetic, he painted an entirely new study of the same situation.[29] Hamlet holds Ophelia's hand tenderly in both of his, a pose for which Shakespeare offers no textual support. There is no sign of the cruel joking that Hamlet directs against her in the play. Ophelia is obviously drawn from Rossetti's memory of Elizabeth, and she is far more prominent relative to the rest of the design than she was in the earlier work. Her bright face and clothes dominate the somber colors of the rest of the canvas. There are only the lovers, the gifts, and Ophelia's book; all of the interjected symbols are absent. It is as if Rossetti were uneasy at having taken up so much of the earlier work with his own self and his problems, and therefore dedicated a new canvas to the celebration of Lizzie's old griefs, which, he felt, he had wrongfully subordinated. Accordingly, Ophelia's reluctant rejection of her lover is painted in a spirit of great sympathy and delicacy. The epigraph chosen is not that of the first design, Hamlet's mordacious "I did love you once," but the later remark whose sting is all self-directed: "What should such fellows as I do crawling between earth and heaven?"

In the meantime, in 1864, there was another painting of Ophelia. The chosen subject was an apt one, *The Madness of Ophelia*, taken from Act IV Scene v, where the crazed girl is strewing flowers, as Horatio[30] leads her away from the bewildered King and horrified Queen. The model for Ophelia was indirectly Lizzie, for there is an undisputed similarity in features, attitude, and dress between the Ophelia and Horatio of this work and the Belle Dame and her "wretched wight" in Rossetti's water-color, *La Belle Dame sans Merci* (the version of 1855), for which Lizzie did pose.[31] The similarity in the two works of different subject has caused speculation upon whether or not the earlier work was originally meant to be a representation of Ophelia and then retitled. This is a matter that need not concern us, but the plain fact that Rossetti associated the two stories is suggestive and important.

The factor common to the two stories is that both Ophelia and the Belle Dame, with her "wild wild eyes," are, if not deranged, at least spiritually estranged from all others. And some of the feeling relevant primarily to the poem of Keats (in which the Belle Dame's frenzy harms her lover, and not, like that of Ophelia, herself) finds its way into the later painting. The conflation of the two heroines gives more significance to the horror in the attitude of the Queen in *The Madness of Ophelia;* the mad girl is not only pitiful but frightful, and one draws back from her in fear of harm. Ophelia becomes something of a femme fatale, if only in Rossetti's guilty mind, just as his destroyed Lizzie, in 1864, was apparently beginning to haunt him. Pity and fear were joined for him too.

This speculation is strongly supported by Rossetti's excellent little ballad, *An Old Song Ended* (1869):

> "*How should I your true love know*
> *From another one?*"
> "*By his cockle-hat and staff*
> *And his sandal-shoon.*"
>
> . . . .
>
> "For a token is there nought,
> Say, that he shall bring?"
> "He will bear a ring I gave,
> And another ring."
>
> "How may I, when he shall ask,
> Tell him who lies there?"
> "Nay, but leave my face unveiled
> and unbound my hair."
>
> "Can you say to me some word
> I shall say to him?"
> "Say I'm looking in his eyes
> Though my eyes are dim."

Rossetti's poem is directly related to *Hamlet*, for the "old song" that constitutes the first stanza is one that the mad Ophelia

The Madness of Ophelia
Courtesy of The Oldham Art Gallery and Museum, Oldham, England

sings in the scene just referred to, Act IV Scene v. Rossetti's continuation of the song makes it clear that he still had Lizzie in mind, much as in his pictures upon *Hamlet*. True to Shakespeare's implication,[32] he gives the "true love" two rings, symbolic of two loves; and Lizzie, like the lady of the song, had had an unfaithful "true love." The lady, like Lizzie, dies in his absence, and perhaps because of his absence. The lady, about to die, calls attention to her "unbound" hair as a mark by which her false lover will know her. In the year that Rossetti wrote the poem, Lizzie was exhumed for the recovery of his poems in manuscript, which he had dramatically buried with her seven years before, and there were rumors after the recovery of how her red hair had grown after death, filling the coffin.[33] The poem's last two lines, which, ironically, come close to being words of comfort, are a prediction of horrible hauntings to the old lover, and similarly the accounts of Lizzie must have tormented Gabriel. Again Lizzie is associated with a heroine who is both Ophelia and Belle Dame sans Merci—that is, both victimized and vengeful.

The frightful stare is even more explicit in the closing lines of "A Superscription" (*House of Life* XCVII), also written in 1869:

> But should there dart
> One moment through thy soul the soft surprise
> Of that winged Peace which lulls the breath of sighs—
> Then shalt thou see me smile, and turn apart
> Thy visage to mine ambush at thy heart
> Sleepless with cold commemorative eyes.

There are hints in the sonnet that indicate the corpse of Lizzie, lying in its coffin, as the imaginary speaker:

> Look in my face; my name is Might-have-been;
> I am also called No-more, Too-late, Farewell
> . . . .
> Mark me, how still I am . . .

William says of the sonnet, "Chiefly, the sense of loss in the death of one supremely beloved is referred to . . . ."[34] The hide-

ous image of a dead one coming maliciously to life lends substance to the threat at the end of the poem. Because of the
implied image there is a frightful concreteness not found in
William's paraphrase, "Sense of loss is spoken of as remaining
comparatively dull and passive . . . but as reasserting itself with
direful force at moments when the soul feels beguiled into happiness or contentment." The specific moment from which his
dead wife was keeping Rossetti was that of love forgetful of her:

> But should there dart
> One moment through thy soul the soft surprise
> Of that winged Peace which lulls the breath of sighs . . .

This is an allusion to Love, Dante's *pace d'amore*.[35] Thus did the
woman victimized by her love retaliate upon love. Ophelia was
joined by the Belle Dame sans Merci to form a conception
worthy to reflect Rossetti's own feelings toward Lizzie: tender
pity, and guilty terror at those "cold commemorative eyes."

A year later Rossetti's "mind was full"[36] with a prose "cartoon" for a long ballad to be called *Michael Scott's Wooing*. He
had already made several drawings with this title,[37] one as
early as 1848–1849. All are scenes in which Michael woos
his maiden by conjuring magical pageants of delight. Rossetti, more taken by the title than the scene (a Michael Scott,
about whom almost nothing is known, appears among the
black magicians in Dante's "Inferno"), failed in several attempts to conceive a satisfactory story suited to the name. In
1870 he succeeded by adapting a story related to him by Theodore Watts-Dunton, who had heard it from a Welsh gipsy
girl.[38] It is easy to see why Rossetti would be interested in the
story: Michael Scott's beloved, Janet, drawn to him by his
magic and her love for him, yet protective of her purity, per-
ishes under "the struggle of her heart." Michael, in the midst
of magical practices upon her love, sees her spirit rush by him
in the night and throw itself to the waves. Janet's dead body
is found in her room, "turned violently round as if in the act
of rising from her bed [to go to Michael], she had again thrown
herself backward and clasped the feet of a crucifix at her bed-

head. . . . " She is another Ophelia to a sexual Hamlet, another lady destroyed by her innocent love for a harmful man. As in all of Rossetti's later portrayals of the victimized woman there are indications of a reflexive destruction: Michael Scott hears a threat similar to those at the end of *An Old Song Ended* and *A Superscription:* "The fiend who whispers this concerning her says also in my ear how surely I am lost."

Finally, in the following year, 1871, Rossetti wrote the poem, \Rose Mary, in which the victimized girl gains a triumph greater than the token one of wreaking vengeance upon the man who has ruined her. Rose Mary is rather an Aloÿse than an Ophelia, for in her love for Sir James she has given herself to him. The two elements of her name indicate that Rossetti is dealing with his old problem, that of reconciling in the same beautiful woman sexual sin with holiness. The plot of the poem turns on the traditional device of the Beryl-stone, a magical globe that tells the truth solely to the pure. Rose Mary's mother, not suspecting her daughter's lapse, causes her to read the stone for news of danger to Sir James. Because of Rose Mary's sin, evil spirits have charge of the stone, and they give false information that leads to Sir James's death. Rose Mary is thus punished for her lapse, even though her sin "was for love alone."

For a change the onus for the downfall of the lady does not rest upon the guilty male entirely. Her enemy is the stone itself, as the first two lines of the poem make clear: "Of her two fights with the Beryl-stone: / Lost the first but the second won." Eventually Rose Mary herself sees the stone to be the villain of the piece:

> And lo! for that Foe whose curse far-flown
> Had bound her life with a burning zone,
> Rose Mary knew the Beryl-stone.

The stone is her enemy because it, or the evil spirits that inhabit it, insist upon the sinfulness of acts of love, and punish them. The evil spirits remark that it is they who "had frought her" with "the soil of sin," and it is they who boast, "Lo! have not We leashed the twin / Of endless Sorrow to Sin . . . ?" They, in short, are responsible for the fact that illicit love means "Death and sorrow and sin and shame," and the Beryl-stone stands for that fact. It is because of the stone, then, that Rose Mary is "held in the hand of some heavy law," which makes life miserable for her on earth, and offers her no better fate after death than that of Paolo and Francesca:

> With him thy lover 'neath Hell's cloud-cover to fly,—
> > Hopeless, yet not apart,
> > > Cling heart to heart,
> And beat through the nether storm-eddying winds together.

Rose Mary might well have exclaimed, with the Wife of Bath, "Alas, alas, that ever love was sin!" But unlike the Wife she does something about it: exclaiming, "Love, for thy sake! In Thy Name, O God!" she cleaves the Beryl with a sword, releasing herself from that "heavy law." The devil's forces are driven out, God is triumphant, and Rose Mary, destroyed by her act, is accorded a martyr's place among the blessed in heaven.

There is a good deal of glissando here, but Rossetti's intent is plain enough: the forces of evil are associated with the whole system of good and evil that considers acts of love to be criminal. With the rebellious stroke of the sword she destroys the old "heavy law," and finds herself in a new order, to be identified with the forces of good, where her old sin becomes an act of righteousness. The God of the Ten Commandments assumes the airs of Cupid, leading her to his "Heaven of Love" with the words,

> > Thee, true soul, shall thy truth prefer
> To blessed Mary's rose-bower:
> Warmed and lit is thy place afar
> With guerdon-fires of the sweet Love-star
> Where hearts of steadfast lovers are:—

In the heaven of the Blessed Damozel, where the acts of true love are the works of saints, the two elements of her name become one in sanctity.

Hardly justified and inevitable, the reconciliation was more

Rossetti's pious hope, or arbitrary act of will. He treated the conclusion of the poem rather cavalierly in a letter to Scott, saying that he found the plot "so consummately tragic that I have been obliged to modify the intended course of the catastrophe to avoid an unmanageable heaping up of the agony."[39] Although the concerns of the poem meant more to him than he would confess to Scott, the letter truly reveals that the conclusion was forced upon the poem in an arbitrary manner. He could permit Rose Mary to wipe out with the stroke of her sword all considerations of sex as sin, but the considerations continued to weigh heavily upon him. His reaction to Robert Buchanan's charges of "fleshliness" that appeared in print almost within hours of the completion of this poem[40] is sufficient evidence of this fact. Rose Mary notwithstanding, his conception of love was just not compatible with his conception of sin, and he had no magical sword to set them right.

In keeping with the pattern of the rest of the works reflecting this fantasy, there may be something of Rossetti's own unfaithfulness in Rose Mary's lover, Sir James, who was secretly escaping to meet another lady when killed. Sir James' sin is a double one, for to the sin of loving is added that of leaving. He is damned according to the new law as well as the old. Rossetti's own feelings of guilt may have helped to decide Sir James' fate.

Rossetti returned in this poem to his old considerations of reconciling sex and sanctity, and envisioning a paradise of love, with good reason. I may anticipate Chapter Eight somewhat to say that the greater part of the poem was written at Kelmscott, where Gabriel was living with Jane Burden Morris in an association that was certainly idyllic and quite probably illicit. With his "regenerate rapture"[41] came the return of his old problems as well.

In summary, it is convenient to distinguish between Rossetti's victimized women who sin sexually and those who do not. The first are found in the earlier and later works related to the fantasy. Without exception these ladies who have given themselves to their lovers have been abandoned by them. All are of the delicate, sensitive, "soulful" type, from which Rossetti chose his Madonnas. His problem was to justify their apparent angelic qualities with their sins. At first he defended their purity by allowing them no strength to resist their lovers and their emotions, and barely any knowledge of the act; later he called into question the system of good and evil that holds the consummation of true love to be sinful. Both justifications are undertaken to preserve his conception of the heavenly woman: in the first the emphasis is upon preserving innocence, and in the second it is upon defending sexuality. The difference was probably Jane Morris, an obvious angel whatever her behavior, and therefore a living answer to Rossetti's original problem. With her advent the concern became one of defending the act rather than denying it, of preserving righteousness rather than innocence in the commission of the act.

Intermediate in time are sexually innocent ladies whose lovers victimize them nevertheless by deserting or tormenting them. Quite obviously Rossetti had his own Lizzie in mind, and found Hamlet and Ophelia to be fictional counterparts remarkably well suited to describe his situation with her. He made some adaptations to bring the story closer to home: his Hamlet is rather more tender, and his concerns are rather more sexual. But Rossetti was entirely too successful in his choice of counterparts; his Lizzie, like Ophelia, became mentally disturbed and committed suicide. After her death he continued to portray her as Ophelia, in a guilty way that reveals his increasingly uneasy concern about his unjust treatment of her. His latest works on the subject show Ophelia to be almost as much of a femme fatale as a victim, for her ghost will haunt the man who abused and destroyed her.

CHAPTER SEVEN

The Femme Fatale

THE later works reflecting the theme of Ophelia give a taste of Rossetti's next fantasy, that of the femme fatale. If the number of works related to a theme is a fair indication of importance, the last fantasy of Rossetti's to be introduced is second only to that of the heavenly woman. The two most prominent fantasies suggest that he was more concerned with the influence of the beloved upon the male than vice versa, or at least that he recognized hers to be a greater power than his. The femme fatale is the precise opposite to the heavenly lady, and hence holds much in common with her, as a negative does with the photograph. Both ladies are powerful attractive forces, drawing the male to his death; both assume the spectra of good and evil, and salvation and damnation; both have access to supernatural realms; both are beautiful. Knowing Rossetti's fascination with the heavenly lady, we cannot be surprised at his interest in the devil's Beatrice, her opposite.

In fact Rossetti's earlier femmes fatales are remarkably like his Madonnas. In *The Card-Dealer* (1849), for example, there are many odd suggestions of *The Blessed Damozel:*[1] the Dealer has "gold that's heaped beside her hand," and the Damozel leans upon the "gold bar of Heaven"; the Dealer has "woven golden hair," and the Damozel's is "yellow like ripe corn"; in the one poem we find "magic stillness," and in the other, "waters stilled at even"; the Dealer's "eyes unravel the coiled night / And know the stars at noon," and the Damozel "saw / Time like a pulse shake fierce through all the worlds" (with this passage compare also, "the instant thrill / Pulse through the lighted rooms"); the poet and Dealer "play together" at cards, and the newly met lovers of heaven "play at holy games"; when the Dealer "shall speak, thou'lt learn her tongue," and the Damozel says, "I myself will teach to him / . . . / The songs I sing here." Going beyond the verbal parallels we find others: the poet says of the Dealer, "rich the dreams that wreathe her brows," attributing to her the Damozel's thoughtful, distant, "soulful" attitude. Most important, the trance into which the Dealer puts her victims is very like the lover's state in the presence of his heavenly lady; there is the same blurring of the eyes, the same destruction of distinctions:

> though its splendour swoon
> Into the silence languidly
> As a tune into a tune . . .
>
> And each [card] as it falls reflects
> In swift light-shadowings,
> Blood-red and purple, green and blue,
> The great eyes of her rings.
>
> A land without any order,—
> Day even as night . . .
> A land of darkness as darkness itself.

Furthermore, there is a bounce to the poem, showing that Rossetti revelled in the imaginative experience with no very grim concept of suffering and destruction. Although the Card-Dealer is ominous, her victims are certainly enjoying themselves; and it is the enjoyment that is more definitely expressed. Even the victims' thrill at the name of Death has its delights. The reversal of "Life" and "Death" at the end (in the later version) reveals Rossetti's easy equation of the two concepts. Destruction meant much the same thing to him as salvation: a fascinating association with a beautiful woman.

The Staff and Scrip (1851) makes no distinction between salvation and destruction either, for the Pilgrim reaches his heaven and his beloved by means of martyrdom. Upon meeting Queen Blanchelys he experiences a *déjà vu;* in her he recognizes a creature of his imagination:

> Right so, he knew that he saw weep
>   Each night through every dream
> The queen's own face, confused in sleep
>   With visages supreme
>   Not known to him.

She is associated with the goal of his pilgrimage, and his salvation: never "had he ever felt / So faint in the sunshine / Of Palestine" as in her presence. He defends her successfully in battle, but at the expense of his life. Love's martyr, he receives the meed of love; years later, at the death of the Queen, she is granted to the Pilgrim in heaven:

> The lists are set in Heaven today,
>   The bright pavilions shine;
> Fair hangs thy shield, and none gainsay;
>   The trumpets sound in sign
>   That she is thine.

Again heavenly bliss means the happiness of lovers, but here it has been earned by submission to suffering and destruction. Thus were Rossetti's two fantasies made one. Incidentally, the *déjà vu* upon meeting, the postponement of bliss, and the Pilgrim's blending worship with helpfulness all suggest the newly met Lizzie as a partial inspiration for the poem.[2]

But certain of Rossetti's traits made the femme fatale a being quite different from the heavenly lady. One trait, which could be associated with the femme fatale only, was a fascination with evil and diabolism. William says that the devil was "a personage of great predilection with my brother ever since his early acquaintance with Goethe's Faust"—that is, since he was six, or shortly thereafter. "That he entered fully into the spirit of a story of *diablerie* is certain."[3] The list of Gabriel's juvenile reading, writing, and drawing supports William's assertion,[4] and such depictors of the infernal as Soulier, Maturin, Bürger, and

Meinhold are usually mentioned by William as Gabriel's favorites.

One work that would seem to have grown out of this childhood interest is *Sister Helen* (1851). Sister Helen casts a spell that kills her Keith of Ewern and damns his soul in spite of the individual pleas of his family. The reason for her vengeance is that he has seduced her ("What else he broke will he ever join? . . . What else he took will he give again?") and abandoned her to marry another. Sister Helen, then, is not only the destroyer that her name suggests, but a victimized lady as well.

The intent of the poem is to make a situation of terror as forceful as possible. The intent is furthered by the gruesome ironies of Sister Helen as she responds to her brother's questions; the close, vivid depiction of scenic features (for example, the wood-coal's shining "red as blood" through the thinned wax of the effigy, and the white and gold hair of the suppliants against the black night); and the incremental effect of the various repetitions of sound and situation. The character of Sister Helen is especially vivid: her relating all the innocent remarks of her brother to her own situation dramatizes her ingestive monomania; and her having to keep her thoughts to herself, her loneliness. Her emotional state is even more frightful than the supernatural machinery that she employs, for she is absolutely vengeful, as remorseless to herself as to her old lover.

The terror of this poem must be clearly distinguished from that evoked, for example, by the last lines (quoted in the previous chapter) of "A Superscription." Both poems are effective, but the intent of each is different. The personages of the ballad remain distant from us, and comfortably distinct from ourselves, whereas we feel that the condition described in the sonnet could be our own. Although there are realistic elements in the ballad, and artificial ones aplenty in the sonnet, the difference is that between terror concocted and terror experienced. All of Rossetti's early works including femmes fatales have *Sister Helen's* distance from reality, a distance that takes the form, in his artistic works, of caricature. For example, *The Laboratory* (1849: Marillier, opp. p. 34), the 1848 sketch of *La Belle Dame sans Merci*, and the devil in *Retro Me, Sathana* (1848: both works Marillier, opp. p. 17), are all somewhat playfully depicted, although their situations are primarily fearful. These works, like *Sister Helen*, lack final seriousness, and their terrors are make-believe ones.[5]

The terrors were kept distant to keep them harmless. It goes without saying that the fantasy of the femme fatale was one that Rossetti was not anxious to have come true. Therefore, while he was painting his heavenly lady as realistically as possible, and looking for her among the ladies of London, he was content to keep his temptress a caricature.

A second trait of Rossetti's that helped to isolate the femme fatale from the heavenly lady was his fascination with death, and especially suicide. His mind turned easily to the subject, as we may infer from his two near-suicides. One often comes upon chance statements by Rossetti's friends that indicate the strength of his interest. For example, the normally sensible, right-thinking Brown finds that he has "talked about suicide and suicides afterward with Rossetti. To bed at 5 A.M."[6] Bell Scott remarks, "About Gabriel—the short ending to his ills, in the worst case, was of course often spoken of by him. . . . I could not strongly dissuade him."[7] Even in 1848, before he had any serious troubles, Gabriel turned automatically to the desire for death. In the *bouts-rimés*, in which he had to write whatever came into his head at the slightest suggestions, he composed the following:

> Death—an arched path too long to see the end,
> But which hath shadows that seem pure and cool.
>
> *An Altar Flame*

> Were't not exceeding well
> To shake my soul out of this tiresome life
> For a call any-whence and any-whither?
>
> *At Issue*

> I dared not cry upon His strength to shield
> My soul from weapons it was bent to wield
> Itself against itself.
>
> *Praise and Prayer*

What I have just said about Rossetti's early interest in diabolism holds as well for his first fascination with death and suicide: he enjoyed an excitement in musing upon them, but preferred keeping them at a distance. His fun was in posing, in reading and spinning these fantasies, not in experiencing them. The style of the three quotations above reveals just how purely "literary" his interest was; and the high spirits which accompanied these awful considerations are seen in a letter of August 30, 1848 to William:

> *Apropos* of death, Hunt and I are going to get up among our acquaintance a Mutual Suicide Association, by the regulations whereof any member, being weary of life, may call at any time upon another to cut his throat for him. It is all of course to be done very quietly, without weeping or gnashing of teeth. I, for instance, am to go in and say, "I say, Hunt, just stop painting that head a minute, and cut my throat"; to which he will respond by telling the model to keep the position as he shall only be a moment, and having done his duty, will proceed with the painting.[8]

The tone would have to change before the consideration could become morbid. What first interested him in death and suicide, as with the devil, was its caricature, and not the thing itself.

Rossetti's interests in diabolism and willful death combined with his interest in womanly beauty to form his fantasy of the femme fatale, and to form it independent of that of the heavenly woman. In a kind of running palinode to his major theme he occasionally drew temptresses throughout the time of his deepest involvement with Beatrice and her counterparts. Besides the works just mentioned there was also the slight pen-and-ink sketch called *Lo Marinaio Oblia . . .* (1853), based on a passage from a *canzone* of Jacopo da Lentino's which Rossetti had translated as follows:

> Sweet, sweet and long, the songs the sirens know.
> The Mariner forgets,
> Voyaging in those straits,
> And dies assuredly.
> Yea, from her pride perverse,
> Who hath my heart as hers,
> Even such my death must be.

There was also *Arthur's Tomb* (1854), the water-color *La Belle Dame* (1855), *A Fencing Scene* (ca. 1855), *Launcelot at the Shrine* (1857), *Joseph Accused by Potiphar's Wife* (1860), and *Lucretia Borgia Administering the Poison Draught* (1860).

In *Launcelot at the Shrine*, treated in Chapter Five, the opposition of femme fatale to heavenly lady was first made explicit. The work also marks the first elaborate, lifelike portrayal of a femme fatale by Rossetti. For the first time a work depicting a femme fatale was treated with entire seriousness, as if there was a genuine relationship between the fantasy and his life. No longer was the fantasy merely held at arm's length for perusal and amusement; there were regular correspondences hereafter between his works on the theme and his own life. For example, the painting of the cool Lucretia Borgia in the act of poisoning her husband was done at the outset of Rossetti's own difficult marriage; it is just possible that he was expressing here, in an exaggerated form, his sense of his own wife's adverse effect upon him.

The death of Lizzie in 1862 seems to have made the fantasy of the femme fatale both immediate and clear: the destruction of his "Beata Beatrix" was to be only the first step in his own destruction, and the women who had driven her to her death— fleshly Fanny was apparently not the only soulless woman to tempt him astray[9]—would destroy him, too. Immediately upon Lizzie's death Rossetti painted a number of femmes fatales, all fleshly and curvaceous. At this time, or perhaps a little earlier, he recalled his Lucretia Borgia, and repainted the central figure entirely, making her "with sinuous and ample curves."[10] In 1863 he painted a small oil of Helen of Troy from Holman Hunt's old fiancée, Annie Miller, whom we have already had occasion to associate with Fanny. Marillier (pp. 129–130) is disappointed with Rossetti's conception of Helen, finding her " . . . sumptuous enough, without, however, much claim to intellectual or imaginative beauty. . . . there is little to suggest that 'daughter of the gods divinely tall and most divinely fair' for whom the towers of Ilium were sacked." The observation is just, but the effect, I believe, entirely intentional and meaningful. For Rossetti's fantasy of the temptress was assuming his old

Helen of Troy
Courtesy of Hamburger Kunsthalle

fantasy of the sinful woman. So to speak, the tug of war in
Found between prostitute and old suitor was being won by the
woman; instead of being raised, the woman of flesh was pulling
the man down into the dirt.

The next year brought another work of a fleshly temptress
with surprisingly little "claim to intellectual and imaginative
beauty." Although the goddess of *Venus Verticordia*[11] is obviously
beautiful and powerful, there is something unreasoning and
animal about her too. Marillier calls her a "tall, massively built
woman—no spiritual goddess of beauty." The model, according
to Allingham, was a recent discovery of Gabriel's, a cook, "a
very large woman, almost a giantess."[12] Venus stands amid
honeysuckles and roses (Rossetti's floral adjuncts to sexual passion), holding the attractive apple in her left hand and the
destructive dart in her right. Her beauty is compelling, yet
frightening in its latent brutal inhumanity. This we see also in
the sonnet written in 1868 to accompany the work:

> A little space her glance is still and coy;
> But if she gives the fruit that works her spell,
> Those eyes shall flame as for her Phrygian boy.
> Then shall her bird's strained throat the woe foretell,
> And her far seas moan as a single shell,
> And through her dark grove strike the light of Troy.

The last line indicates Rossetti's association of the work with the
previous *Helen of Troy*. He continued throughout the 1860's to
revise the painting and paint replicas.

Naturally Fanny Cornforth loomed large as a femme fatale
at this time. In *Fazio's Mistress* (1863) she was painted plaiting
her hair before a mirror. In Chapter Four I quoted a part of
the *canzone* of Fazio degli Uberti, translated by Rossetti, that
inspired the work. The setting for the painting was taken from
the poem's first lines:

> I look at the crisp golden-threaded hair
> Whereof, to thrall my heart, Love twists a net.

Although Fazio immediately drops the sinister suggestion that

Venus Verticordia
Courtesy of Russell-Cotes Art Gallery, Bournemouth, England

his mistress is a trap, to praise in a spirited manner the "every earthly joy" that abides in her, Rossetti, a year after his wife's death, chose for illustration the two lines out of ninety that imply disaster.[13]

Lady Lilith, the best of the works portraying bodily beauty as destructive, was done from Fanny a year later. Its disposition is almost exactly that of *Fazio's Mistress*, for the voluptuous Lilith also sits coldly regarding herself in a mirror while she combs out her long blonde hair. Perhaps the association between Lilith and Fazio's mistress was brought about by Rossetti's reading in Goethe's *Faust* the passage on Lilith that he translated in 1866 as follows:

> Hold thou thy heart against her shining hair,
> If, by thy fate, she spread it once for thee;
> For, when she nets a young man in that snare,
> So twines she him he never may be free.

In the sonnet called "Body's Beauty" (*HL* LXXVIII), written to illustrate this picture, Rossetti introduced the following lines, reminiscent of both Fazio and Goethe:

> And subtly of herself contemplative,
> Draws men to watch the bright web she can weave,
> Till heart and body and life are in its hold.[14]

In the discussion of Rossetti's early association with Fanny I remarked that her body's soulless beauty had attracted him to her, although he had been unwilling to deny her a soulfulness, or see evil in her. But after Lizzie's death he consciously made the distinction between "Body's Beauty" and "Soul's Beauty," and recognized the first to be a powerful, evil snare from whose harmful attractions he could not escape. The simple mistress, Fanny, had become, probably without her knowledge, a femme fatale.

At this time Lilith was a particularly apt counterpart to Fanny. Lilith was made of earth, and Fanny was of earth. Lilith was the first wife of Adam, and, I presume, Fanny was the former mate of Gabriel in the sense that she was his sexually before Lizzie. According to rabbinical mythology, Lilith was

Lady Lilith
Photograph of the painting in its original state, with Fanny
Cornforth as model
Courtesy of The Wilmington Society of the Fine Arts, Delaware
Art Center (Samuel and Mary R. Bancroft Collection)

transformed, after the creation of Eve, into "a night spectre especially hostile to newly-born infants."[15] Rossetti, still regretting the loss of Lizzie's stillborn child, would not have failed to make the application to his own situation. Lilith's flowers are the usual rose, and the poppy, symbolizing perhaps Rossetti's own sin of forgetfulness toward Lizzie into which he had been lured by Fanny's "elemental power of carnal loveliness."[16] Finally Fanny, like Lilith, held her man to earth in her net, preventing him from rising to his prelapsarian blessedness, which Rossetti, forgetting his wife's shortcomings, would associate with his wife. As Lilith subjugated the youthful Adam, so Fanny (I quote "Body's Beauty") left Rossetti's "straight neck bent"—a phrase with religious as well as sexual and psychological implications.

But in life Fanny was as incapable of being Lilith as Lizzie was of playing Beatrice. Whatever her bodily glories, Fanny was hardly a deceiver, hardly "subtly of herself contemplative." In associating her with the supernatural, serpentine aura of Lilith, Rossetti was revealing his own guilty feelings rather than her character, and hence was not really painting from Nature. Professor Baum, in speaking of her later reputation, points out that students of Rossetti have incorrectly inferred her character from this portrayal: "Fanny has suffered from her equation with Lilith. . . . She was neither so maleficent nor so cunning nor so cold."[17] The fact that Rossetti later settled into a long, easy, and somewhat condescending relationship with her indicates a change in his own characterization of her. Another sign of his changed opinion was the revisions of his paintings of her. In 1872–1873 he had *Lady Lilith* returned to him, and he repainted the face from another model, Alexa Wilding[18] (see Marillier, p. 133). The result, it is generally conceded, was an inferior characterization, but he was happy with it. It is almost as if he were saying that he had changed his mind; that Fanny was no Lilith. Although the elements of evil and fleshliness could be attributed to her, she existed to be saved rather than to destroy. She belonged basically to a different fantasy. In the retouching Rossetti regained his thematic consistency, and implied that Fanny was no destroyer of Lizzie and himself.

Even earlier he had tried to have the name, *Fazio's Mistress*, changed. In a letter of August 1869 to Mr. Rae, the owner of the picture, in searching for reasons for the change, he showed his uneasy dissatisfaction: "It was always an absurd misnomer in a hurry; and the thing is much too full of queer details to embody the poem quoted, which is a thirteenth-century production. Do have the writing on the frame effaced, and call it anything else. *Aurelia* would do very well for the golden hair."[19] The associative series that includes Fazio, Goethe, Lilith, and Fanny belies the assertion that the work was an "absurd misnomer in a hurry"; and never before or after did he show special concern for the faithfulness of a design to the literary work illustrated. In 1855 he had thought that an illustrator should "allegorize on one's own hook on the subject of the poem, without killing, for oneself and everyone, a distinct idea of the poet's";[20] and we have seen how well he did observe laissez-faire in this matter. A better reason for his wish would be an anxiety to dissociate the portrait of Fanny from the story upon which it was built, and to save Fanny from the imputation of being a femme fatale. In short, he wanted to make amends.[21]

One reason for the passing of the coarse, fleshly femmes fatales was probably that he began to see Lizzie as destructive. I have already marked her change, in his works, from a simple victim to an avenger. Besides the works depicting her as an avenger discussed under the theme of the victimized woman,[22] there was also the water-color, *The Merciless Lady* (1865). The blonde lady—the merciless one—plays her lute, holding the man's undivided attention from the second, dark-haired lady, who tries unsuccessfully and jealously to catch his heart. Lizzie had already been drawn "sans Merci" in 1855, and here the lute-player bears a close resemblance to her. She has the same light, fluffy hair that Rossetti was in the habit of giving to portrayals done from Lizzie's memory.[23] As the girl makes her bewitching music with a shallow mock-soulfulness, she keeps both the man and the dark-haired girl from mutual happiness. One hesitates to suggest a counterpart from Rossetti's life—the memory of Lizzie keeping him and another from happiness—but "A Superscription" seems to suggest the same thing.

The Merciless Lady
Reproduced by Fogg Art Museum, Harvard University,
from Marillier's *Dante Gabriel Rossetti* (1899)

The dark-haired lady with whom Rossetti hoped to find his "winged Peace" was probably Jane Morris, whose association with Rossetti is the subject of the next chapters. All that need be said here is that the fantasy of the femme fatale did not die with the birth of his close friendship with her. In fact the fantasy was more active than ever; from 1868 through 1870 at least sixteen works on the theme were produced.[24]

The fantasy of the femme fatale, like that of the victimized woman, turned upon Rossetti's self-supposed ill treatment of Lizzie, and her suicide. It shared with the other fantasy of degradation the dominant place in his imagination throughout the 1860's, becoming at the time even more obsessive than the theme of the heavenly lady, which ruled his earlier imaginative life. His femme fatale was as old as his Madonna, and at first was sometimes confounded with her. She had her birth in the tales of terror and wonder that he read as a youth, and inherited their improbabilities and exaggerations. The humor and caricature in his early works related to the fantasy show the high spirits with which he approached them. Given as he was to seeking out striking coincidences between literature and his life, he believed, when he saw his life take a sinister turn, that the temptress of his imagination had assumed actuality. His pity for the dead Lizzie led him to look first for the femme fatale in Lizzie's rival, Fanny, by whom he found himself sexually enthralled. When the guilty memory of Lizzie refused to fade, pity yielded to fear and annoyance, and the ghost of the vengeful wife, rather than the fleshly Fanny, assumed the role of femme fatale. Both attempts at finding a counterpart were extensions of the two chief fantasies of the 1850's, for Fanny had been his sinful woman, and the pathetic Lizzie, his Madonna.

CHAPTER EIGHT

Jane Morris and the
Conflict of Fantasies

ROSSETTI's association with Jane Burden Morris and his works inspired by her deserve special consideration, because he saw in her "The meaning of all things that are" ("Heart's Compass," *HL* XXVII). Unlike Lizzie, who came into Rossetti's life as the embodiment of his imaginary Beatrice, and unlike Fanny, his Jenny, Janey herself was the "given," who led him to seek out a suitable literary situation for her. During 1867–1872—the time of his closest association with her—all the old dreams were recast and the old problems restated. In fact she served as a nexus for all of his fantasies.

Implicit in those fantasies, as we have seen, are divergent and even contradictory attitudes toward sexuality. In that of the Madonna, the love-embrace is the way to heaven, and heaven's primary activity. In that of the sinful woman it is a venal peccadillo, more than redeemed by generous kindness. In those of the victimized woman and femme fatale it is a damnable sin. The moral and metaphysical differences account for the "discordant phases of profession"[1] so irritating to Rossetti's interpreters. But to Rossetti they must have served as a comfort, for even as he felt himself drawn to the bodily beauty of some Lady Lilith, he could still harbor hopes of encountering, finally, some Blessed Damozel, beautiful of soul, who would save him.

When he fell in love with Janey, the discord was made manifest. No longer moving from one woman to another, he was now obliged to address himself to moral and metaphysical unification. Now, with her dominating his imaginative flights, an unwelcome consistency was demanded of him. As a result there was, especially, a clash between Janey seen as heavenly lady and Janey seen as femme fatale. The result was an emotional crisis in his life.

We owe to Professor Doughty the piecing together of the "consistent and persistent design" with its "thousand details"[2] all revealing an illicit relationship of mutual passion between Rossetti and Jane Morris. Professor Doughty discusses the many indications of the love for her in Rossetti's poems, many of which take on special meaning when the love is assumed; the unintentionally ostentatious obscurantism of Gabriel and his contemporary biographers, that of his brother especially; the joint dwelling of Rossetti and the Morrises, and the long trips that William Morris undertook alone, seemingly to leave Janey and Gabriel to themselves; the hints of marital disappointment in William Morris's own writings and conversation; the coincidence of the fluctuations in Rossetti's health and temperament with his removals to and from the presence of Janey; the innuendoes of scandal current at the time; and Rossetti's remarks of affection for Janey that have come down to us. I shall not repeat Professor Doughty's work, which needs no advocate, although I shall make use of it.

The mention of a few names, dates, and places is in order, however. Gabriel first met Janey, the daughter of a groom, at Oxford in 1857 during the "Jovial Campaign." He discovered her at the theatre (in church, according to another account), and, as was his wont, persuaded her to sit to him for Guenevere. They seem to have engaged in some short-lived adventure of the heart,[3] but soon he returned to his ailing Lizzie, and, in 1859, Janey was married to the doting William Morris. What evidence we have indicates a pleasant, easy association thereafter between the two couples. Soon after Janey's marriage Rossetti painted her twice more: not as the seductive Guenevere but as Beatrice in *The Salutation of Beatrice* (1859), a work in two panels painted on a cabinet for the "Red House," the Morrises' new home at Upton; and as the Virgin Mary in *The Seed of David* (1859–1864), a triptych commissioned by the Llandaff Cathedral in Cardiff.[4] So even from the first he seems undecided whether to see her as Guenevere or Beatrice, seductress or savior.

Because of intervening distance and the Morrises' preoccupation with their two young daughters, the family saw little of Gabriel during the early '60's, for him the time of Lizzie's death and his degrading attraction to fleshly femmes fatales. But in 1865 the Morrises moved to the Bloomsbury section of London, and the old friendship was of course resumed. In June 1866 he began a portrait of Janey in a blue dress, seated before a table with a glass of roses. In the spring of 1868 he made studies of her for *La Pia*, and, in the summer, for *Aurea Catena*. There were occasional separations thereafter—his visits to Penkill in 1868 and 1869, and her trip to Ems with Morris in the summer of 1869—but from early 1868 on she was frequently his model and guest at Cheyne Walk. In July 1871 the Morrises and Rossetti undertook the joint possession of Kelmscott Manor, on the Thames near rustic Lechlade. To this retreat came Janey with her two daughters, and Gabriel, while Morris set off for Iceland. Henceforward there were occasional, painful separations (including a long one, from early October 1871 till late September 1872, during which time Rossetti suffered a mental collapse and attempted suicide), but the two were most often together until July 1874. After this time Gabriel relinquished his share in Kelmscott Manor and never returned, although Janey still made "rare and valued visits"[5] to him during the rest of his life.

Janey's appearance, according to all contemporary accounts, was wondrous. She was a tall, pale, somber, beautiful, silent woman—"a figure cut out of a missal," said Henry James, half in awe, and half in amusement:

> . . . when such an image puts on flesh and blood, it is an apparition of fearful and wonderful intensity. . . . Imagine a tall lean woman in a long dress of some dead purple stuff, guiltless of hoops (or of anything else, I should say), with a mass of crisp black hair heaped into great wavy projections on each side of her temples, a thin pale face, a pair of strange, sad, deep, dark Swinburnian

Portrait of Mrs. William Morris (1866–1867)
Courtesy of The Society of Antiquaries of London

eyes, with great thick black oblique brows . . . tucking themselves away under her hair, a mouth like the "Oriana" in our illustrated Tennyson,[6] a long neck, without any collar, and in lieu thereof some dozen strings of outlandish beads—in fine complete.[7]

William Rossetti described her more worshipfully:

> Her face was at once tragic, mystic, passionate, calm, beautiful, and gracious—a face for a sculptor, and a face for a painter—a face solitary in England, and not at all like that of an English-woman, but rather of an Ionian Greek. It was not a face for that large class of English people who only take to the "pretty," and not to the beautiful or superb. Her complexion was dark and pale, her eyes a deep penetrating grey, her massive wealth of hair gorgeously rippled, and tending to black, yet not without some deep-sunken glow.[8]

James, William Rossetti, Watts-Dunton, and Graham Robertson all give independent testimony that Gabriel's many portrayals of her were accurate and not exaggerated or idealized.[9] William Rossetti said, of portraying her face, "For idealizing there was but one process—to realize."[10] All found her appearance impressive, and if later observers such as James, George du Maurier, Bernard Shaw, Richard le Gallienne, and Graham Robertson seasoned their self-conscious worship of her with wit, it was because the postures of the Pre-Raphaelite movement itself were becoming embarrassing, and not because Janey's appearance failed its fame.

The personality behind the silent "face of arcane and inexhaustible meaning"[11] has remained enigmatic. It is as hard to accept Watts-Dunton's assertion that she was "superior to Morris intellectually"[12] as it is to credit those who thought her silence to be due to mindlessness. The vignettes of Janey feeding the vegetarian Shaw pudding with suet in it, Janey proffering a jar of quince jam to le Gallienne, and Janey eating strawberries from the hand of the solicitous Rossetti are not very revealing. Robertson's fancy that "her mystic beauty must have weighed rather heavily upon her," that "she would have preferred to be a 'bright chatty little woman' in request for small theatre parties and afternoons up the river,"[13] is based more on down-to-earth

Aurea Catena
Courtesy of Fogg Art Museum, Harvard University (Bequest of
Grenville L. Winthrop)

surmise than on close observation. Watts-Dunton's statement that the groom's daughter was "very shy and retiring, almost fearful in her attitude toward others,"[14] is likely true, simply because uneasiness is so often the cause of social silences. A somewhat critical estimation of her underlying personality is given by a biographer of her husband:

> Perhaps unresponsive by nature or through the inhibitions of her upbringing, perhaps spoilt by the attention of poets and painters, it seems that she had allowed herself to fall into a character of inaccessible beauty, and to wear not only the Pre-Raphaelite draperies designed by Morris, but also the airs of a Guenevere. . . . For many years she was the victim of unexplained ailments, which seem to have had some nervous origin. Her letters (the few which are published, or are open to inspection) reveal no more than an ordinary concern for the details of life, with an undertone of dissatisfaction, occasionally of self-pity. . . . Janey, it seems, was not the kind of person to take much blame on herself. . . . As she grew older her personality seems to have grown less, rather than more, sympathetic, and her air of aloof discontent to have become more marked.[15]

What we know of her behavior with Rossetti supports the suggestions of an all-consuming self-concern. A passage from Rossetti's "Heart's Haven" (*HL* XXII), written in 1871 and evidently inspired by her, is further evidence of her fearfulness and immaturity:

> Sometimes she is a child within mine arms,
> Cowering beneath dark wings that love must chase,—
> With still tears showering and averted face,
> Inexplicably filled with faint alarms . . .

This is the woman who came to be for Rossetti "the one necessary person."[16]

But working with correspondence unavailable to earlier students, Rosalie Glynn Grylls, in *Portrait of Rossetti*, can add more favorable touches: she sees in Janey "a good brain" and "an unusually developed normality" (p. 118), a sense of humor, and warm feelings. Janey was "a tomboy imprisoned in the cast of

Guinevere. . . . sorry for herself when no longer able to romp but still generous with her sympathy to others" (p. 180).

Although it seems impossible to construct a character-sketch upon which all would agree, it is not difficult to explain her attractiveness for Rossetti. In Janey he found at last the union of the physical and spiritual elements of his original ideal. In spite of the difference in features she was very like Lizzie in that she was richly "soulful" (as the word has been used throughout this study). Not only was she beautiful, but her appearance suggested hidden emotions too sacred for utterance, "thoughts too deep for words." She seemed (to repeat William's expression) a very shrine of "arcane and inexhaustible meaning." A "Delphic Sibyl," Robertson called her. Furthermore, her long silences of themselves must have encouraged Rossetti to exercise his ready imagination in searching her arcane face for glimpses of his old fantasies. If we are to judge from his poetic accounts, their friendship was quiescent rather than animated, characterized by long silent trancelike "spells":[17]

> This close-companioned inarticulate hour
> When twofold silence was the song of love
>
> *HL* XIX

>   Beneath her sheltering hair,
>   In the warm silence near her breast,
>   Our kisses and our sobs shall sink to rest,
>   As in some still trance made aware
>   That day and night have wrought to fulness there
>   · · · · · · · · · · · · · ·
>   And closed lips and closed arms a silence keep,
>   Subdued by memory's circling strain,—
>
> *The Stream's Secret*[18]

> What word can answer to thy word,—what gaze
> To thine, which now absorbs within its sphere
> My worshiping face, till I am mirrored there
> Light-circled in a heaven of deep-drawn rays?
>
> *HL* XXVI

The last passage, whether Rossetti intended it so or not, is really most self-revelatory. In exploring her eyes for residual deep meaning, he discovers instead his own reflected image; similarly, the universal notions that he seeks in her oracular face always turn out to be his own old thoughts, somewhat "light-circled" for their reflection from her.

Rossetti's works executed in the first years of their reborn friendship consistently indicate frustration or deprivation. The portrait begun in 1866 of Janey in a blue dress seated before a jar of roses is probably more than mere portrait, for blue is the color of faithfulness, and roses are for Rossetti the flower of physical passion. Janey sits within reach of the roses, but, with a melancholy look and a display of her wedding ring, she ignores them. There may even be a hint of rivalry between husband and artist in the inscription, *Conjuge clarâ poeta, et praeclarissima vultu, / Denique picturâ clara sit illa meâ*. The suggestion here of conflict between passion and marital troth appears more likely in the light of paintings that follow, namely, several preliminary studies for *La Pia*, and the oil, *Aurea Catena*. The former studies[19] portray the unfortunate wife of Nello della Pietra of Siena, who was left to die by her husband in a fortress overlooking the lethally pestilential Maremma marshes. She sits in a blue dress (in the subsequent oil), fingering her wedding-ring, the cause of her poisonous death-in-life. Rossetti translated the relevant passage from Dante's "Purgatorio," Canto V, as follows:

> Remember me who am La Pia. Me
> Siena, me Maremma made, unmade.
> He knoweth this thing in his heart—even he
> With whose fair jewel I was ringed and wed.[20]

The thought of William Morris, permissive to a fault, as a cruel and fatally restrictive husband is outrageously unfair; yet Rossetti in his fantasies might well have seen the story as analogous to Janey's actual situation: that of a woman bound by marriage to drag out her days in a loveless, miasmic existence.

Aurea Catena tells much the same story. Janey, leaning upon the top of the wall in a pose similar to that of the Blessed Damozel's upon the gold bar, is depicted as enclosed within an elevated garden. Instead of the wedding-ring as a symbol of bondage there is a golden chain about her neck. A heart hangs from the chain, as well as a closed locket, containing (the heart suggests) a picture or memento of a loved one. Ivy, symbolic of memory,[21] is clinging to the wall in the foreground, and in the background there are two rivers that flow on in the same direction but do not join. The obvious implication is that the two rivers are the lives of Gabriel (the secret love) and Janey, constrained to continue in their separate ways.[22] If there are specific memories alluded to, they could be those of their first friendship, during the "Jovial Campaign" of 1857.

A few succeeding works continue the concern with marital bonds and love-sequestered ladies. *Mariana* (Marillier, opp. p. 158), begun in 1868,[23] takes its subject from the very beginning of Act IV of *Measure for Measure*. Mariana (painted from Janey), long frustrated in her love, is seated within the "Moated Grange," listening to the Boy's teasing song of a still attractive love that seems beyond reach (quoted text from Kittredge edition):

> Take, O, take those lips away
> That so sweetly were forsworn;
> . . . .
> But my kisses bring again, bring again;
> Seals of love, but seal'd in vain, seal'd in vain.

There is no analogy between the reluctant Angelo and the apparently all too willing Gabriel, unless Rossetti's rumored early rejection of Janey for Lizzie is referred to. But the love-longing, the betrayal, and even the moat carry out the association between Mariana and La Pia, and from thence to Janey. Another work in this group (although Janey did not serve as model) is a crayon *Penelope* (1869; Marillier, opp. p. 154). The faithful wife sits in a reverie at her idle loom. It is rather surprising, under the circumstances, that Rossetti would choose to concern himself with a subject endorsing fidelity rather than adultery. Yet even here the heroine's situation is much like that of the other works just discussed, for again we find illicit temptation, and sequestration from the lover. Janey, like Penelope, must only remember and wait.

At some moment the golden chain was finally broken, it

would seem, and the restricted love temporarily found free expression. Perhaps the rapprochement was celebrated in the four sonnets, almost certainly written in December 1868,[24] entitled "Willowwood" (*HL* XLIX–LII). They dramatize an emotional meeting of lovers—a catharsis of love—and a pensive depression that follows.[25] The poet, sitting with Love "upon a woodside well," listens to the song of Love,

> and that sound came to be
> The passionate voice I knew; and my tears fell.
> And at their fall his eyes beneath grew hers;
> And with his foot and with his wing-feathers
> He swept the spring that watered my heart's drouth.
> Then the dark ripples spread to waving hair,
> And as I stooped, her own lips rising there
> Bubbled with brimming kisses at my mouth.

The beloved's hair like "dark ripples" calls Janey to mind,[26] and other phrases in the sequence ("The shades of those our days that had no tongue"; "For once, for once, / For once alone!" "Her face . . . as grey / As its grey eyes") also suggest their situation or Janey's appearance. The mirrored image that assumes substance is greatly reminiscent of early works of Rossetti's such as *Hand and Soul*, *St. Agnes of Intercession*, and *The Mirror*,[27] works that revealed his concern with the association between the lady of his imagination and the lady of flesh and blood. But the consummation is only momentary—perhaps a measure of the change in his fancies since his youth.

After the kiss, when "her face fell back drowned," Love

> Pressed on my neck with moan of pity and grace
> Till both our heads were in his aureole.

Love grants the poet a momentary comfort or blessing. Yet the "soul-wrung implacable close kiss" is hardly an altogether happy meeting. The lovers' miserable lives apart in Willowwood, interrupted by the one kiss, are to be resumed for "one lifelong night." And the basic gesture of the poem, that of stooping to kiss an image in a pool, is obviously the self-destructive gesture of Narcissus. In following the bidding of the god Love and seeking his blessing, the poet may instead be destroying himself. This uncertainty as to outcome is not resolved in the poem. Janey, Rossetti's new "image of thine own soul within thee" (to recall the early passage from *Hand and Soul*), is somehow both the promise of the soul's rebirth[28] and the insubstantial "last hope lost," driving the lonely soul to its destruction.[29]

Two myths, which Rossetti treated at the time in his art and poetry, also seem to have a bearing upon the reunion between Gabriel and Janey and its attendant concerns. *Orpheus and Eurydice*,[30] a design in pencil of 1869, with Eurydice apparently drawn from Janey, also depicts a momentary meeting of two lovers separated and soon to be parted again. As in *La Pia* and *Aurea Catena* the lady has been imprisoned; as in *La Pia* and *Mariana* she resides in dismal circumstances. The difference between *Orpheus and Eurydice* and the situations in the earlier works is that an attempt is made to rescue the heroine from her incarceration. To put the difference in the terms of this study, the fantasy changes from that of the victimized woman to that of raising the fallen woman (although for once the lady's fall is not a sexual one). As in "Willowwood" the lovers meet and are quickly parted again.[31]

The second myth is that of Pandora, of which two crayon studies were made in the spring and summer of 1869, an oil in 1871, and a somewhat different chalk replica in 1879. Again the model was Janey. Pandora stands with straightforward gaze, closing the box upon Hope after having released the winged evils that wreathe her head in a red smoke. Engraved on the box is *nescitur Ignescitur* (*Ultima manet Spes* in the 1879 version). The gown is not the blue one of the early portrait, *La Pia*, and *Mariana*, but one of vivid red. The accompanying sonnet, written in March 1869, establishes the association between the legend and Rossetti's own situation:[32]

> What of the end, Pandora? Was it thine,
> The deed that set these fiery pinions free?
> Ah! wherefore did the Olympian consistory
> In its own likeness make thee half divine?
> Was it that Juno's brow might stand a sign

Pandora (1871)
Courtesy of The Art Museum, Princeton University

Pandora (1879)
Courtesy of Fogg Art Museum, Harvard University (Gift of Grenville
L. Winthrop)

For ever? and the mien of Pallas be
A deadly thing? and that all men might see
In Venus' eyes the gaze of Proserpine?
What of the end? These beat their wings at will,
The ill-born things, the good things turned to ill,—
Powers of the impassioned hours prohibited.
Aye, clench the casket now! Whither they go
Thou mayst not dare to think: nor canst thou know
If Hope still pent there be alive or dead.

The line, "Powers of the impassioned hours prohibited," has nothing to do with the legend, but it is a good description of adulterous moments. Professor Doughty points out that " . . . even the mythology assumes a more or less personal symbolism":

> Pandora has been made half divine in order to anger Juno (Hera, the goddess of marriage and of women), bring a frown to the brows of Pallas (Athene) the goddess of wisdom, and infuse "In Venus' eyes the gaze of Proserpine"; that is, her love must be perplexed by difficulties such as those of Proserpine, the unhappy wife doomed to divide her life between the brightness of the upper world of freedom and the sadness of her existence with an unloved husband below.[33]

The rings, chains, and prisons of previous works give way to the opened box and fiery pinions, symbolic of release and freedom. The release has been accomplished by a lady made "half divine" by the gods, who have endowed her with their own several characteristic virtues. This last could be both an imaginative compliment to Janey and yet another statement of belief in the more-than-human status of the beautiful woman. But here, as in the "Willowwood" sonnets, there is uncertainty verging on despair as to what the lady has accomplished. She may be a heavenly lady in her gesture of release and preservation of Hope, but the poet is more inclined to see her as femme fatale, the unwittingly maleficent agent of destruction. The many question marks of the sonnet are faithful, if rhetorical, indicators of Rossetti's own confusion and hesitation.

We have seen in these various works of release or fulfillment that there is, surprisingly, more of painful uncertainty and fear for the consequences of the action than there is of pleasure. Apparently the breaking of the chain brought about something other than what was expected. What probably happened in fact was that Janey, afraid that she had overstepped herself, fled for a time from the illicit liaison tempting her. At least I infer so from the fading face in "Willowwood" and *Orpheus and Eurydice*, and the belated clenching of the casket in *Pandora*. The effect on Rossetti must have been a strengthening of his uncertainty with respect to her. From their first association he did not know whether she was a Beatrice or a Guenevere, a bearer of hope or evil; her vagaries at this time must have made her seem even more a Pandora, a questionable composite of the two.

Other works likewise expressed uncertainty with respect to Janey's true nature. Even the titles, *Dark-lily* (later changed to *Love-lily*), *Rose Mary*, and *Perlascura* ("Dark Pearl")[34] suggest the ambivalence with which he regarded her. But after the initial expressions of confusion just indicated, he customarily segregated, at least in his works, his fantasies of Janey the heavenly lady from Janey the femme fatale. I shall examine the nature of the two fantasies separately.

CHAPTER NINE

Jane Morris and the
Heavenly Lady

ROSSETTI plainly desired to make Janey into the Beatrice that he had not found in Lizzie. This time, however, the equation required an effort of the will and an active exercise of the imagination, for no startling coincidence established it. Instead of the earlier confrontations (for example, those in *Hand and Soul*, *St. Agnes of Intercession*, *Ecce Ancilla Domini*, and *How They Met Themselves*) he now very masterfully portrayed pursuits:

> that Lady Beauty, in whose praise
> Thy voice and hand shake still,—long known to thee
> By flying hair and fluttering hem,—the beat
> Following her daily of thy heart and feet,
> How passionately and irretrievably,
> In what fond flight, how many ways and days!
>
> *HL* LXXVII (ca. 1866)

In 1870 he considered painting "Love in black; and Beatrice in white walking away, back view"[1]—an attitude that must have distressed him. The equation between Janey and Beatrice was made more difficult by Janey's dark curly hair, for, as has been noted, the lady of courtly love was always blonde. This was no small discrepancy, especially to a painter, but, as had happened before with Lizzie, the past accommodated itself to the intractabilities of the present. A second difficulty was that both Janey and he were no longer young, and had married; their past experiences in love did not render them suitable doubles for Dante's pure young lovers. The coincidences that had led Gabriel twenty years before to believe himself a latter-day Dante were now not obvious, although it must have pleased him to recall that the historical Beatrice was married at twenty-one to Simone de' Bardi, and that Dante himself, according to Boccaccio, had had loves other than Beatrice.

Occasionally Rossetti would draw Janey merely as a near-Beatrice, or type of Beatrice. One of the last paintings depicting Janey, now entitled *The Daydream* (1880; see Marillier, opp. p. 198), was first called *Monna Primavera*,[2] presumably in reference to the passage in the *Vita Nuova* in which Guido Cavalcanti's love, named Primavera ("Spring"), precedes Beatrice into Dante's presence. Dante then declares that God had caused her to be so named because, as spring precedes the full summer, so she serves as a precursor, giving promise of Beatrice herself. So, perhaps, Rossetti hoped to move from Janey, the mere promise of his eventual Beatrice, to that ultimate Beatrice. The ameliorative process is entirely consistent with Rossetti's sonnet, "The Love Moon" (*HL* XXXVII, ca. 1868), in which he is apparently justifying the transference of his devotion from the dead Lizzie to Janey:

> Nay, pitiful Love, nay, loving Pity! Well
> Thou knowest that in these twain I have confess'd
> Two very voices of thy summoning bell.
> Nay, Master, shall not Death make manifest
> In these the culminant changes which approve
> The love-moon that must light my soul to Love?

The great Victorian concept of progress is clearly recognizable behind the astrology and Dantesque personifications.

Rossetti also likened Janey to a second near-Beatrice, the "Donna della Fenestra" or "Lady of Pity" of the *Vita Nuova*. Dante looks up from his mourning the death of Beatrice to see

> a young and very beautiful lady, who was gazing upon me from a
> window with a gaze full of pity, so that the very sum of pity

appeared gathered together in her. . . . whensoever I was seen of this lady, she became pale and of a piteous countenance, as though it had been with love; whereby she remembered me many times of my own noble lady, who was wont to be of a like paleness.[3]

For a time Dante is tempted to love this new lady, but finally he returns to the service of the dead Beatrice. Rossetti had been interested in Dante's Lady of Pity long before his liaison with Janey. In a footnote to his translation of this passage he had suggested that the Lady was Gemma Donati, to whom Dante was married about a year after the death of Beatrice.[4] And in his water-color, *Dante Drawing the Angel* (1853), he had drawn a sympathetic lady whom he also saw as Gemma Donati. Like the Lady of Pity, Janey came to the poet after the death of his first love. Furthermore the Lady's remarkable paleness of countenance was reflected in Janey, whose color Georgiana Burne-Jones described as that of a statue.[5] These similarities are perhaps enough to support the suggestion that Janey and the Lady of Pity were counterparts. In 1870 Rossetti made two chalk studies from her as *La Donna della Fenestra* (Marillier, p. 160),[6] and in 1879 he painted the work in oil (Marillier, opp. p. 196). The studies associating Janey and La Donna were especially appropriate in that, like earlier works drawn from Janey, they expressed her ambiguous nature: La Donna might be one whom Love "set in my path that so my life might find peace" (to quote the *Vita Nuova*), but she might also be the object of a base and misleading desire.[7]

Dante's subsidiary heroines may have offered the apter analogies to Janey, but Beatrice still promised the richest rewards. Rossetti painted Janey as Beatrice several times in the 1870's, although perhaps less frequently than we might have expected. There were two gigantic canvases, plus numerous studies, reproducing in oils the water-color of 1856, *Dante's Dream* (cf. Marillier, opp. p. 73 and opp. p. 166). In a vision Dante, led by Love, is shown the dead Beatrice, who is attended by two mourning maidens. When the great size (7′ 1″ x 10′ 6½″) of the picture of 1871 proved inconvenient to its first owner, a somewhat smaller version was painted to replace it. One study

for the figure of Beatrice (Marillier, opp. p. 160) is more satisfactory than the Beatrice of the painting itself. We also find
Janey as Beatrice in the unfinished *Boat of Love* (ca. 1874;
Marillier, p. 177), and, in 1880–1881, in a new oil study (plus a
replica) of an old theme, *The Salutation of Beatrice* (Marillier,
opp. p. 200). All of the works are large, and therefore ambitious
undertakings. But perhaps size was an unconscious substitute for
qualitative virtues. The works have often been criticized for
executive failures, and dexterity was never Rossetti's forte. Even
more damning is the evident lack of meaning, of thought, in
their conception. Rossetti merely chose designs from his youth,
or painted Janey with only the most obvious and inert of Dantesque trappings. The ingenious symbolism by which he customarily related his best works to his own situation is simply not to
be found here. The result is flatness and mannerism, not meaning.
The fact that most of the depictions of Janey that do not represent
her as Beatrice seem to be "deeply symbolic" analogues to his
own life suggests that he found the equation of Janey to Beatrice
particularly difficult or disturbing, too improbable, perhaps, for
a whole-hearted effort.

Rossetti attempted to make Janey into a Madonna more
assiduously in his poetry[8] than in his art. In the poetry his
intent was somewhat less extreme than in his art; he did not
insist upon identifying Janey with Beatrice or any other Dantesque figure, but rather saw her as a mere type, or latter-day
redaction, of Beatrice. Janey was like Beatrice only in that she
was a heavenly lady, leading the man's soul to heaven; there
was no need, in this looser relationship, for her to look just like
Dante's beloved, or to lead a coincident life. Furthermore the
looser relationship gave Rossetti greater freedom to develop his
peculiar heretical opinions, already indicated in Chapter Two,
that the primrose path was the way to heaven. Although he borrowed freely from Dante in his poetry, his religion of love was his
own, and Janey was herself.

Most of the sonnets in *The House of Life* were written from
1868 to 1873, the time of Rossetti's greatest attachment to Janey.
Rossetti clearly had Dante in mind when writing them: like
Dante in the *Vita Nuova* he chose the sonnet to celebrate each

stage of his particular romance, and like Dante he tried to discern a divine comedy behind the incidents of his romance. This intent might be disregarded in a reading of *The House of Life*, especially in the light of the "Fleshly School" controversy; but the truth is that the poems address themselves to grand speculations far more than to frank descriptions of acts of love.

In *The House of Life* Rossetti treats the lady as a micro-heaven, in whom may be discerned the answer to all ultimate mysteries. The lady here and now is like heaven after death (this simple two-stage analogy may be contrasted with Dante's elaborately graduated universe):

> Sometimes thou seem'st not as thyself alone,
> But as the meaning of all things that are;
> A breathless wonder, shadowing forth afar
> Some heavenly solstice hushed and halcyon;
> > "Heart's Compass," *HL* XXVII (?1871)

>   of that face
> What can be said,—which, like a governing star,
> Gathers and garners from all things that are
> Their silent penetrative loveliness?
> > "Gracious Moonlight," *HL* XX (?1871)

The repetition of the phrase "all things that are" shows how important it was for Gabriel to find inclusiveness in her. The passages indicate also that the "meaning" which he sought in her was to include loveliness, and, quite specifically, the old "heavenly solstice" envisioned in *The Blessed Damozel*.

To the poet falls the task of communicating the meaning that he was discovering in this oracular creature: he addresses his lady,

> Yea, in God's name, and Love's, and thine, would I
> Draw from one loving heart such evidence
> As to all hearts all things shall signify . . .
> > "Heart's Hope," *HL* V (?1871)

Like Dante he is lover, poet, and prophet. He is permitted his vision only by grace of the god Love. Because he loves he is privileged to see all meaning:

> O Singer! Magic mirror thou hast none
> Except thy manifest heart; and save thine own
> Anguish or ardour, else no amulet.
>> "The Song Throe," *HL* LXI (1880)

> And shall my sense pierce love,—the last relay
> And ultimate outpost of eternity?
> Lo! what am I to Love, the lord of all?
> One murmuring shell he gathers from the sand,—
> One little heart-flame sheltered in his hand.
> Yet through thine eyes he grants me clearest call
> And veriest touch of powers primordial
> That any hour-girt life may understand.
>> "The Dark Glass," *HL* XXXIV (1871)

All of these passages implicitly envision the lady as an oracular shrine and the poet as her priest. The inconsistency as to whether it is the lady's face or poet's heart that is the "magic mirror" does not affect the basic fact that the lady is the source of vision, and the poet's love for her the means to vision. The metaphor of the loving poet as a seashell, in which the sound of the whole great sea is audible, reiterates the assumption that love is a microcosm answerable to heaven, an assumption on which Rossetti's poetic venture depends.

Seeing Janey as a faithful miniature of the heavenly afterlife, Gabriel read his own salvation into her smile. Janey actually meant heaven to him, and his thoughts under her influence constantly turned toward it. When young he had hoped to find the counterpart to the heaven of his imagination in everyday life, with Lizzie. But now in his forties, and having found a heaven-on-earth in his love for Janey, he hoped to find it the counterpart to a heaven beyond, to be enjoyed eternally after death. The first was a longing for the extension of an imaginative situation into reality; the second, a longing for the extension of a real situation into an imagined situation presumably or hopefully to be realized. While love-passion and eternal life were elements together important to both youthful and mature desires, eternal life became the paramount consideration in the latter:

> blest were he
> With youth forevermore, whose heaven should be
> True Woman . . .
>
> .   .   .   .
>
> Were Paradise all uttermost worlds among.
>
> .   .   .   .
>
> Yet shall Heaven's promise clothe
> Even yet those lovers . . .
>> "True Woman: Her Heaven," *HL* LVIII (1881)

> Lo! Love yet bids thy lady greet thee once:—
> Yea, twice,—whereby thy life is still the sun's;
> And thrice,—whereby the shadow of death is dead.
>> "The Morrow's Message," *HL* XXXVIII (?1868–1869)

> when we are dead,
> Our hearts shall wake to know Love's golden head
> Sole sunshine of the imperishable land;
>> "Love and Hope," *HL* XLIII (?1871)

> Howbeit athwart Death's imminent shade doth soar
> One Power, than flow of stream or flight of dove
> Sweeter to glide around, to brood above.
> Tell me, my heart,—what angel-greeted door
> Or threshold of wing-winnowed threshing-floor
> Hath guest fire-fledged as thine, whose lord is Love?
>> "Through Death to Love," *HL* XLI (1871)

> But lo! what wedded souls now hand in hand
> Together tread at last the immortal strand
> With eyes where burning memory lights love home?
>> "Stillborn Love," *HL* LV (1869)

> City, of thine a single simple door,
> By some new Power reduplicate, must be
> Even yet my life-porch in eternity,

Even with one presence filled, as once of yore:
Or mocking winds whirl round a chaff-strown floor
Thee and thy years and these my words and me.
                    "Memorial Thresholds," *HL* LXXXI (1874)

Finally, the poet asks if the soul may, after death

          at once, in a green plain
Stoop through the spray of some sweet life-fountain
And cull the dew-drenched flowering amulet?
Ah! when the wan soul in that golden air
Between the scriptured petals softly blown
Peers breathless for the gift of grace unknown,
Ah! let none other alien spell soe'er
But only the one Hope's one name be there,—
Not less nor more, but even that word alone.
                    "The One Hope," *HL* CI (1869)

Even this extensive quotation does not exhaust the passages relating the beloved to the poet's salvation. The attitude may vary from triumph to doubt to bitter hopelessness, but the preoccupation is ever the same.

Once Rossetti's metaphysical preoccupation is recognized it becomes easier to appreciate his manner in these poems. One device—the continual personification and deification of Love—can seem like an arbitrary elaboration, an unpleasant mimicking of Dante: "Then, how I hate 'Love,' as a lubberly naked young man putting his arms here and his wings there, about a pair of lovers; a fellow they would kick away in the reality."[9] Robert Browning's amusing criticism has good common sense to recommend it, but ignores the fact that in introducing Cupid, Rossetti was expressing his belief that love extended beyond the five senses that compose common sense. Cupid is truly functional in these poems:

          my Lady stood at gaze and smiled
When her soul knew at length the Love it nursed.
. . . at her heart Love lay
Quickening in darkness, till a voice that day

Cried on him, and his bonds of birth were burst.
Now, shadowed by his wings, our faces yearn
Together, as his fullgrown feet now range
The grove, and his warm hands our couch prepare;
Till to his Song our bodiless souls in turn
Be born his children, when Death's nuptial change
Leaves us for light the halo of his hair.

"Bridal Birth," *HL* II (1869)

An unadorned paraphrase of these lines might be, "The new love that the Lady once sustained for me now serves us both, and will 'father' and sustain us in the Afterlife." The audacious sentiment is made palatable by the underlying analogy of Cupid ("Love") as Christ, who was also born of a woman, and went to "prepare a place" for his mother and those she loves. In another poem Love is spoken of as "our light at night and shade at noon" ("Heart's Haven," *HL* XXII, 1871). This is at once a succinct way of saying that love (pictured as a Cupid with wings that are both fiery and sheltering) brings both ardor and soothing rest where there is else none; and also a way of implying the bolder sentiment that Love is like the Biblical "cloud by day and pillar of fire by night," a supernatural guide to the Promised Land.[10] Although the god Love is occasionally nothing but the conventional "lubberly naked young" archer, he is usually a more awesome, Christian "lord of all" ("The Dark Glass," *HL* XXXIV), sitting on his throne,[11] overseeing his shrine,[12] or harvesting souls.[13] Rossetti introduced his Christian Cupid to express the religious, basically Christian, nature and function of his love.

Perhaps the most revealing of Rossetti's poetic manners is his use of the word "soul." It occurs sixty-eight times in the sonnets, and the kindred "spirit," nine times. It is a revealing semantic study to go through the poems, paraphrasing his meaning wherever the word appears. Usually it must be taken in its modern, post-Kantian sense of "innermost feeling"—"the heart's affections," or, as Rossetti describes it ("Love Sweetness," *HL* XXI, 1870), "the confident heart's still fervor." The following passages assume this definition:

the soul-wrung implacable close kiss.
"Willowwood-2," *HL* L (1868)

Her breath and all her tears and all her soul
"Willowwood-4"

She loves him; for her infinite soul is Love,
· · · · · · · · · · · · · · · ·
... her soul to answering ardors fanned
"True Woman: Her Love," *HL* LVII (1881)

Even of her inner self the perfect whole:
The very sky and sea-line of her soul.[14]

In the last quotation Rossetti actually defines the word, using it
in apposition to "her inner self." A second, more august usage
has the inner self indicating, primarily, holiness rather than the
heart's affections. It is paraphrased in "Equal Troth," *HL*
XXXII (ca. 1871), as the "heart's elect alcove":

Breathe low her name, my soul, for that means more.
"Her Gifts," *HL* XXXI (ca. 1871)

her soul's immediate sanctuary
"True Woman: Her Heaven," *HL* LVIII (1881)

How strange a thing to be what Man can know
But as a sacred secret! Heaven's own screen
Hides her soul's purest depth and loveliest glow ...
"True Woman: Herself," *HL* LVI (ca. 1881)

Often Rossetti meant the word in both senses, thus joining the
two different ideas of passion and holiness:

And as she kissed, her mouth became her soul.
"Secret Parting," *HL* XLV (ca. 1868–1869)

The double meaning is especially helpful in describing Janey's
"soulful" face, and it is also what is usually meant in the several
passages in which the soul is contrasted with the body.[15]

Sometimes, too, the soul becomes a being quite independent of the human host, leaving its inner sanctum and assuming a life, personality, and mobility of its own. In the following passages the soul behaves much like those in Donne's *The Ecstasy:*

> Hour after hour, remote from the world's throng,
> Work, contest, fame, all life's confederate pleas,—
> What while Love breathed in sighs and silences
> Through two blent souls one rapturous undersong.
> > "Youth's Antiphony," *HL* XIII (1871)

> two souls softly spanned
> With one o'erarching heaven of smiles and sighs
> > "The Lovers' Walk," *HL* XII (1871)

> Her soul sought / My soul . . .
> > "The Love-Letter," *HL* XI (1870)

> And my soul only sees thy soul its own . . .
> > "Lovesight," *HL* IV (1869)

Of course this language can be considered "a manner of speaking" only, but if we respect Rossetti's intention to make a true religion of love we cannot discount the metaphysical activity that these passages intimate.

Turning from passages in which the context is primarily amorous to some that are religious, we find that Rossetti uses "soul" unequivocally to mean the part of man's being that lives on after the body's death:

> Alas! but who
> Shall wrest a bond from night's [i.e., Death's] inveteracy,
> Ere yet my hazardous soul put forth, to be
> Her warrant against all her haste may rue?
> > "Cloud and Wind," *HL* XLIV (ca. 1871)

> And now Love sang, but his was such a song . . .
> As souls disused in death's sterility
> May sing when the new birthday tarries long.
> > "Willowwood-2," *HL* L (1868)

Alas, the soul! how soon must she
Accept her primal immortality . . . ?
"The Heart of the Night," *HL* LXVI (1873–1874)

Shall Peace [i.e., the heavenly reward] be still a
                    sunk stream long unmet,—
Or may the soul at once in a green plain
Stoop through the spray of some sweet life-fountain . . . ?
"The One Hope," *HL* CI (1869)

Thus "soul" runs the gamut of meaning from inner feeling, to inner holiness, to an active metaphysical entity, to an immortal spirit.

The word's tendency to soar almost imperceptibly in meaning made it valuable to Rossetti, for it permitted him to bridge the flaw in his religion of love. With the help of the word he could leap from Janey's strong inner feelings to his own afterlife. The best example of this technique is "Bridal Birth" (the relevant passage is quoted above, p. 144). There is a balance to the poem: what the Lady once did for Love, that shall Love soon do for her and the poet. The balance is emphasized (and the sentiment aurally condoned) by the repetition of the word "soul." But the meaning of the word has drifted from "heart's affections" to "immortal spirit."

A final example of Rossetti's use of the shifting meaning of "soul" is from "Love's Testament," *HL* III (1869):

O what from thee the grace, to me the prize,
And what to Love the glory,—when the whole
Of the deep stair thou tread'st to the dim shoal
And weary water of the place of sighs,
And there dost work deliverance, as thine eyes
Draw up my prisoned spirit to thy soul.

In the context of the whole sonnet this is saying very little more than, "you give me a lift." The octave establishes that the occasion described is merely a lovers' embrace, occurring "at Love's hour." The ambitious analogy in the sestet is therefore describing another Donne-like union of amorous souls, in which the Lady's dominant soul ("inner feeling") raises the poet's from his "place of sighs"—in short, from the doldrums. But, as often happens in Rossetti's poetry, the analogous situation is more significant than the actual one. It is that of the descent of the blessed shade of Beatrice to the shores of hell to "work deliverance" upon Dante's spirit. In this context the souls are traditional, Christian ones, and the salvation is divine rather than psychological. One may question the blasphemy in describing the act of love as the act of salvation, or the reversal of Milton in likening small things to great, but we must grant that Rossetti was true to his own terms. In his universe of heaven and micro-heaven the one kind of union and salvation of souls was but the type and promise of the other on its grander scale. Again the drifting meaning of the words "soul" and "spirit" enabled him to give a sense of propriety to the analogy.

Probably all of the sonnets just mentioned were written with Janey in mind. Beatrice, Orpheus, and Christ are alluded to in passing as types of Janey, but for once Rossetti was finally at a loss for the fictional analogue to support his liaison. There was no set plot to follow, and it is easy to see how his poetry could become complicated and elaborate in consequence, as he tried to narrate the story of his heavenly progress solely from the cues taken from the various moments of his relationship with her. With heaven resting on her smile, and hell on her froward glance, it is easy to see how dependent upon her he could become—how truly she could become "the one necessary person." When we recall the many partings and reunions in the course of their romance—changes probably instigated by the unstable and self-centered Janey—we can imagine how often Rossetti had to tailor his fantasies of his fate to reconcile them to Janey's latest mood. In the astrological terminology of the sonnet-sequence, he was ever recasting and accommodating his horoscope to the latest aspect of Janey, whom he likened frequently to the moon,[16] an object of inconstancy as well as pale beauty.[17]

The analogy between Rossetti's love-life and afterlife held true even when the failure of the love promised nothing better for the future than hell. We find, accordingly, that sonnets of despondency, such as "Death-in-Love" (XLVIII) and "Love's Fatality" (LIV), are preceded by sonnets such as "Severed Selves" (XL), "Parted Love" (XLVI), and "Without Her" (LIII)[18] announcing the absence of the beloved. And as the titles indicate, severance meant more than present sorrow; it meant death, as surely and for the same reasons that the lovers' ecstasy meant heavenly bliss. Only after the poet's time is divided between his lady and loneliness does he express doubts about his heavenly meed ("Love and Hope," XLIII; "Cloud and Wind," XLIV; and "Secret Parting," XLV); and only after her absence becomes the rule do we find depictions of hell ("Vain Virtues," LXXXV; and "Lost Days," LXXXVI), as vivid as any of his visions of heaven. The sonnets are not arranged in chronological order, but rather in a rough order of increasing pessimism, with a durable "One Hope" yet remaining at the end.[19]

One can see how a potential heavenly lady, in absenting herself, could become a kind of *femme fatale malgré elle*. Except for her lack of desire to do harm she would be a complete femme fatale, for she is clearly one in effect. In the sonnets apparently inspired by Janey's absence, Rossetti was reluctant to describe the Lady as a willful destroyer. There are no reasons given for the Lady's departures, except for occasional hints that they were beyond her control;[20] and "Change and Fate," the title to the second section of the Sequence, shows where he placed the blame for his prospective ills. Fate's role in these sonnets may be so large partly because he wished to attribute Janey's flights to something other than her own volition.

In fact he found an apt analogue to describe just such an unintentional femme fatale: Hero (see "Hero's Lamp," *HL* LXXXVIII, ca. 1875) was the unwilling destroyer of Leander, who thought he saw salvation and happiness in her lamp, but found death instead. The association between the lamp and Rossetti's own love, pursued as if it were a beacon, is obvious. He also transported the theme to his painting; an oil of Janey holding a lamp, eventually named *La Ricordanza* or *Mnemosyne* (Marillier, p. 190), was originally intended as a study of Hero.

The work was completed in 1876, a year after the composition of the poem.[21]

In only two sonnets of *The House of Life* that could refer to Janey is the Lady presented as a voluntary bearer of death.[22] "Newborn Death" (*HL* XCIX, 1868–1869) personifies Death as follows:

> wilt thou stand
> Fullgrown the helpful daughter of my heart,
> What time with thee indeed I reach the strand
> Of the pale wave which knows thee what thou art,
> And drink it in the hollow of thy hand?[23]

Although the "daughter" brings about the death of the man, and does so deliberately, she does not necessarily do mischief thereby; and therefore she does not qualify as a thoroughgoing femme fatale. There is doubt as to whether she is working the man's damnation or salvation. Even the blessed must die before they can find salvation, as Rossetti indicated in the title of another sonnet, "Through Death to Love" (*HL* XLI). The "helpful daughter of my heart" may prove to be a Beatrice in disguise, and the poet, in "Newborn Death," is careful to be neither reconciled to the lady, Death, nor resentful of her.

The other sonnet that presents deliberately deadly ladies is "Death's Songsters" (*HL* LXXXVII), and here, too, the half-promise of heaven lies behind the fatal seduction. The first twelve lines of the poem describe two incidents in the life of Ulysses in which he resists sexual temptation and consequently furthers his aims. In the first incident Helen is brought to the wooden horse by the dubious Trojans so that she may coax out any warriors that may be hidden there. Ulysses then holds his comrades' lips to prevent their replies to her seductive songs. In the second, Ulysses, after ordering himself bound to his mast, sails unharmed past the singing sirens. The final two lines of the sonnet turn from the stories to some self-questioning:

> Say, soul,—are songs of Death no heaven to thee,
> Nor shames her lip the cheek of Victory?

The plain meaning of the lines is difficult to come by, let alone their relationship to the rest of the poem.[24] But I may note that both lines are reversals of what would ordinarily be expected in the context: the poet does *not* say, "are songs of Heaven no death to thee?" ("are you not fatally betrayed by songs of heavenly bliss?"); and he does *not* say, "nor shames her cheek the lip of Victory" ("does not the lying lip of the false, deceptive Victory that Ulysses forwent shame her beautiful appearance?"). His converse meaning seems to be, "will not the promise of Heaven in the song of the seductress, Death, hold true?" and, "is not the Victory that Ulysses gained so paltry (in comparison with the attractions of Death) that she blushes for shame even as she shouts in triumph?" Rossetti thus sets himself in opposition to Ulysses, urging himself to embrace as the greater good the deadly sexual temptation that Ulysses shunned. Again the femme fatale is seen as a savior in disguise. Again heavenly bliss is not distinguished from the throes of dying, for both states are envisioned as the enjoyment of an attractive lady.

It proved difficult for Rossetti to relate Janey to Beatrice in his paintings in any direct or rewarding way; so he tended to versify his fantasies of her as a heavenly lady. Now, in the late 1860's and early 1870's, seeing Janey as a micro-heaven or preview of heaven, he tried repeatedly to find signs in her attitude toward him that figured forth the salvation of his soul. His constant metaphysical speculation, his frequent recourse to Dante, and his ingenious adaptations of Christian language and concepts indicate that sex was now subordinate in his mind to salvation. But his peculiar divine comedy was threatened in two ways: first, the Lady sometimes left him, and thereby forecast his damnation. Second, even when the Lady smiled, it was possible that her promise of salvation was a false promise—that he was following a wandering fire of love rather than love's beacon, and that what seemed to be a heavenly kiss was really the kiss of spiritual death. Regarding the first threat Rossetti was careful to assume the good intentions, at least, of the Lady; regarding the second he took a desperate comfort in the similarity between the state of dying and the heavenly state, for he envisioned them both as the embrace of a beautiful woman. Thus a hope of salvation was doggedly preserved throughout *The House of Life.*

The range of feelings, far greater than that in any other work of Rossetti; the breadth of consideration, and the fervor with which the speculation is pursued; and the imaginative and verbal ingeniousness in translating particular incidental occurrences into ultimate truths all help to make *The House of Life* Rossetti's finest and most representative work. It is his one production that figures forth his own life without confusing it with an analogue. It is the one work to which all his others can be conveniently appended.

La Donna della Fiamma
Courtesy of City of Manchester Art Galleries, England

CHAPTER TEN

Jane Morris and the

Femme Fatale

DURING the time of Rossetti's greatest involvement with Jane Morris, he produced more works describing femmes fatales than at any other time of his life.[1] Several considerations point to her as the source of inspiration. In the years 1868–1872 Janey was, to the best of our knowledge, the only woman of any importance to him. The extent of his involvement with her would seem to have precluded further ventures. At this time he made many protracted visits—to Kelmscott, Penkill, Scalands—changing and circumscribing his acquaintance, and thereby making it difficult to sustain a clandestine relationship with anyone other than his frequent companion, Janey. He may have had his encounters, but could hardly have developed a relationship of any significance. Fanny was carefully kept at bay, and although the dead Lizzie was much on his mind as a vengeful femme fatale, he could not have seen her as destroying him by means of her sexual attraction. Thus Janey becomes the inspiration for his seductive femmes fatales by default, as it were.

There are positive indications as well. I have already observed that Rossetti's earlier attitude toward Janey was ambivalent, for he saw her as Perlascura and Pandora, both composites of heavenly lady and fatal lady. It may be significant that two of the femmes fatales who played a large part in his works in the years under discussion—namely, Helen and Guenevere—were married and adulterers. Also, the crucial gesture of the fantasy of the femme fatale—the passionate coming together of lovers—is exactly the same as that of the fantasy of the heavenly lady. The difference between the fantasies lies in the outcome of the embrace, its meaning, and the moral order that finds it good or evil—not in the embrace itself. There is no reason to suppose another incident's giving rise to Rossetti's sinister works, for Janey could have encouraged both fantasies with the same attractive smile.

The likelihood is increased with the recognition of a curious double use of symbols and gestures by Rossetti. Not only is a situation common to both fantasies, but the terms of one find their way into the other. For example, there is the little scene, from which Rossetti borrowed, at the beginning of Canto XXIII of the "Paradiso": *Come l'augello, intra l'amate fronde* . . . Beatrice in suspense and longing is likened to a mother bird who protects her young through the night, and awaits the dawn *con ardente*, when she may see and nourish them. The image, beautiful in itself, is easily related to the protective love-longing that is the typical attitude of the Blessed Damozel, and of the Madonna in general. Rossetti, in his uses of the simile, preserved its comforting quality:

> Each dawn until we meet is as a bird
> That wings from far his gradual way along
> The rustling covert of my soul,—his song
> Still loudlier trilled through leaves more deeply stirred.
> "Winged Hours," HL XXV (?1868–1869)

> Next day the memories of these things
> Like leaves through which a bird has flown,
> Still vibrated with Love's warm wings . . .
> The Portrait

But in the time of Rossetti's friendship with Janey, the bird in the leafy boughs became a symbol of disaster as well. *The Sea Spell*,[2] an oil of 1877 that depicts a singing siren, is described in an accompanying sonnet as follows:

A Sea Spell
Courtesy of Fogg Art Museum, Harvard University (Gift of Grenville
L. Winthrop)

Her lute hangs shadowed in the apple-tree,
While flashing fingers weave the sweet-strung spell
Between its chords; and as the wild notes swell,
The sea-bird for those branches leaves the sea.

The painting shows a dazed bird, the sea behind him, emerging from a jungle of leaves. In an especially sinister touch Rossetti chose for some of the foliage that of the Venus Fly Trap, which has "a symbolism made apparent in the name itself."[3] Thus were the longing bird and the beloved boughs subverted in meaning to serve the femme fatale.

A second example—a reversal of the first—is that of the lady in a tree, one of Rossetti's favorite dispositions. It appears first in the design of 1857 for the Oxford Union, *Launcelot at the Shrine of the Sanc Grael*. I have already given Rossetti's description of Guenevere, standing with arms extended in the branches of the apple tree, preventing Sir Launcelot from seeing the Grael by interposing the apple, symbolic of sin. The situation is not only that of Guenevere, but also that of Eve tempting Adam into her sin, and of the serpent tempting Eve. Since the stance is obviously crosslike, it is possible that a suggestion of an infernal redemptrix or devil's Christ is intended as well.[4] With the renewal of friendship with Janey came the re-employment of this artistic situation. In the ballad *Eden Bower* (1869), Lilith persuades the snake to lend her his form so that she may bring about man's fall:

In these coils that tree will I grapple,
And stretch this crowned head forth by the apple.

Her conversation with the snake is rather a seduction than an argument, for she addresses him in an erotic manner consistent with her previous life with Adam and her subsequent career as Lady Lilith:

Look, my mouth and my cheek are ruddy,
And thou art cold, and fire is my body . . .
Then bring thou close thine head till it glisten
Along my breast, and lip me and listen . . .

In thy sweet folds bind me and bend me,
And let me feel the shape thou shalt lend me . . .
Then ope thine ear to my warm mouth's cooing
And learn what deed remains for our doing.

Again the elements of temptation, sex, sin, and damnation are joined in the primordial apple proffered from the tree. And again, in *The Orchard Pit*, a prose tale of 1869, the elements and situation are the same:

> . . . all my life I have dreamed one dream alone—I see a glen whose sides slope upward from the deep bed of a dried-up stream, and either slope is covered with wild apple-trees. In the largest tree, within the fork whence the limbs divide, a fair, golden-haired woman stands and sings, with one white arm stretched along a branch of the tree, and with the other holding forth a bright red apple. . . . Below her feet the trees grow more and more tangled, and stretch from both sides across the deep pit below: and the pit is full of the bodies of men.

The sin involved in taking the apple is sexual sin, for

> at the heart of the apple was a red stain like a woman's mouth; and as I bit it I could feel a kiss upon my lips.[5]

The tale ends with the narrator about to enact his dream.[6] With all of these arboreal temptresses in at least the back of his mind, and Janey the model for the first of them, Rossetti yet painted her in one of his serenest canvases as sitting among the branches of a sycamore tree. *The Day Dream* (Marillier, opp. p. 198), executed in 1880 but projected at least eight years earlier, is described as follows in the accompanying sonnet:

Within the branching shade of Reverie
Dreams even may spring till autumn; yet none be
Like woman's budding day-dream spirit-fann'd.
Lo! tow'red deep skies, not deeper than her look,
She dreams; till now on her forgotten book
Drops the forgotten blossom from her hand.

Clearly the work has none of the feeling of the others, and possibly Rossetti himself never associated them; yet all that is needed is an apple or outstretched hand to reveal the implications of the situation.[7]

A third example of interplay between the fantasies is Rossetti's treatment of the fires of love. Flame is a frequent image in *The House of Life*, occurring in at least a third of the sonnets. In accordance with the fantasy of salvation the flame is beneficial, holy, and sacramental:

> Two bosoms which, heart-shrined with mutual flame,
> Would, meeting in one clasp, be made the same
> > "Severed Selves," *HL* XL (1871)

> love's emulous ardours ran,
> Fire within fire, desire in deity.
> > "The Kiss," *HL* VI

> And as I took them [i.e., Love's baubles], at her
> > touch they shone
> With inmost heaven-hue of the heart of flame.
> > "Love's Baubles," *HL* XXIII (?1868–1870)

> Far in your eyes a yet more hungering thrill,—
> Such fire as Love's soul-winnowing hands distil
> Even from his inmost ark of light and dew.
> > "Soul-Light," *HL* XXVIII (?1871)

The last image is that of the flame-colored band of the rainbow, but the spelling of "ark" permits reference as well to the altar-fires of the Sanctum Sanctorum.[8] Fire is also associated with the femme fatale, but in her hands it becomes painful and destructive. The troubles that Pandora looses are painted, as Rossetti describes them in the sonnet, with "fiery pinions"; Circe's table is "lit with fragrant flame"; Cassandra cries,

> O Paris, Paris! O thou burning brand,
> Thou beacon of the sea whence Venus rose,
> Lighting thy race to shipwreck! Even that hand

Wherewith she took thine apple let her close
Within thy curls at last, and while Troy glows,
Lift thee her trophy to the sea and land.

Cassandra (a double sonnet for a drawing; 1869)

The refrain of *Troy Town* is, "O Troy's down, / Tall Troy's on
fire"; at the climax of *The Orchard Pit* the Siren appears in the
fork of the tree, "blazing now like a lamp beneath the moon."
Hero's disastrous lamp has already been mentioned, as has *La
Donna della Fiamma*.

A last example of an image that crosses lines of fantasy is
that of the lady's song. Rossetti had customarily indicated soul
in his drawings by portraying the lady as singing, or playing a
musical instrument.[9] Now, ten years later, with Janey's arrival,
again he filled his canvases with music. In 1867 he painted an
oil *Christmas Carol* (Marillier, p. 146), an entirely different subject
from that of 1857. In the new work a lady plays upon a lute.
The lady in *Veronica Veronese*, 1872 (Marillier, opp. p. 168),
attempts to repeat the song of a canary upon her violin. In the
Bower Meadow, 1872 (Marillier, opp. p. 170), a group of ladies
are singing, playing, and dancing. *La Ghirlandata*, 1873 (Marillier, opp. p. 172), "represents a lady playing upon a garlanded
harp, in the midst of a forest clearing, where angel faces peer
down upon her rapt in wonder of her music, and mystical blue
birds cleave the air."[10] And the soulful *Roman Widow*, 1874
(Marillier, opp. p. 177), plays a dirge upon two citherns before
her husband's tomb. In all of the works there is a kind of com-
munity with the heavens, revealed in the various religious rites,
the birds, angels, and rapturous upward glances. But even this
sacred activity can be seen as sinister by Rossetti, for he turns
to the depiction of sirens, whose traditional occupation is singing.
Helen in "Death's Songsters," and the several temptresses in
Ligeia Siren, *The Sea Spell*, *The Orchard Pit*, and *The Doom of the
Sirens* all destroy with their deceptive songs.

Thus the two different fantasies divided between themselves
the same woman, the same situation, and even the same terms.
Occasionally Rossetti indicated his own recognition of the per-
plexity: in a fragment of verse based upon his prose tale, *The*

Orchard Pit, and written in the same year, he described, in a grotesque image, the lady in the tree as having

> Life's eyes . . . gleaming from her forehead fair,
> And from her breasts the ravishing eyes of Death.

Nowhere else in his work is the confusion between the women of the two fantasies so graphically presented. That both salvation and damnation can seem to emanate from the same object or situation is admitted also in the progressively vivid lines of "Inclusiveness" (*HL* LXIII):

> May not this ancient room thou sitt'st in dwell
> In separate living souls for joy or pain?
> Nay, all its corners may be painted plain
> Where Heaven shows pictures of some life spent well;
> And may be stamped, a memory all in vain,
> Upon the sight of lidless eyes in Hell.

To a seer practiced in culling arcane meanings from his lady's eyes, such ambiguity and relativism is finally disruptive. It is a sign that his prophetic venture and his basic assumptions are in danger.

The confusion between the two fantasies was not fortuitous, being based upon what was finally a moral confusion. Janey recalled for Rossetti two "discordant phases of profession," neither of which he was able to relinquish. Behind the heavenly lady was the assumption, already described sufficiently, that human, sexual love is good and leads to heaven. Behind the femme fatale was the contradictory assumption that sex is sinful, and leads away from spiritual salvation to damnation. The same relationship with the same woman was thus subject to two conflicting moral systems: one of his own making, which he desired but could not bring himself to believe utterly; the other the orthodox one of his youth, which he had disowned but could not drum out of his system. The confusion of fantasies indicated an emotional conflict between desire and guilt, and a moral conflict between adopted beliefs and basic feelings upon the subject of sexual behavior.

Perhaps, in my efforts to describe the religious system of

Rossetti's own making, I have not emphasized sufficiently the power that orthodox morality exerted over him. Although he rebelled against the early religious and moral training received from his mother, he could not rid himself of it completely. The traditional Christian morality would make its mark upon one with such an acute feeling for the traditional Christian rewards and punishments. In his early works treating the sinful woman (*Found* and *Jenny* are two examples) we have seen him apply the conventional moral code to the prostitute, regarding her sexual acts as spiritually self-destructive. So even in his early manhood he was influenced by conventional morality, although he did not then apply it to erring males, and harbored it in a fantasy comfortably removed from that of the Madonna. The traditional morality was also operative in the mid-1860's, when he was dealing with fleshly femmes fatales (relevant works include *Fazio's Mistress, Lady Lilith, and Venus Verticordia*). In this dissolute time he treated succumbing to sexual temptation as damnable, even of himself; but he cultivated a distinction between ladies with "body's beauty" and those with "soul's beauty," a distinction that permitted him to preserve the fantasy of the heavenly lady from the morality underlying the theme of the femme fatale. Thus even in his degeneracy he had a hope that if he could find the Blessed Damozel he could still be saved. It remained for Janey, rich in body and soul, to confound the fantasies and force the moral conflict.

Rossetti was not successful in facing the conflict of moral judgments which I have related to his love for Janey. His usual response was to vacillate between them. For instance he made simultaneous plans in 1869–1870 for writing *The Harrowing of Hell*, in which (as we have seen) ". . . the redemption wrought by Christ [was] to be viewed as an elevation of the conception of love from pleasure into passion, hence entailing the redemption from Hell of Adam and Eve, David and Bathsheba, *etc., etc.*"[11] and *God's Graal*, which he epitomized rather ruefully in a letter to Swinburne as "the loss of the Sangraal by Lancelot—a theme chosen to emphasize the marked superiority of Guenevere over God."[12] In the one projected work, love-passion meets with God's approval; in the other, with His punishment. Thus did "vain desire . . . and vain regret / Go hand in hand," to take from the closing sonnet of *The House of Life* Rossetti's description of his own state at the time.

In only two works did Rossetti actually bring the two moral systems to bear upon each other. *Rose Mary* (1871) was discussed in Chapter Six. There I observed that the Beryl-stone, with its ban upon fornication, represented the traditional moral system; and that Rose Mary's destruction of the stone and its "heavy law" revealed Rossetti's desire to do the same. The happy "Heaven of Love" to which Rose Mary was finally led was governed solely by Rossetti's invented moral code. Yet, as I pointed out, the battle of moralities was fought rather crudely and inappropriately with the sword. The cleaving of the stone represented Rossetti's great desire for the victory, but not the victory itself.

The second work was *The Doom of the Sirens* (*Works*, pp. 610–613), Rossetti's prose outline, written in 1869, of a projected "Lyrical Tragedy." Again conventional morality is operative, as a Prince and then his son come to the "Siren's Rock" to confront the temptress, Ligeia, who promises love but dispenses death to those who succumb to her. Orthodox morality constitutes the rules of the tourney, so to speak, and the contending forces are paganism and illicit temptation versus Christianity and marital troth—Guenevere versus God again. Rossetti emphasizes that it is for the cause of Christianity that the Christian Prince attempts to resist (and thereby destroy) the pagan beauty. But Ligeia woos the Prince from his wife, and paganism is triumphant. After a twenty-one year interim the son of the Prince returns to the rock and repulses Ligeia; his father is thereby avenged, and the power of Christianity tardily affirmed. Yet, in his victory, the son finds himself "physically absorbed into the death-agony of the expiring spell; and when, at his last word of reprobation [to Ligeia], the curse seizes her and her sisters, and they dash themselves headlong from the rock, he also succumbs to the doom . . . ." The similarity of his death-in-victory to that of Rose Mary's extends even further, for his bride dies with him, joining him, we are to infer, in an eternity of lovers' bliss. The son's reward for resisting sexual temptation is his removal from the old order that demanded his resistance. As in *Rose Mary*, it is Rossetti's own lovers' morality that governs heaven; as in *Rose Mary*, the defeat of evil means the downfall of the concept of sex as sin.

In one respect *The Doom of the Sirens* is more satisfying than *Rose Mary;* its hero conquers the "heavy law," not by swinging a sword, but by fulfilling the law. By confronting it and satisfying its unpleasant requirements, he proves himself its master, worthy to rise above it to his reward. The conquest makes good sense dramatically, but unfortunately Rossetti in his own life could not follow suit, apparently. Everything indicates his inability to resist the siren's song; according to the terms of his projected play he would have been damned. Perhaps this consideration prevented him from writing it.

Rossetti was as unsuccessful in his life as in his works in reconciling the two conflicting moral systems that underlay his two dominant fantasies. In fact, his failure to do so took an extreme and dramatic form. It can be argued that his emotional collapse and attempted suicide during the first days of June 1872 were largely due to this very conflict of moralities.

The event which initiated his collapse was a virulent review of his poetry. "The Fleshly School of Poetry—Mr. D. G. Rossetti" appeared in the October 1871 *Contemporary Review*, and its effect on Gabriel was violent and permanent. He flew into great rages, composing unprintable replies, assiduously searching out the true name of the author of the pseudonymous review, even considering challenging him to a duel. William Bell Scott mentions Gabriel's "visibly breaking down under the paltry infliction of 'an article,' "[13] and describes the offended poet's arrival at a dinner as follows:

> At last we heard a tremendous peal at the bell, and knocking, a great noise ascended the stair, and he burst in upon us, shouting out the name of Robert Buchanan, who, it appeared, he had discovered to be the writer of the article in the *Contemporary Review* which was so distracting him. He was too excited to observe or to care who were present, and all the evening he continued unable to contain himself or to avoid shouting out the name of his enemy.[14]

Both Scott and Gabriel's brother attest that the review contributed directly to his breakdown; William writes, of the expanded article by Buchanan, published in pamphlet in May 1872,

> In my brother's life it was deplorably prominent. . . . It is a simple fact that from the time when the pamphlet had begun to work into the inner tissue of his feelings, Dante Rossetti was a changed man, and so continued till the close of his life.[15] Certain it was that when the pamphlet appeared . . . his fancies now ran away with him, and he thought that the pamphlet was a first symptom in a widespread conspiracy for crushing his fair fame as an artist and a man, and for hounding him out of honest society.[16]

Robert Buchanan's part in the affair was not a noble one. His motives were jealousy, revenge, and a desire to steal some light from Rossetti's rising star. His means were devious and cowardly, and his attitude willfully prejudiced. As an apostle of morality he was a hypocrite. When the reaction of contemporary poets and critics proved overwhelmingly unfavorable to him, [17] he changed course to flow with the stream, composing a series of recantations as shallow as his original charges. We may well wonder why the words of this pretentious, mean man, who was regarded with contempt and amusement by Rossetti's friends Meredith and Swinburne, had such a profound ill effect upon him.

Although Buchanan's character and motives were small, his accusations still had to be met of themselves, and they struck Rossetti where he was the most unsure of himself. The chief charge, which was the most upsetting to Rossetti, was a moral, rather than purely literary, indictment.[18] Adopting for the nonce the attitude toward public mention of sexuality that has come to be called "Victorian," Buchanan equated sensuality with sinfulness, and the fulfillment of human love with revolting lust; and asserted righteous indignation at Gabriel's frankness on the subject:

> . . . so sickening a desire to reproduce the sensual mood, so careful a choice of epithet to convey mere animal sensations, that we merely shudder at the shameless nakedness. . . . It is flooded with

sensualism from the first line to the last; it is a very hotbed of nasty phrases. . . . Sonnets XII to XX are one profuse sweat of animalism. . . . [Rossetti] pursues the metaphor to the very pit of beastliness. . . . there is a veritably stupendous preponderance of sensuality and sickly animalism. . . . abnormal types of diseased lust and lustful disease. . . . It is simply nasty.

It will be clear to the reader that not all of the sweat and nastiness in these sibilant remarks emanates from Rossetti's poems. Some truly immoral person or some single-minded apostle of the morality of *The Blessed Damozel* could have shrugged off Buchanan's contemptible utterances, and, judging the traditional morality by its champion, might well have felt justified in flouting it. Gabriel differed greatly from Buchanan in admitting that a naked woman has her attractions. But, as we have seen, there was a part of himself that felt sex to be as degrading and sinful as Buchanan asserted. He, too, in his fantasy of the femme fatale, associated submission to sexual temptation with the horrors of charnel pits, strangulation, hell-fire, "quag-water," and bestiality. Buchanan was merely echoing, with more directness and stridency, the charges that Rossetti was half-heartedly bearing against himself.

Rossetti's retort to Buchanan, "The Stealthy School of Criticism," was published in the *Athenaeum* in December 1871 (republished in *Works*, pp. 617–621). His most relevant reply to Buchanan's principal indictment was that the presence of "soul" in a sensual situation made everything all right, and that the amorous relationships that he celebrated included "soul":

> . . . one charge it would be impossible to maintain against the writer of the series in which ["Love-Sweetness"] occurs, and that is, the wish on his part to assert that the body is greater than the soul. For here all the passionate and just delights of the body are declared—somewhat figuratively it is true, but unmistakably—to be as naught if not ennobled by the concurrence of the soul at all times.

> . . . a beauty of natural universal function, only to be reprobated in art if dwelt on (as I have shown that it is not here) to the

exclusion of those other highest things of which it is the harmonious concomitant.

That I may, nevertheless, take a wider view than some poets or critics, of how much, in the material conditions absolutely given to man to deal with as distinct from his spiritual aspirations, is admissible within the limits of Art,—this, I say, is possible enough. . . . But to state that I do so to the ignoring or overshadowing of spiritual beauty, is an absolute falsehood, impossible to be put forward except in the indulgence of prejudice or rancour.

Whereas Buchanan applied the "Victorian morality" indiscriminately to Rossetti's works, Rossetti answered by applying the morality of *The Blessed Damozel* with equal indiscrimination. He disregarded his works dealing with femmes fatales—his Liliths, Gueneveres, Helens, et al.—and made his stand upon the works dealing with heavenly ladies—*The House of Life* in particular. Perhaps the whole matter of femmes fatales was too highly charged for Rossetti to permit himself to argue upon the distinction between evil and the depiction of evil, between life and literature. For whatever reason, he let "soul" come to the rescue of fleshliness in both literature and life.

According to William, Buchanan's pamphlet of May 1872 had an even more adverse effect upon Gabriel than the original review. It was largely a repetition, in expanded form and even stronger language, of the previous charges. Throughout most of the pamphlet he ignored Rossetti's defense, continuing to accumulate examples that he considered salacious from Rossetti's poetry, and attacking by any means that he could. The body of the book is despicable pulp, but toward the end he does come entirely to the point: challenging Rossetti's defense, he claims, in what is a direct questioning of the moral system related to Rossetti's heavenly lady, that Rossetti

... does not, in fact, discriminate between passion and sensuality. . . . No one can rejoice more than I do to hear that Mr. Rossetti attaches a certain importance to the soul as distinguished from the body, only I should like very much to know what he means by the soul; for I fear from the sonnet he quotes [i.e.,

"Love-Sweetness,"] that he regards the feeling for a young woman's person, face, heart, and mind, as in itself quite a spiritual sentiment. In the poem entitled "Love-lily" he expressly observes that Love cannot tell Lily's "body from her soul"—they are so inextricably blended. It is precisely this confusion of the two which, filling Mr. Rossetti as it eternally does with what he calls "riotous longing," becomes so intolerable to readers with a less mystic sense of animal function.[19]

The tenor of these remarks is supported by several jibes challenging specifically Rossetti's notions of soul and salvation:

. . . to treat the body and upholstery of a dollish woman as if, in itself, it constituted a whole universe . . . [20]

. . . religion outraged, in one gibbering attempt to apotheosize vice . . . [21]

. . . finding religion distorted into lust, and lust raving in the very language of religion . . . [22]

I do not admire [the Flesh's] absurd manner of considering itself the Soul.[23]

What Rossetti calls soul is thus flatly reduced to flesh or "animal function," and the assumptions underlying his Madonna are scouted. To the attack upon his Holy of Holies he gave no reply.

This line of criticism, not found in Buchanan's earlier article, is telling, and substantially fair, being aimed at the point in Rossetti's assumptions with respect to the heavenly lady that most needed elaboration; yet it should have served as the beginning of discussion rather than its end. It would not be hard to play Rossetti's advocate, composing responses that he might have made to Buchanan's remarks. One could say that Rossetti's position relative to Buchanan is that of one with perfect sight trying to explain color to the color-blind; that the skeptic's failure or refusal to see soul in sexuality does not prove its absence. One could say that "soul" and "body" are truly felt to be one only in a state of conceptual innocence; that the use of the terms introduces a distortion of truth that is difficult to think away thereafter. One could object to Buchanan's introduction of debasing terms for Rossetti's own terms (i.e., "confusion" for Rossetti's unity of body and soul, and "animal function" for "love"), thereby causing further distortion. After these preliminaries one would be obliged, in behalf of Rossetti, to explain what soul does mean. His multiple sliding concept that was examined earlier would be inadequate, of course; so one would do well to adopt or revise some post-Kantian system that treats consistently of the soul as man's "inner" feelings.

I do not mean to assert by this hypothetical rebuttal that the ethos implied in Rossetti's fantasy of the heavenly lady is ultimately sound. It is enough to argue that, first, the ethos stands the test of the healthy heart: Buchanan notwithstanding, a human beloved can inspire many exalted emotions customarily considered religious. And, second, whatever its ultimate defensibility, Rossetti's ethos is at least capable of further defense and development in the face of Buchanan's criticism of it.

Nevertheless Rossetti had nothing to reply, as the pamphlet worked "into the inner tissue of his feelings." He could not answer Buchanan successfully because, again, the critic echoed one phase of his own attitudes and beliefs. In truth he could *not* tell soul from body; and although some simple lover of the Blessed Damozel, living entirely within the universe of that poem, would not feel compelled to do so, Rossetti was so compelled, for he had been living upon the discrimination ever since he first divided his love and fancies between Lizzie and some "Jenny." If he could not distinguish between body and soul, then he had no grounds for delimiting the jurisdiction of the two moralities. Furthermore, any defense of the heavenly woman would have been especially half-hearted now, for he and Janey were in the midst of a long separation (October 1871 to September 1872), which, if due to Janey's turning from him, meant damnation anyway. Just as his reaction to the earlier review had been primarily *ad hominem*, against its pseudonymity, so also now he treated the pamphlet—with considerable justification—as a personal attack rather than an ethical challenge.

He now believed that there was an elaborate conspiracy under-foot to destroy him.[24] The excessiveness of his reaction strongly suggests that he was using the pseudonymity and purported conspiracy as red herrings, to draw his thoughts away from his own moral confusion.

Within the month Rossetti experienced a mental crisis and attempted suicide. Several factors contributed to his continued demoralization—the strain, perhaps, of his relations with the absent Janey, illness, insomnia, and the drugs and spirits that he imbibed to counteract it—but a guilty conscience certainly contributed its share. Perhaps his fearful, paranoid suspicions, now habitual, that a vast corps of enemies was attacking him was the projection to the social realm of his moral probing of himself.

The event that finally brought on the crisis was Rossetti's reading Browning's recently composed *Fifine at the Fair*. The poem gave substance to his fears of a conspiracy, and focus to his guilty feelings. Probably written with Rossetti somewhat in mind,[25] although presumably not intended to vilify him, it is certainly applicable to him. Browning once declared that it was intended "to show morally how a Don Juan might justify himself partly by truth, somewhat by sophistry";[26] and, as Professor Doughty observes, it ridicules the notion that "sense" is sanctified by "soul." The similarity in moral criticism between *Fifine* and Buchanan's pamphlet is strong, and it is easy to see how the poem could feed Rossetti's suspicions of a hostile conspiracy. An additional blow was given him in the final pages: Gabriel "at once fastened upon some lines at its close as being intended as an attack upon him, or as a spiteful reference to something which had occurred, or might be alleged to have occurred, at his house."[27] At the end of the poem we learn that Don Juan leaves his home and wife one evening to go philandering with the ropedancer, Fifine. Upon his return he finds his wife dead or dying. In the "Epilogue" she returns to haunt him in his miserable degeneracy. The events are similar to those rumored to have occurred upon the night of Lizzie's death ten years before. Even the haunting suggests Gabriel's life, and the "old house— / Every crumbling brick embrowned with sin and shame!" could easily be a luridly colored reference to gloomy old 16 Cheyne Walk. It is little wonder that Rossetti was upset.

Don Juan's illicit love caused his wife's death—a stroke by Browning that must have been particularly hard on Rossetti's well-being. Ever since Buchanan's articles, Rossetti's guilty feelings for his behavior in love would have been painful enough already. Now *Fifine* helped to remind him of a consequence of his philandering that he had been trying to forget for ten years. It reminded him of evidence straight from his life that his amorous adventures were vicious and disastrous. To one habituated to searching literature for patterns of his life, and who was having a discouraging time trying to see himself as a Dante, the thoroughly apt analogy between Browning's Don Juan and his own life would not have gone unnoticed. And the aptness of the analogy would serve as a kind of proof that sex was evil and damning rather than holy and saving. Even though he had probably not been pursuing some Fifine on the night of Lizzie's suicide, the fact remained that his infidelities had tormented the already depressed and disturbed wife. Thus *Fifine at the Fair* must have reinforced Rossetti's guilty feelings about sex, intensifying them and focusing them upon the single incident of Lizzie's suicide.

Within a day or so of reading *Fifine*, Rossetti's "seizure" began. To give William's account: "from his wild way of talking—about conspiracies and what not—I was astounded to perceive that he was, past question, not entirely sane."[28] He was in the process of completing the sale of a picture, and he suggested to the dealer, Lefevre, that the agreement be canceled if the price for the picture be thought too high—a strange offer from "the paragon of artists at making a bargain,"[29] and a sign that his guilty conscience was at work. He grew fearful and suspicious of others, accusing Dr. Maudsley, a specialist on mental diseases, of trying to do him ill, and (succumbing to auditory delusions) charging an astonished cabman (who was transporting him, for the sake of seclusion, to Dr. Gordon Hake's home in Roehampton) with ringing an annoying bell throughout the trip. During a walk near Dr. Hake's home he believed that a band of gypsies that he encountered were gathered to work his harm.[30]

On the evening before Whitsunday "he sat up late in conversation with his brother on various family-matters,"[31] and then,

> having gone to bed . . . my brother heard (this was of course a further instance of absolute physical delusion) a voice which twice called out at him a term of gross and unbearable obloquy—I will not here repeat it [Professor Doughty believes that the term was "murderer"]. He would no longer endure a persecution from which he perceived no escape. He laid his hand upon a bottle of laudanum which, unknown to us all, he had brought with him, swallowed its contents, and dropped the empty bottle into a drawer. Of course his intention was suicide . . . .[32]

And his weapon, the drug that had killed his wife.

Perhaps there was, in Rossetti's attempted suicide, an unconsciously felt duty to his old assumption that he was living a part; a duty to live out the analogy and, now that his Madonna had failed him, to make the fantasy of the femme fatale, at least, come true. Although his act seems to make Janey a femme fatale after all, the fantasies were still of his own devising, the confusion of his own creating, and his downfall, therefore, his own making. Janey's greatest disservice to Rossetti was her meaning too many things to him.

CHAPTER ELEVEN

The Attenuation of Fantasy

ROSSETTI's attempt at suicide did not clear the air. The old problems were still present at his recovery, and in his physically and emotionally weakened condition he was even less prepared to master them. The ten years after the attempt were not an unbroken gloom, of course, for there were many moments of pleasure and laughter. But all who knew him agree that he never regained his old health and spirits. He also never resolved his moral dilemma.

His old desire was still present. Within four months, as soon as he was recovered from the physical consequence of his act, he was back in Kelmscott, in search of "peace"[1] with "the one necessary person." This was one of his sunniest times. His letters, filled with tales of his playful escapades with Janey's two daughters and the household dogs, testify to his well-being. Janey and he were together almost constantly until July 1874, when she departed from Kelmscott. A perturbed Gabriel left shortly thereafter. He continued thenceforth to receive the "rare and valued visits" of which Hall Caine spoke,[2] and to use Janey as the model for several new paintings. Now his life was usually empty of her presence, although she seems to have been ever welcome as a guest. Meanwhile his preoccupation with the heavenly lady kept pace with his attraction to Janey. There was the *Boat of Love* (ca. 1874; Marillier, p. 177), in which Janey was portrayed as Beatrice; and several other Dantesque replicas, in which Janey figured as heavenly lady: *La Donna della Fenestra* (1879);

Dante's Dream (1880); and the unfinished *Salutation of Beatrice* (1880). There were also works in which some face other than Janey's served as model for the Madonna: a new version of the *Damsel of the Sanc Grael* (1874; Marillier, opp. p. 176); an unfinished replica of *Beata Beatrix* (1877); *Sancta Lilias* (1879; Marillier, p. 198); and two versions and several studies of *The Blessed Damozel* (Marillier, opp. p. 188, p. 189, and opp. p. 190); for the early subject was now transferred to the poet's other medium. In these works the usual alternative to Janey was Alexa Wilding, a kind of "Mrs. Morris for beginners."[3] In Rossetti's poetry the old desire was repeated (I omit sonnets written for *The House of Life*) in three modest but moving lyrics. It is found in *Insomnia* (1881):

> Is there a home where heavy earth
> Melts to bright air that breathes no pain,
> Where water leaves no thirst again
> And springing fire is Love's new birth?
> If faith long bound to one true goal
> May there at length its hope beget,
> My soul that hour shall draw your soul
>   For ever nearer yet.

It is repeated as well in *Alas, So Long* (?1881), where the beloved seems to be Lizzie rather than Janey:

> Ah! dear one, you've been dead so long,—
> How long until we meet again,
> Where hours may never lose their song
>   Nor flowers forget the rain
> In glad noonlight that never shall wane?
>   Alas, so long!

We find it again in *Spheral Change* (1881):

> O nearest, furthest! Can there be
> At length some hard-earned heart-won home,
> Where,—exile changed for sanctuary,—
> Our lot may fill indeed its sum,
> And you may wait and I may come?

The "heart's one Hope" had survived the crisis.

Unfortunately the old guilt had survived too. Only a few works portray the theme of the femme fatale, notably *Ligeia Siren* (1873) and *The Sea Spell* (1877), but the guilty conscience showed itself in other ways. All accounts of Gabriel's later years disclose his continual wild suspicions of a conspiracy against his name. He broke with many of his friends, believing them to have turned against him. He now refused—quite wisely, considering his state—to read unfavorable reviews of his work. And the persecuting voices were not all human: William remembers, of Gabriel's later years, that " . . . there was once a thrush hard by, which, to my hearing, simply trilled its own lay on and off. My brother discerned a different note, and conceived that the thrush had been trained to ejaculate something insulting to him. Such is perverted fantasy. . . ."4 Dr. Hake wrote to Theodore Watts-Dunton upon a different occasion, "I have been obliged today to see about hiring a man to keep off birds and such noises from the studio so as to enable [Gabriel] to work. He is very depressed."5 This from a man with the reticence to say of Rossetti's attempted suicide merely, "his night was the most troubled one that he had hitherto passed through," is saying much. The voice that Gabriel heard in the birds' notes was likely that of the dead Lizzie; for earlier, in the midst of negotiations for the opening of her grave, he had taken the notes of a chaffinch to be her voice prophesying his misfortune.6 In the 1860's he had frequented seances, probably to wrest the secret of Lizzie's death from the grave, but now, in the 1870's, he attempted to dissuade Hall Caine from attending one, saying, " . . . they're evil spirits—devils—and they're allowed to torment and deceive people."7 It was thus that he continued to ascribe to human and inhuman beings the accusations with which he must have been persecuting himself. In the words of his house-companion,

> . . . the solitude of his last years—with its sleepless nights and its delusions born of indulgence in the drug—was not wholly, or even mainly, the result of morbid brooding over the insults of pitiful critics, but of a deep-seated, if wholly unnecessary sense as of a curse resting on him and on his work, whereof the malignancy of criticism was only one of many manifestations.8

There were as well more direct manifestations of a guilty conscience. In 1881, as he entered upon his last illness, he wished to confess his sins to a priest. When the insensitive Bell Scott pointed out to him that he was not Roman Catholic, he replied, "I don't care about that. . . . I can make nothing of Christianity, but I only want a confessor to give me absolution for my sins. . . . What I want now is absolution for my sins, that's all."[9] Perhaps no other comment shows so well the stubborn inconsistency of the man, and the power of the rejected religion over him. "Even the ringing of the church bells on Sunday seemed . . . to give him pain."[10] In his moral probing of himself he searched every corner of his life: "Matters of very old as well as more recent date agitated his mind; even so old as the year 1847 or 1848, when his desultory habits of work, or lack of filial deference, used to annoy our father. . . . "[11] Rossetti's feelings of guilt, no less than his amorous desires, had survived the attempted suicide. The conflict of desire and guilt remained unresolved.

Its effect upon Rossetti was a pathetic eagerness to have his works considered morally sound, and yet a helplessness or dependency in dealing with moral issues. A characteristic common to the young friends that he made relatively late in life was a moral reassurance, before which he became remarkably amiable and compliant. One such friend was Theodore Watts-Dunton, who nurtured moral fiber in more than one poet: Rossetti seemed

> . . . strangely liable to Mr. Watts' influence in his critical estimates. . . . [The jealous rival, Caine, then quotes Rossetti as saying,] "in a question of loss or gain to a poem, I feel that Watts must be right." . . . Mr. Watts took the view (to Rossetti's great vexation at first) that ["Nuptial Sleep"], howsoever perfect in structure and beautiful . . . , was "out of place . . . in a group of sonnets so entirely spiritual as *The House of Life*," and Rossetti gave way.[12]

Another such friend who emphasized the "entirely spiritual" in Rossetti was Hall Caine himself, who owed his friendship with the poet to the position he had taken in a lecture defending Rossetti before they had ever met. The point to the lecture was that Rossetti's poetry was

> . . . unconsciously making for moral ends . . . Every thought . . . mixed with and colored by a personal moral instinct that was safe and right. This was perhaps the only noticeable feature of my lecture . . .

> . . . knowing Rossetti's nature as I afterward learned to know it, I see that such pleading for the moral influences animating his work was of all things most likely to enlist his sympathy and engage his affections. . . . [Rossetti] jumped with eagerness at a wholehearted defense of his . . . impulses, as a writer who had been prompted by the highest of spiritual emotions, and as a man to whom the passions of the body were as nothing unless sanctified by the concurrence of the soul.[13]

Upon receiving a copy of the lecture, Gabriel had written to his mother that Caine's lectures were done "in the spirit I most wish,"[14] and to the young Caine himself, urging him to correspond, and to visit him when in London. Thus did Rossetti attempt to drown out the tormenting inner voices by surrounding himself with soothing ones from without.

In these last years three gradual changes overcame him, and they are easily related to his trying to move away from his unresolved conflict. The first is the fading of his old desires and inspirations, even a dissatisfaction with his old themes. Aging and sickly, he was understandably less ready than he once was to answer to his old muse, Erato, and the moral pangs that he now felt in her presence must have made him a somewhat restive votary. In the fall of 1877 he wrote to Shields, "My power of work is not essentially impaired at present I believe, but I must confess that enthusiasm no less than encouragement seems other than it was."[15] In 1876 he wrote to Fanny, "I . . . feel so little interest in everything that I can hardly push on my work at all."[16] To Skelton he complained that he could now make no new departure in art, " . . . finding myself, as I grow older, more than ever at the mercy of my first sources of inspiration."[17] For the most part he toiled for gain over replicas of his old paintings. Now he crudely referred to *The Blessed Damozel*, the most ambitious of his newer designs of a Madonna and once the symbol of his optimistic idealism, as the "Blasted Damozel," or the "Bloody Dam"[18]—"chaff" again, to keep the heart on the sleeve from showing, but perhaps, this time, indicating the restiveness of disillusionment as well. "I shouldn't wonder, now," he teased the young Hall Caine, "if you imagine that one comes down in a fine frenzy every morning to daub canvas."[19] Such, at least, was not the practice of the weary Rossetti. His fresh visions of heaven were now fairly restricted to little lyrics.

A second change to overtake Rossetti was a profession of skepticism or agnosticism on questions of religion and metaphysics. Prior to the 1870's he did not profess Christian beliefs, of course, but neither did he feel compelled to deny their validity, or even to think about their validity. He seems always to have held a secretive, filmy half-faith in his peculiar conception of heaven, a faith that he was careful not to analyze lest it disintegrate. But in 1879, with complete lack of insight, he wrote to Edmund Bates, "I myself was never gifted with implicit faith in things not undeniably proved."[20] The new attitude is seen in his large pencil drawing of 1875, *The Sphinx*, or *The Question*. A dying youth, a resolute man, and a feeble old man toil up the cliff of life to a Greek sphinx, a female emblem of the mystery of life and death. But their questions are not answered, for her lips are shut and her gaze is fixed beyond them. "This design," says Frederic Stephens, "Rossetti characteristically wrote of as being meant to be a sort of painted *Cloud Confines*. . . ."[21] The last-mentioned work declares,

> But no word comes from the dead;
> Whether at all they be,
> Or whether as bond or free,
> Or whether they too were we,
> Or by what spell they have sped.

In 1871, just before his disturbance, Rossetti sent the following verses to Scott:

> Let no priest tell you of any home
> Unseen above the sky's blue dome.
>
> .   .   .   .
>
> To have loved and been beloved again
> Is nearer heaven than he can come.[22]

The Sphinx or *The Question*
Permission of The Birmingham Museum and Art Gallery, England

This is not saying, as Rossetti had said many times before, that mortal love has the power of salvation after death, for here the poet denies all metaphysical knowledge whatsoever.

Perhaps the professions of agnosticism were sops to the conscience. In shunning all metaphysics Rossetti dissociated himself from the Blessed Damozel's heaven, but he escaped from the hell of the femme fatale as well. Since the traditional morality would lose its terrors if its traditional sanctions could be denied, he may have sacrificed prospective bliss in order to assuage his present torment at the prospect of damnation.

I have already given evidence that his metaphysical agnosticism was merely sporadic. His brother accurately describes Gabriel's beliefs as periodic and nebulous: "His opinions on the subject were highly indefinite; his utterances often negative, sometimes positive; his interior and essential feelings, a mixture of the two, highly coloured by passion and the imagination, hazily distinguishable by himself, and by no means to be neatly ticketed by others."[23] The profession of agnosticism may be seen as a third profession, taking its place, in the 1870's, against those associated with the heavenly lady and the femme fatale.

A third change of Rossetti's last years was his attempt to dissociate his personality and experiences from his works.[24] Although he could still write, in 1880, "By thine own tears thy song must tears beget, / O Singer!" ("The Song-Throe," *HL* LXI), most of his proclamations now emphasized impersonality and technique, and deprecated "fine frenzy" on the part of the artist. Hall Caine reports his saying, one night in 1880, "Now I paint by a set of unwritten but clearly defined rules, which I could teach to any man as systematically as you could teach arithmetic. . . . Painting, after all, is the craft of a superior carpenter. The part of a picture that is not mechanical is often trivial enough."[25] On a later date he extolled "fundamental brainwork" as the key to good poetry.[26] Although this quality had always been a characteristic of his own work, he had never vaunted it above passionate self-expression. Again Caine tells us that "Rossetti used to say . . . that he would never again write poems as from his own person."[27]

Certainly a good part of Rossetti's advocacy of impersonality was due to the flagging of the emotions upon which he had built his principal works. Now he had to reconcile himself to the realization that his inspiration was no longer what it had been once. When a poet can no longer fly, he praises the pedestrian. Rossetti was doing more, however, than calling lost grapes sour, and sweet the lemons at hand. Impersonality extended to outright denial of any connection between himself and the situations of his earlier works: "To speak in the first person is often to speak most vividly; but these emotional poems [i.e., *The House of Life*] are *in no sense* 'occasional.' The life involved is life representative . . ."[28] (italics mine). He even changed indications of Janey's dark hair in four of his sonnets, substituting references to the blonde of his dead wife.[29] In this light his newly assumed impersonality may be seen in part as an attempt to mislead the ignorant from discovering the actual intimacy that inspired most of his mature works.

Rossetti's assumed impersonality was an attempt to fool himself as well. In 1881 he retouched his great painting, *Dante's Dream*, changing the color of Beatrice's hair from Janey's dark tint to "a golden hue . . . not wholly exempt from a pinkish tendency."[30] Another time (William is unsure of the date) he lightened the Virgin of his Llandaff triptych, for which Janey had also sat.[31] As it was no secret that Janey was the model for the heroines, Rossetti must have made the alterations for his own satisfaction. By depicting the Virgin and Beatrice as blonde, he made them less like Janey. His purpose would seem to have been a dissociation of himself from the fantasy of the heavenly lady, or at least a dissociation of Janey from the ideal ladies represented. For reasons of prudence, guilt, or disenchantment Rossetti now denied his "heart's one Hope." Thus do faltering visionaries grow old.

In keeping with Rossetti's new professions, the poetry of his last years expresses a new impersonality. He himself believed that he was now developing a greater dramatic instinct, with a greater range of sympathy and knowledge of life.[32] He wrote sonnets in praise of other poets,[33] and composed historical ballads. In the latter he introduced narrators—in *The White Ship* (1878–1880) a butcher, in *The King's Tragedy* (1881) a lady-in-waiting—with points of view very different from his own. The shame of Fitz-Stephen, the pilot, at failing the King and the impulsive bravery of Kate Barlass are far removed from the lovers' embrace, the usual focal point for Rossetti's dramatic situations. The poems were a new departure for him. They were not, however, so impersonal as he pretended. And it is well that they were not, for where the later poems owe something to his own life they are the most successful.

Because his paintings now were spiritless pot-boilers, we may regard the narrative poems as the most ambitious works of his last years. Although the ballads were greeted enthusiastically by the poet's friends as signs that his poetic spark had been renewed, they are generally ignored today. Yet they deserve better.

There are reasons for their present unpopularity, one being that they are guilty of aimlessness. The plots proceed forthrightly, but coherence extends no further. Both ballads are composed of successive little episodes rather than one story, and, although the form of the ballad sanctions such an arrangement, it does not exempt a poem from unity. The trouble is, finally, that the stories have no fixed core. Rossetti's earlier works formed themselves around one great *ego*, which lent them unity. But in *The White Ship* our attention vacillates among King Henry, the Prince, Fitz-Stephen, and Berold. In *The King's Tragedy* it wanders among King James, Queen Jane, and Catherine Douglas. Lacking a dominant figure, the ballads rely upon plot and *sententia* ("Lands are swayed by a King on a throne. / The sea hath no King but God alone"; "To be born a King! . . . Alack the Day!"); but the plots are not sturdy enough, and the general principles are not pervasive enough, to serve as unifying agents.

Furthermore, the stories gain little by being transmitted through Berold and Kate, who utter few worthwhile observations of their own[34] and sometimes intrude, thrusting their own little concerns into situations of greater moment. Dramatic relief is a valid effect, to be sure, but the narrators offer little contrast, because the entire poems are routed through their meaner sensibilities. As a result, the episodes lack both immediacy and an interesting perspective, and yet another character is added to each poem to vie for the role of central figure. If Rossetti introduced Berold and Kate to ensure the poems' impersonality, he achieved it at a cost.

Nevertheless, the works—*The King's Tragedy* in particular—reward overcoming these obstacles to enjoyment, for many of the episodes are based upon very meaningful situations. For instance, in *The White Ship* there is the plight of the Prince, a bad man destroyed in nobly trying to save a good woman; and that of the presumptuously proud King Henry, who loses his life's one great hope and "never smiled again." Characteristically, both situations reach down into Rossetti's own life and earlier fantasies for their deeper meaning. The charitable impulse that moves the Prince to rescue his sister is the same that underlies the fantasy of the sinful woman. We have seen in the early works of the theme that the lady is treated very like a sister.[35] But here, in accordance with Rossetti's own later life, the elevation of the woman gives way to the degradation of the man. As the weaker vessel (here, alas, quite literally), he partakes of the doom of the lady, who becomes an unwilling femme fatale. And the situation of King Henry can also be made into a personal parable of Rossetti's presumption, lost hopes, and last years.

The situations are basically rich in meaning from Rossetti's life, but they have been cut off from that meaning and left to make their own way. The relationships drawn in the previous paragraph are valid, I believe, but—in the context of the poem—improper and irrelevant. Rossetti does not encourage us to make the personal application, as he almost always does. As a result, the incidents of *The White Ship* seem weak and thin. Rossetti, avoiding significance from his own life, is hard pressed to find it elsewhere, and the disembodied verse is a little too set and lifeless:

> He was a Prince of lust and pride;
> He showed no grace till the hour he died.
>
> . . . .
>
> God only knows where his soul did wake,
> But I saw him die for his sister's sake.
>
> "O wherefore black, O King, ye may say,
> For white is the hue of death today . . . ."

Full many a lordly hour, full fain
Of his realm's rule and pride of his reign:—
But this king never smiled again.

With conventional antitheses employed in place of the more characteristic gropings after ultimate mysteries, the ballad seems trivial by comparison.

One passage must be excepted, however. Berold's account of his "moment's trance 'neath the sea alone" has often been praised; it ends with the couplet,

And when I rose, 'twas the sea did seem,
And not these things, to be all a dream.

Although the style is again antithetical, the passage describes exactly and vividly Berold's confused perception—his private thoughts and the peculiar workings of his mind. The lines of intimate psychological revelation come as a surprise in this poem, which is otherwise content to remain on the surface of things. Again an analogue from Rossetti's own life is at hand, for, like Berold, he had sunk near death and then regained consciousness. We do not know his imaginings upon waking from his frustrated suicide; they were probably not at all like those he ascribes to Berold. Yet the similarity in situation would have been apparent to him, and may have led him to compose the most insightful passage of the poem.

My interest in the passage is not in unearthing yet another artistic reflection of Rossetti's life, but rather (in addition to simply appreciating the verse) in observing that for once the relationship between poem and poet is irrelevant. The passage does not call for biographical interpretation; it possesses its own terms, and Berold need not be an extension of Rossetti. Although the poet's own sensations must have inspired the lines, the lines are emancipated from them. In this passage Rossetti succeeded, perhaps for the first time, both in employing his own meaningful feelings and memories in a poem's behalf, and yet in dissociating himself from it.

The King's Tragedy is also largely impersonal, but in this later ballad Rossetti has made poetic use of his own feelings more readily. For example, he translates within the ballad some lines from *The King's Quair*, composed by the historical King James I of Scotland. Rossetti selects passages expressing sentiments strangely close to his own leading concerns:

> Ah sweet, are ye a worldly creature
> Or heavenly thing in form of nature?
>
> . . . .
>
> But unto my help her heart hath tended,
> And even from death her man defended.

The lines are poignant in the light of Rossetti's disappointed quest for a heavenly lady; and yet they have a poignancy quite aside from this consideration, a pathos of their own that is ensured by the dramatic situation. We know beforehand that nothing the heavenly Queen Jane can do will spare the King from his impending murder. Although the feelings and terms are related to Rossetti's life, they are just and entirely accounted for within the situation of the poem. And the situation is sufficiently removed from his own to discourage the personal application.

Twice more Rossetti recalls old themes, but both are now rid of the sexuality that originally governed them. The first recollection is a translation from *The King's Quair*, where King James sings of the pit under Fortune's wheel:

> "And under the wheel beheld I there
> An ugly Pit as deep as hell,
> That to behold I quaked for fear:
> And this I heard, that who therein fell
> Came no more up, tidings to tell:
> Whereat, astound of the fearful sight,
> I wist not what to do for fright."

We think of *The Orchard Pit* (see p. 159), over which presides, not Fortune, but a temptress offering an apple that holds a kiss. Rossetti makes the pit of *The King's Tragedy* an actual one: King James is killed in a vault beneath his chamber, and the obvious association is made explicit:

> Through the dusk I saw where the white face lay
> In the Pit of Fortune's wheel.

The second echo of Rossetti's past work is the powerful description of Queen Jane,

> And how she dealt for her dear lord's sake
> Dire vengeance manifold.

The episode suggests *Sister Helen*, where Helen also remains fixed in stern prayer until her betrayal has been avenged. But the one lady is a bereaved wife, and the other, a betrayed love. Queen Jane is not moved by sexual jealousy. In a way, what Rossetti meant by "impersonal" poetry was poetry without sexual considerations.

The Queen's revenge is presented more impressively than the pit of Fortune. The pit does not seem so terrible to us as it apparently did to Rossetti. His making the symbolic pit an actual one does not succeed in inducing a horror greater than what the simple murder inspires of itself. The Orchard Pit of the earlier work is far more meaningful, in part because the narrator's attitude toward it is richer; longing and revulsion are joined in a fearful fascination, and the victim is led against his will to destroy himself through his own desire. The struggle of emotions makes the pit terrible. But in *The King's Tragedy* James is driven rather than charmed into his place of death, and the situation is correspondingly less effective.

The vengeance of Queen Jane, however, is moving. Throughout the story she has been called flowerlike; in James's first sight of her she was "like a lily amid the rain." But in her revenge the lily is gone, having given way to an impersonal agent of fire and froth. The "furnace-flame" that burns within her and shows through her eyes is consuming her as well as the traitors. Like Sister Helen, she burns with love and hate together; her words, whispered in the ear of the corpse of her husband at the death of the last traitor, "James, James they suffered more!" are the more terrible because of the loving tones in which they are uttered. The episode is far more concise than *Sister Helen*, and more effective, because it marks the change in Queen Jane from flowerlike wife to widow "with fire-drawn breath." It succeeds whereas the pit of Fortune fails because it uses the terms proper to the poem rather than drawing upon those proper to other artistic works or the life of the poet.

Thus Rossetti, in the works of his later years, did achieve a more conventional balance between detachment and involvement, and occasionally with substantial artistic success. It is therefore with somewhat less justification than before that I trace in his works a parable of his own life. Nevertheless, there does seem to be something of Rossetti in the King. James—like Gabriel a man of the heart—is deeply in love. Like Gabriel he is love's poet. And James was betrayed by his seeming friends, as Gabriel in his paranoid delusion was convinced that he had been. Moreover, Rossetti was not too modest to imagine himself a king; in fact he was nicknamed "The Sultan" by his intimates in his later years,[36] and Whistler called him king.

In the poem three ladies try to oppose the force of the King's faithless friends, and all three fail. The first is "a woman tattered and old," a witch who has foreseen the King's death, and who tries thrice vainly to persuade him to beware. The second is Kate Barlass, the Queen's chambermaid. When the traitors are about to burst upon the King's chambers, she substitutes her arm for the absent bar, but her bravery goes for nothing. And the Queen, although she helps to hide James, and refuses at sword's point to reveal him, is also helpless before the determination of the enemy. Three would-be savior ladies fail before the superior power of the King's adverse destiny and his foes. Surely there is something here of Rossetti's faded trust in the successive Madonnas who once gave meaning to his life. And Queen Jane, who fails as a savior, yet comes to her greatest power as a lady of destruction, is suggestive of another queenly Jane.

Finally I mention *Jan Van Hunks*, even though the greater part of the work was composed thirty-five years before Rossetti's death. It was begun in 1846 or 1847, and nearly completed. Then, on his deathbed, he took it up again, and put the finishing touches.[37] It is a grimly humorous narrative of a smoking-contest between Jan and the Devil. Jan smokes himself to death, and thereby loses the contest. The "shrieking wretch" is dragged off to hell, according to the terms of the wager, where

> They've sliced the very crown from his head,—
>> Worse tonsure than a monk's,—
> Lopped arms and legs,—stuck a red-hot tube
>> In his wretchedest of trunks;
> And when the Devil wants his pipe,
>> They bring him Jan Van Hunks.

The diablerie and unexpected humor are actually quite in keeping with the high spirits of Rossetti's youth. The humor comes about largely through that element of caricature (amply illustrated in the stanza quoted here) that is discussed in Chapter Seven in my account of his early femmes fatales.

Rossetti resumed his old tale to do Watts-Dunton a favor. In a characteristic fit of generosity he proposed writing a joint volume of verse with the younger man, and in casting about for ways to fulfill his promise he remembered "The Dutchman's Pipe" (as it was first called). But then something about the old poem captured his fancy to a degree remarkable for an exercise of friendly duty. Watts-Dunton reports that " . . . he enjoyed writing the ballad, for he frequently laughed over it while reading it to me, a few verses at a time, every evening."[38] Hall Caine tells us that "Rossetti himself had never smoked in his life, I think, but his enjoyment of the Dutchman's agony, as he recited or dictated . . . the stanzas he had composed in bed, made the place ring with laughter."[39] These accounts of death-bed levity are corroborated by Lily Hall Caine (Hall Caine's niece) and William.

I propose an analogy that is, I trust, not merely fanciful: like Jan Van Hunks, Gabriel had "played with fire"—the fires of love.[40] Like him he had tried to beat the devil at his game, and had lost. At least this was his fear. The story might well have pleased the old sinner Gabriel, even though it deals with death and damnation, for it made a caricature of his sober fears, and thereby made them more bearable. To have a vivid vision of the devil as "a little old man / In broidered hosen and tocque," and his retinue as "a knot of fiends / Red, yellow, green and blue," is to divest hell of verisimilitude, and hence of deepest terror. So the poet returned at the last to the caricature of his youth, taking comfort, perhaps, in that distance between literature and life that he had disregarded throughout most of his years to his eventual distress.

Rossetti's conflict of fantasies—his conflict of sexual desire and sexual guilt—remained unresolved in his last years, although it underwent attenuation. He surrounded himself with friends who soothed his conscience; he lost interest in creating ambitious or sustained works dealing with either a heavenly lady or a femme fatale; he now emphasized manner rather than matter, and impersonality rather than passionate involvement with his characters; he sometimes propounded an agnosticism on metaphysical matters that was antagonistic to both of his primary fantasies, and hence a defense against their conflict. The most ambitious poetic works of his last years dramatize the helplessness of man and woman as savior, and the power of woman as destroyer. All three of his later ballads depict the death of a hero, and in all three the death is brought on by the hero's willful or presumptuous behavior. Perhaps, at the end, Rossetti was repenting of his own presumptuous and ultimately self-destructive fantasies, his visions of fair ladies of heaven and hell. If so, then he was repenting of the governing principle of his imaginative life.

CHAPTER TWELVE

An Assessment

I

UNTIDINESS was a fundamental trait of Rossetti's nature. From the beginning this quality was present in him, for we have seen him blur his eyes intentionally and equate the resultant giddiness with the pleasures of heaven. His whole life was a clutter, be it of paintings, pots, professions, fancies, or moralities, and he delighted in the disorganization. John Ruskin, with remarkable insight in view of the date, criticized his friend indirectly by criticizing the narrator of *Jenny*: "altogether a disorderly person," he called him, ostensibly for leaving gold strewn in Jenny's hair, but also, by inference, for disorderly emotions: "I don't mean that an entirely right-minded person never keeps a mistress: but, if he does, he either loves her—or, not loving her, would blame himself, and be horror-struck for himself no less than for her, in such a moralizing fit."[1] At the time Rossetti's fantasies were moving apart, so to speak, and he could afford to ignore the warning; but when the dreams came into conflict over the person of Janey, and were haled before his conscience by Buchanan, Rossetti paid the penalty in full.

The works of the man do not share in this personal failure, however, precisely because poems have endings and pictures have frames. No one poem or picture, not even *The House of Life*, expresses the sum of the man, for his discordant phases did not form a whole; but a given work is often a meaningful and profound expression of one side of the author, or of the discord itself.

One reads Rossetti for the sadly second-best reason that one reads all poets today: to appreciate the experiences he describes rather than the meanings that he has found; to learn his truths of perspective rather than the eternal ones. Rossetti's world was untidy, but the compensatory virtue was richness. Heaven, earth, and hell; love, guilt, and hate; rarefied and base emotions; and facts and fantasies all crowded into his consciousness. He tried to find in the persons of various fair ladies a grand harmony comprehending all these elements, and even though he ultimately failed, his attempts were various, ingenious, and profoundly self-expressive.

I have already described at length how Rossetti probably conceived his works; how he tried to assume the roles and live the lives of certain literary or historical characters. The resultant works might be called "method" poems and paintings. Because of his self-identification with his characters and their situations, he would probably admit to few if any differences between his idea of a character and the original. His Beatrice was *the* Beatrice, his Hamlet was *the* Hamlet, and so forth. For him the value of his conception must have resided in its faithfulness to the parental conception, in the coincidence between the two. We, on the other hand, are more willing and able to appreciate differences between his imaginative situations and their originals, and to recognize his imaginative expressions as unique artistic conceptions. To put the matter another way, Rossetti may be regarded as a translator. His earliest achievement was his successful translation of the early Italian poets, and indeed almost all of his works are translations in the general sense, for they are reconstructions of old stories in the terms of his own life. Like all good free translations they are unified combinations of the present situation and the original story, existing somewhere between the two, bridging and accommodating them both.

Because Rossetti's works characteristically lie between his own situation and an adopted, given situation, it is as important in understanding his work to know the story of his life (colored as it was by his fantasies) as it is to know the traditional situations that he was depicting. If we bear in mind the traditional story only, we shall sometimes find his works, in their deviations from their originals, to be annoying because apparently purposeless and inexplicable; but when we see them as ingenious accommodations of one man's life and another man's story, we can understand and appreciate them more readily.

The worth of Rossetti's work lies in his conception of the Blessed Damozel, too lifelike for Beatrice and too loving for Lizzie; in his Virgin Mary, a simple, everyday girl frightened yet resolute in the knowledge of her future responsibilities; in his Hamlet with no political or ancestral problems, who focuses rather upon considerations of love; Ophelia, with her sinister suggestions of La Belle Dame Sans Merci; Launcelot, clumsily making a fool of himself at the tomb of Arthur; Guenevere, redolent with the tempting fruit of Eve; Venus, gross and barbaric, and crass Helen of Troy; and Pandora, more loving than one might expect of a bearer of mischief.

When he did not resort to fictional analogy, but chose to describe instead an incident from his life or figment of his fancy, he depicted, directly or indirectly, those moments that were personally meaningful and vivid: the eerie sense that he was regarding his double in Dante; the visitations from the dead Lizzie; his rescuing Janey from her marital bondage; and her showing him the way to heaven. The moments, although implicit in his works, are not always clearly presented. For example, it may not occur to the reader that the personification, "Might-have-been," in "A Superscription" recalls the vengeful corpse of a dead wife, or that such vague talk as, "A shaken shadow intolerable, / Of ultimate things unuttered the frail screen," probably refers specifically to the memory of Lizzie's face, silent upon the reasons for her suicide. In accordance with his "method" writing Rossetti portrayed his own experiences; but it was frequently unwise, for various reasons, to refer forthrightly to those experiences. Consequently his works are sometimes without a dramatic situation, full of sesquipedalian utterances suggesting an infinitude of ultimate meanings, but growing out of a kernel of specific truth. A knowledge of his life and fantasies often gives one power to penetrate the clouds, and to realize the specific dramatic situation that gave rise to the work. Good, vivid conceptions can be discovered within vague verses.

There is another kind of vagueness, I hasten to add, that is meaningful, poetically effective, and precisely suited to Rossetti's state of mind. In his general abstractions lies the drama of the life that he led but did not mean to lead. At the last he was not the Dante that he desired to be—the visionary poet who comprehended the universe and spoke of it coherently and clearly. He was rather a retrograde Dante of darkness, who had glimpsed a vision, and then had lost it in its pursuit:

> such a small lamp illumes, on this highway,
> So dimly so few steps in front of my feet,—
> Yet shows me that her way is parted from my way . . .
> Out of sight, beyond light, at what goal may we meet?
> *The Song of the Bower* (1860)

> the beat
> Following her daily of thy heart and feet,
> How passionately and irretrievably,
> In what fond flight, how many ways and days!
> *"Soul's Beauty,"* HL LXXVII (1886)

Although he struggled constantly (and poignantly, as in these verses) to discern the answers to life's mysteries, what he ultimately saw and expressed was the vast incomprehensibility of things. His poems, like his life, begin with sharp imagery and end in great hollow sounds. The long words indicate what he did not envision and know, while the frequent words that presume and appeal to the reader's experience and understanding, or to the universe at large (e.g., *such, so, how, what,* and *how many* in the quotations above), indicate his continued faith that the great answers do exist. It would have been dishonest for him, at this stage in his pursuit of his old vision, to speak in sharp images and clear relationships. The struggling verses—expressively inarticulate—have their own impressiveness.

Rossetti's complementary virtue as a poet and painter was his ability to express his fantasies in all their vividness and immediacy. His visions of heavens warmed by love are always moving, whether set down at nineteen or fifty-three. His hells are made to seem as nightmarish to us as they must have been to him:

> but after death
> God knows I know the faces I shall see,
> Each one a murdered self, with low last breath.
> "I am thyself,—what hast thou done to me?"
> "And I—and I—thyself," (lo! each one saith,)
> "And thou thyself to all eternity!"
>
> "Lost Days," *HL* LXXXVI (1858)

What makes his scenes vivid to us is less the painter's eye than the forceful, primary emotions expressed: great desire for a woman; great longing for heaven; terror of hell and the dead; pity for a woman; guilt for sins. There is often sophistication in the adjustment of an old story to his situation, or in a turn of phrase, but the thrust or purport of a work of Rossetti's is governed by a child's simplicity and fervor.

His greatest weakness is equally related to his "method" composition. He saw himself as various great figures—Dante, Hamlet, Launcelot, and Ulysses—but it was the mountains that had to come to Mohammed. Unless there was a coincidence between his life and that of the old hero, he could not relate himself to him; he could not leave the confines of his own skin and situation. It is no wonder that his works are filled with mirrored images of himself looking back at himself. Rossetti was a supreme egoist, revealing empathic powers very late in life only. He was concerned with *la condition humaine* only insofar as he himself represented it. Considering his self-confinement, we must wonder at the diversity and scope that he actually did achieve in his works. Yet there was an obsessive sameness to his considerations throughout his life, a circling charm of thoughts from which he could not break free.[2]

II

The view of Rossetti's life and works that I have presented differs in some ways from the usual view. For example, it is customary to see him almost exclusively with respect to his heavenly ladies, to consider him simply in his role as a second Dante. Although it is an injustice to think him merely a visionary spinner of Dantesque situations, merely the author of *The Blessed Damozel*, *Dante at Verona*, *Beata Beatrix*, and *Dante's Dream*, even Doughty takes out of dramatic context Rossetti's verse from *The Orchard Pit*, "All my life I have dreamed one dream alone" (which refers, as we have seen, to a fantasy of destruction), and applies it to Rossetti's own Dantesque dream of salvation.[3] So difficult it is to dissociate Rossetti from his greatest conception. I have elaborated three additional "dreams," and shown their places relative to the primary dream.

Second, although it is commonplace to say that Rossetti succeeded in harmonizing the elements of spirituality and sensuality, I must conclude that finally he did not. There is no denying his desires, attempts, and assertions concerning such a harmony, and one sees that both elements are simultaneously present in some of his works. But taken as a whole, his works are based on contrary moral systems, in which sensuality and spirituality are often opposed. The systems taken together would seem to reveal uncertainty and confusion, not success. Rossetti is to be commended for his enterprise and imagination rather than for any actual ontological achievement.

Third, I believe that he was aware and interested in what was going on around him, whereas he is frequently described as the prototypical aesthete, living for his dreams alone.[4] His brother was quite right, although unsuccessful, in trying to confute " . . . a current misconception that Dante Rossetti could be adequately described as a sentimentalist, a dreamer, a mystic, an aesthete, and the like, without allowance being made for a considerable counterbalance of attributes of a very opposite character."[5] The statements quoted in the notes do not take into account Gabriel's being, to some extent, the confrere of Hunt and Millais; like them he "followed Nature," painting from living models and actual landscapes, even to the end of his career. They do not account for his hearty humor, his "chaffing" and Joe Millerisms[6] that did not always stop short of bawdry, nor for his preference for Cockney words and slang. They do not account for his acumen in financial dealings, nor for his skill as a "booster," both in his own behalf and in that of his friends. They do not account for his gaining a multitude of fervent and loyal friends. They especially do not account for his continual attempts to find a palpable counterpart to his ideal Beatrice, and to his ideal Jenny. They do not account for his entanglements with femmes fatales of flesh and blood, and their effect upon him. He did not live exclusively in dreamland; it would have been utterly out of character for him to say with his artistic friend, Edward Burne-Jones, "Of course imagining doesn't end with my work: I go on always in that strange land that is more true than real."[7] Rossetti's dreams were his guide to life, not his alternative to life.

Fourth, I treat Rossetti's artistic and poetic expressions as if he meant them; as if he were serious about his holy and diabolical ladies. The emotions that I hold to be dominant in him are a desire for a lady, a wish for heaven, and a guilty conscience. The latter two are old-fashioned, and rather surprising in a dissolute and professedly unchristian man, yet they give a unity to his life and a consistent meaning to his works that are indiscernible without them. The alternative is to see Rossetti as a poseur, who wrote and painted for the sake of art or effect merely. Although the latter view of him was taken by his younger admirers, forerunners or disciples of the Aesthetic Movement who recognized his influence upon them, Rossetti himself discouraged the view. For example he disliked Pater and Wilde despite their praise of him, and was ever irritated by a writer's tendency "to set the manner of a work higher than its substance, to glorify style as if it were a thing apart from subject."[8] Rossetti's worship was genuine, and he worshiped, not Art, but the ladies he depicted.

In fact I can think of no better way to indicate summarily Rossetti's worth and uniqueness than through a comparison of him with several of those who admired and borrowed from him. For, although his later followers and apologists remade him in their own image, I regard him as an early Victorian rather than a precocious member of the Utter School. Two biographers have called him in their titles a "Victorian Romantic,"[9] and the two words taken in their stereotypical senses form a discordant composite that handily epitomizes my conception of the man. The Romantic in Rossetti is his fantasy of the heavenly lady, reflecting his tendency to build an ideal, faultless other-world upon his own terms, and to let his trances serve as a protection from and corrective to the "cold hill's side." The Victorian in Rossetti is his fantasy of the femme fatale, which reflects his implicit acceptance of established morality, his preoccupation with guilt, and his advancement of *luxuria* to the head of the list of deadly sins.

Like Rossetti, his followers were poets and artists who customarily slighted the "world of men"—of battle, politics, business, science, and the rest. Like him they frequently adopted medieval, Roman Catholic, or Eastern lore and paraphernalia. Like him they dreamed, yearned, and pined. They could be dissolute and Bohemian, exploring thrilling vices, and yet flirt with religion. Nevertheless there is a consistent difference between him and them. They borrowed much from Rossetti, but they left behind the heart of his attitude, and the omission defines their difference.

In the paintings of Rossetti's early admirer, Edward Burne-Jones, one can recognize the beginnings of the change. The women of his works are half translated beyond the fact of their own physical being, as Rossetti's women typically are not. The basic difference is one of blood content. John Dixon Hunt has recently put the distinction very well: Burne-Jones' "particular role . . . seems to have been to etherealize, to make paler, the image of the beautiful woman. She no longer seems to have the sensual life and passionate warmth of Rossetti's creations; for Burne-Jones she may inhabit a world of mysteries, allegory and suggestion . . . but she has discarded any real physical presence and reveals directly the noumenous world where she exists with no pretentions to any phenomenal existence."[10]

The outset of the change is also observable in Arthur O'Shaughnessy, another disciple of Rossetti:

> You may feel, when a falling leaf brushes
> Your face, as though someone had kissed you;
> Or think at least some one who missed you
> Hath sent you a thought,—if that cheers;

Or a bird's little song, faint and broken,
May pass for a tender word spoken:
—Enough, while around you there rushes
That life-drowning torrent of tears.
from *The Fountain of Tears* (pub. 1870)

The passage is in clear imitation of *The Blessed Damozel*, where a
leaf blown across the face and a bird's notes are momentarily
taken as communication from the dead Damozel. But in
O'Shaughnessy it matters not at all if the kisses and tender
words are delusions. It is doubtful whether the lady's presence
would bring happiness anyway, for the poet chooses not to be
disturbed in his melancholy. She would only be in the way of
his tears. The lady is subordinate to the poet's emotion and
indeed irrelevant to it.

Emotional self-sufficiency like O'Shaughnessy's acquired justification with Walter Pater, another precursor of the Aesthetic
Movement, who found every man (including the lover) to be
hopelessly out of touch with the innermost soul of every other
being, and within reach of his own dreams and sensations only:
"Experience . . . is ringed round for each one of us by that thick
wall of personality through which no real voice has ever pierced
its way to us. . . . Every one of those impressions is the impression
of the individual in his isolation, each mind keeping as a solitary
prisoner its own dream of a world."[11] According to his view a
woman can be little more than a rather pleasing set of sensory
impressions.

Again and again we find that a lady is not seen as a person
of flesh and feelings, but is abstracted, turned into a symbol,
and kept at a distance. Arthur Symons followed Pater in recog-
nizing stimuli only, and not—in Symons's phrase—"the com-
radeship of things"; what he says of flowers would apply to
women as well:

I have loved colours, and not flowers;
Their motion, not the swallows' wings . . .
Amends to Nature (pub. 1906)

If a man can know only his sensory impressions, his pleasure is
cherishing and playing with *them:*

And the only world is the world of my dreams,
And my weaving the only happiness.

The Loom of Dreams (1900)

Similarly, Oscar Wilde's characters can associate with one another only through a protective aesthetic medium. Dorian Gray rejects Sibyl Vane, madly in love with him, for being herself and ceasing to act a part. In so doing she has destroyed his illusion and violated his artistic sensibilities. Heart-broken, she commits suicide. Sir Harry then gives Dorian the following advice:

> You must think of that lonely death in the tawdry dressing-room simply as a strange lurid fragment from some Jacobean tragedy, as a wonderful scene from Webster, or Ford, or Cyril Tourneur. The girl never really lived, and so she never really died. To you at least she was always a dream, a phantom that flitted through Shakespeare's plays and left them lovelier for its presence. . . . The moment she touched actual life, she marred it, and it marred her, and so she passed away. Mourn for Ophelia, if you like. Put ashes on your head because Cordelia was strangled. Cry out against Heaven because the daughter of Brabantio died. But don't waste your tears over Sibyl Vane. She was less real than they were.[12]

Although this speech may not have reflected Wilde's personal opinion, it was his vision, and his earlier works are faithful to it. Whereas Rossetti was drawn to his Jennys for what remained inviolably human in them, Wilde was fascinated by the harlot (the victim of overmuch relationship with other human beings) for becoming, ironically, nothing but an inanimate, artistic *objet:*

> Like strange mechanical grotesques,
> Making fantastic arabesques,
>
> . .   .   .
> We watched the ghostly dancers spin . . .
>
> Like wire-pulled Automatons,
> Slim silhouetted skeletons
> Went sidling through the slow quadrille . . .

Sometimes a horrible Marionette
Came out and smoked its cigarette
Upon the steps like a live thing.
                    The Harlot's House (1883)

In John Addington Symonds's sonnet sequence, *Stella Maris*,
again we find intimacy with the woman thrust aside. It tells
how the narrator

> . . . yields to a passion which overmasters the man at first, how
> his acquired habits of self-analysis necessitate doubt and conflict
> at the very moment of fruition, and how he becomes aware of a
> discord not only between his own tone of feeling and that of the
> woman who attracted him, but also between the emotion she
> inspired and his inalienable ideal of love.[13]

Once more the lady is rejected to preserve an emotional cast.
And finally, in Yeats, too, the lady herself is ultimately dispens-
able.

> Woman herself was still in our eyes, for all that, romantic and
> mysterious, still the priestess of her shrine, our emotions remember-
> ing the *Lilith* and *Sybilla Palmifera* of Rossetti. . . . It could not be
> otherwise, for [Lionel] Johnson's favourite phrase, that life is
> ritual, expressed something that was in some degree in all our
> thoughts, and how could life be ritual if woman had not her
> symbolical place.[14]

Here (to disagree with Yeats) the lady is not the priestess or
intermediary that she was for Rossetti, but an ikon merely, a
symbol rather than an agent, a personification rather than a
person. The personality of the lady is lost in a universal feminine
composite:

> I find under the boughs of love and hate
>
> . . . .
>
> Eternal beauty wandering on her way.
>   *To the Rose upon the Rood of Time* (pub. 1893)

> Who dreamed that beauty passes like a dream?
>
> . . . .

We and the labouring world are passing by:

. . . .

Under the passing stars, foam of the sky,
Lives on this lonely face.

The Rose of the World (pub. 1893)

The lady's own sweet self is ignored, as the poet in his escapist
vision would live in the bee-loud glade of Innisfree "alone."[15]

For almost all the Aesthetes and their immediate precursors
one was a company, two, a crowd. Their view of life may be
described broadly as Rossetti's Pre-Raphaelitism with the Pre-
Raphaelite woman dropped out of it—or, rather, present "in
spirit" only. Although their postures and vestments were often
similar to his, the likeness is misleading, for the difference the
woman made was great indeed. Fleshly and spiritual, exalting
or degrading, powerful or helpless, but always human and always
beautiful, the Pre-Raphaelite woman—a company of real
beings—was always present in Rossetti's life, works, and imagination. She, too, was a Victorian Romantic, and Rossetti is un-
thinkable without her.

Notes

Preface

1. I omit from my calculations Rossetti's occasional poems, poems on art, poetry, or their creators, juvenile paintings and drawings, occasional and familial portraits, and designs for stained glass. Rossetti's maxim for this last medium was, "Anything will do for stained glass." Quoted by Ford Madox Brown in a letter to Frederick Shields, July 22, 1880. In *The Life and Letters of Frederick Shields*, ed. Ernestine Mills (London and New York, 1912), p. 261.

2. Two of the feminine types that I treat—the femme fatale and the victimized woman—are reminiscent of (although not derived from) Mario Praz's "Fatal Lady" and "persecuted maiden" (*The Romantic Agony*, trans. Angus Davidson, 2nd ed. [London, New York, etc., 1951]). I would certainly not deny Rossetti a place in the mental climate or line of tradition described by Praz. Rossetti was particularly drawn to a surprising number of the earlier writers whom Praz treats, and assumed much of their stock-in-trade. Moreover, he furnished his full share of inspiration to the *fin de siècle* forms of the Romantic Agony. But I find Praz's emphasis upon "the less mentionable impulses of the man-animal" (p. ix) to be misleading when applied to Rossetti. To be sure, sexual matters furnished an important impetus with respect to his imaginative works, and, to be sure, perversities must have been latent in Rossetti's sexual nature, even as (I piously assume) they lurk in the natures of us all. But the basic sexual concerns that primarily preoccupied him and informed his works were really quite ordinary. True representatives of the Romantic Agony would have found him unadventurously bourgeois. For better or worse, then, the meaning I find in his feminine types is very different from that found by Praz.

3. *Victorian Studies*, X (1966), 220–222.

4. This point is well argued in two recent essays on Rossetti: Francis Noel Lees, "The Keys are at the Palace: A Note on Criticism and Biography,"

College English, XXIII (1966), 101–108; reprinted in *English Institute Essays*, 1967, pp. 135–149. And William E. Fredeman, "Rossetti's 'In Memoriam': An Elegiac Reading of *The House of Life*," *Bull. of John Rylands Libr.*, XLVII (1965), 298–341. Lees is the more concerned with protecting the integrity of the work from the incursion of biography: "Biography . . . is merely a supplement to the dictionary, which will never do more than furnish the correct parts for the machine" (107). " . . . a house of life which comes on offer in the mode of art can only be opened up satisfactorily from within the art itself" (108). Fredeman, on the other hand, questions "the critical acceptability of using the poem to substantiate biographical speculation" (315), and employs the sonnet sequence *The House of Life* to show that Rossetti "by selection, rearrangement, and grouping . . . has upset the biographically sequential ordering of experience" (323).

  5. "The Truth about Rossetti," *Nineteenth Century*, XIII (1883), 417.

  6. Paull F. Baum, ed. *Dante Gabriel Rossetti: An Analytical List of Manuscripts in the Duke University Library* (Durham, N.C., 1931), p. 29.

ONE: *The Cloak of Fantasy*

  1. *Letters of Dante Gabriel Rossetti*, ed. Oswald Doughty and John Robert Wahl, 4 vols. (Oxford, 1965–1967), I, 255–256. Hereafter cited as *Letters*. The letter is dated July 4, 1855.

  2. Rossetti's confusion of life and literature, and his thrusting himself into the fictive situation, are also indicated in the following observation by Theodore Watts-Dunton: " . . . so powerful (that is to say, so childlike), was Rossetti's imagination, so entirely did it dominate an intellect of unusual subtlety, that these stories interested him just as much as real adventures, and though he knew them to be gossamer fictions woven at the moment of telling, he would be as much affected by an unhappy catastrophe *as though they had been incidents of his real life*, and would sometimes beg for the catastrophe to be altered." "The Truth about Rossetti," *The Nineteenth Century*, no. 73 (March 1883), 419. Italics mine.

  3. *Family Letters*, ed. William M. Rossetti (London, 1895), I, 89. Hereafter cited as *Family Letters*.

  4. *Family Letters*, I, 83.

  5. *Family Letters*, I, 83. For another account of the incident see Thomas Hall Caine, *Recollections of Dante Gabriel Rossetti*, 1st ed. (Boston, 1883), pp. 5–6.

  6. Here is a typical effusion: "Alas the mighty Wells! What has it profited him to have been born the greatest English poet since Shakespeare?" *The Ashley Library: A Catalogue of Printed Books, Manuscripts and Autograph Letters Collected by Thomas James Wise*, [ed. Thomas J. Wise], IV (London, 1923), 141.

  7. Caine, *Recollections*, 1st ed., p. 6. Val Prinsep ("Rossetti and his Friend," *Art Journal*, 1892, p. 130) called the mature Rossetti "nothing of a bruiser."

  8. At this time, when Gabriel was not yet six, his father took him and his

sister walking. "On the way they were delighted at meeting a steam carriage and a squadron of life guards. Maria liked the steam carriage best, and Gabriel the soldiers." Quoted in R. D. Waller, *The Rossetti Family: 1824–1854* (Manchester, 1932), p. 122.

9. *Family Letters*, I, 86.

10. *Family Letters*, I, 87.

11. The poem may be found in *Ashley Catalogue*, IV, 109.

12. *Family Letters*, I, 93.

13. *Family Letters*, I, 92.

14. William Rossetti described his brother's mind as "in a mist as to religious doctrines . . . ." *Family Letters*, I, 382.

15. William says of Gabriel that " . . . his fine intellect dwelt little in the region of argument, controversy, or the weighing of evidence; it was swayed by feelings, and not by demonstrations or counterdemonstrations." *Some Reminiscences* (New York, 1906), I, 129.

16. See Browning's "Parting at Morning," l. 4. See also Maurice Valency, *In Praise of Love: An Introduction to the Love Poetry of the Renaissance* (New York, 1958), pp. 1–19.

17. In the following passage Rossetti describes an actual blurring of his eyesight, as he gains pleasure in willful, active achievement of confusion. He writes to Brown May 23, 1854, "I lie often on the cliffs which are lazy themselves. . . . Sometimes through the summer mists the sea and sky are one; and, if you half shut your eyes, as of course you do, there is no swearing to the distant sail as boat or bird, while just under one's feet the near boats stand together immovable, as if their shadows clogged them and they would not come in after all, but loved to see the land. So one may lie and symbolize till one goes to sleep, and that be a symbol too perhaps." *Letters*, I, 201.

18. "Sloth, alas, has but too much to answer for with me . . . ." Rossetti in a letter to Caine. *Family Letters*, I, 421.

19. In a letter to Brown, May 23, 1854. *Letters*, I, 200.

20. Henry Treffry Dunn, *Recollections of Dante Gabriel Rossetti and his Circle: (Cheyne Walk Life)*, ed. Gale Pedrick (New York and London, 1904), pp. 35–36. Cf. Caine, *My Story* (New York, 1909), p. 126: "the inner room was dark with heavy hangings around the walls, as well as about the bed . . . , and thick velvet curtains before the windows, so that the candles we carried seemed unable to light it, and our voices sounded muffled and thick."

21. *Family Letters*, I, 66.

22. See Henry Currie Marillier, *Dante Gabriel Rossetti: An Illustrated Memorial of his Art and Life* (London, 1899), p. 213. Hereafter cited as Marillier. Because I shall frequently have occasion to refer to the illustrations in this fine book, I hope that the reader will have it at hand. Mrs. Virginia Surtees' book, in press as I write, should be an even better source for many of these illustrations.

23. *Family Letters*, I, 84.

24. *Family Letters*, I, 103.

25. *Letters*, I, 17.

26. *Letters*, I, 23.

27. William says of Gabriel, "His faults were his own. He neither would nor could be a leopard without leopardine spots. To avoid being a jackal or a hyaena was what he could do, and that he did" (*Family Letters*, I, 405).

28. William Holman Hunt, "Memories of Rossetti," *Musical World and Dramatic Observer*, LXX, no. 27 (July 5, 1890), 526.

29. Arthur Symons, *Studies in Strange Souls* (London, 1929), p. 46.

TWO: *The Heavenly Lady: Literature*

1. Edward Shanks, in "Dante Gabriel Rossetti," *The London Mercury*, XVIII, no. 103 (May 1928), 71, says that "the obsolete words in Rossetti are not very many, and his chief individuality in the point of style was the employment of turns of speech which it is hard to call obsolete, simply because one cannot trace them to the usage of earlier times . . . . It gives the impression of archaism without anything that, on analysis, justifies it."

2. " . . . it was hardly necessary to describe [the lady of medieval song]. Her face and figure were to be seen everywhere in the Middle Ages, pictured in miniatures and tapestries, sculptured on the porches of cathedrals, described over and over in the same terms precisely in the songs and romances of chivalry. She was the medieval glamour-girl, blonde and slender, round-armed, straight-nosed, grey-eyed, white-skinned, with her small red smiling mouth, her sparkling teeth, her small firm breasts and slim waist . . . ." Maurice Valency, *In Praise of Love: An Introduction to the Love Poetry of the Renaissance* (New York, 1958), p. 173. The homogeneity of the medieval literary beauty is remarkable. Lewis A. Haselmayer, Jr., writing on "Chaucer and Medieval Verse Portraiture" (Yale University Doctoral Thesis, 1937), declares (p. 204), "We have no feeling or knowledge of what a person looked like, we have only the impression of extreme beauty. The particularization of humanity is entirely absent from medieval poetry." Adelade Evans Harris, in a study of "The Heroines of the Middle English Romances," *Western Reserve University Bulletin: Literary Section Supplement*, n.s. XXXI, *Western Reserve Studies*, II, no. 3 (August 1928), 14–15, is also unequivocal, stating that "no heroine of romance has dark hair," and (of the typically gray eyes), "no other color is mentioned."

3. In the order of their appearance the quotations, all translations by Rossetti, are from the following poems: *His Lament for Selvaggia* by Cino da Pistoia; *Of Three Girls and of Their Talk* by Giovanni Boccaccio; *For a Renewal of Favours* by Ruggieri di Amici; *Of his Lady in Heaven* by Jacopo da Lentino; *His Portrait of his Lady Angiola of Verona* by Fazio degli Uberti; *His Lament for Selvaggia; His Portrait of his Lady; A Message in Charge for his Lady Lagia* by Lapo Gianni; *His Portrait of his Lady; He Will Praise his Lady* by Guido Guinicelli; *His Lament for Selvaggia;* and *His Portrait of his Lady.* The titles of these poems, both here and in the text, are Rossetti's. See *The Works of Dante Gabriel Rossetti*, ed. William M. Rossetti (London, 1911). Hereafter cited as *Works*.

4. William Sharp, *Dante Gabriel Rossetti: A Record and a Study* (London, 1882), p. 297, mentions, of these speeches of Chiaro's Soul, " . . . their specially affecting the personality of Rossetti himself. In fact these passages may be regarded as directly personal utterances applicable to himself as an artist, and this I know from his own lips as well as from every natural evidence . . . . "

5. See Oswald Doughty, *A Victorian Romantic: Dante Gabriel Rossetti*, 2nd ed. (London, 1960), p. 27, for an indication that old Gabriele, too, saw himself as Dante. This work cited hereafter as Doughty.

6. Both in *Works*.

7. Rossetti stated that his immediate inspiration for *The Blessed Damozel* came from reading *The Raven:* "I saw . . . that Poe had done the utmost . . . with the grief of the lover on earth, and [so] I determined to . . . give utterance to the yearning of the loved one in heaven." Reported by Hall Caine, *Recollections of Dante Gabriel Rossetti*, 1st ed. (Boston, 1883), p. 284. *The Raven, The Blessed Damozel*, and the *Vita Nuova* all have basically the same dramatic situation.

8. *Sic.* first 1870.

9. In his last years Rossetti said, in a letter to Harry Buxton Forman (Feb. 10, 1880), that Keats's " 'Kisses four' has a suggestiveness of undermeaning which is no gain." Rossetti, *John Keats: Criticism and Comment*, [ed. Thomas J. Wise] (London, 1919), pp. 14–15. The remark, whether just or not, is equally applicable to *The Blessed Damozel*.

Apropos of this matter, Jerome J. McGann's stimulating and persuasive essay, "Rossetti's Significant Details," *VP*, VII (1969), 41–54 (which I have only recently read), argues that " . . . none of [Rossetti's] religious details will symbolize. . . . On the contrary, the very refusal of the traditional materials to operate in an expected way is so startling that it forces us to see the importance which Rossetti attaches to the pure, and non-symbolic, detail. . . . Saved from their overlay of traditional symbolism, the items of experience can again be, as it were, simply themselves." My only qualifications, which, I believe, McGann himself would grant, are, first, that the process he describes does not hold for *all* of Rossetti's works. And, second, that although Rossetti may have wished to purge his details of conventional symbolic content, he was desirous of retaining the *aura* traditionally attaching to them. He wished to discard meaning while retaining concomitant significance or importance.

10. XXXI, 91–93. *Paradiso*, Italian text with English translation by John D. Sinclair, Galaxy Book (New York, 1961), p. 450.

11. Wendell Stacy Johnson, in "D. G. Rossetti as Painter and Poet," *VP*, III (1965), 9–18, relates the poem to the painting with notable freshness of insight.

12. Miss Nicolette Gray, *Rossetti, Dante, and Ourselves* (London, 1947), p. 34, is most explicit on the first difference: "he has not grasped that Dante had a precise idea, and so there is a constant tendency to blur the thought . . . . " And (p. 38), "Rossetti was not really interested to know . . . Dante's intricate and fantastic analogies; what interested him profoundly was Dante's image."

The second difference has led to even greater condemnation, and often confusion, for Rossetti's human heaven destroys the distinction between the flesh, with all its traditional connotations of evil, and the spirit. William Sharp (p. 249), in talking of *The Blessèd Damozel*, apologizes for Rossetti:

> The working out of this idea naturally involves very materialistic treatment . . . yet not withstanding this the general effect is eminently spiritual . . . .

Walter Pater ("Dante Gabriel Rossetti," in *Appreciations: With an Essay on Style*. 5th ed. of 1910, London, 1924, p. 207) recognizes the problem, but hesitates to condemn:

> One of the peculiarities of *The Blessed Damozel* was a definiteness of sensible imagery, which seemed almost grotesque to some, and was strange, above all, in a theme so profoundly visionary.

Miss Gray (p. 40) is bolder in branding the heretic:

> Love is known in his lady, his lady is to be worshipped. Is it just idolatry? Is the Blessed Damozel not Beatrice, only Francesca? . . . Is not this a soul choosing union with another soul before union with God and is not that rejection and idolatry and Hell?

F. W. H. Myers ("Rossetti and the Religion of Beauty," *Cornhill Magazine*, XLVII [1883], 217; also in *Essays: Modern*, London, 1883) says it all succinctly: "Rossetti is but as a Dante still in the *selva oscura*."

13.   Further examples are to be found everywhere in Rossetti. A number of them are collected below (in Chapter IX, pp. 143–144, and Chapter XI, p. 175).

14.   See Rossetti's letter of June 1848 to his Aunt Charlotte Polidori, printed in *Letters*, I, 39.

15.   "Introduction to Part I" of *Dante and his Circle*, in *Works*, p. 297.

16.   Rossetti's trans. of *La Vita Nuova*, *Works*, p. 343n.

17.   William Rossetti in *Ruskin: Rossetti: Preraphaelitism: Papers 1854 to 1862*, ed. William M. Rossetti (London, 1899), p. 262.

18.   From William's diary for Dec. 10, 1869, in *Rossetti Papers: 1862 to 1870*, ed. William M. Rossetti (London, 1903), p. 417.

THREE: *The Heavenly Lady: Art and Life*

1.   See *Family Letters*, I, 91. Also, Esther Wood, *Dante Rossetti and the Pre-Raphaelite Movement* (New York, 1894), pp. 23–25, gives several anecdotes pertaining to Rossetti at Cary's Art Academy as reported by his fellow-pupil, J. A. Vinter.

2.   See Wood, p. 23.

3.   It should be noted that Rossetti executed and conceived other works as well under Brown, and most of them seem to have been of women. See, for example, *Family Letters*, I, 119.

4.   See William Holman Hunt, *Pre-Raphaelitism and the Pre-Raphaelite Brotherhood* (London and New York, 1905), I, 107–110.

5. *Family Letters*, I, 116.

6. Hunt is generally conceded credit for this dictum of the early Pre-Raphaelites. It is also generally allowed that Hunt formed his notions on painting without copying them from Ruskin's *Modern Painters*, which he had read before Rossetti attached himself to him. Certainly he was the only Pre-Raphaelite who pursued his own precepts consistently and faithfully; in fact they became a creed to this single-minded man, whom William Rossetti described with a trace of irony as having "tenacity of thought" (*Some Reminiscences*, I [New York, 1906], 66).

I find one occasion when Rossetti used the precept before he met Hunt: writing to William on Jan. 22, 1845 of a young would-be artist he remarks, "Certainly, as long as he keeps to Nature, his powers are perfectly gigantic" (*Letters*, I, 30). The proper inference is not that Rossetti invented the term, but that Hunt was taking over a precept that was common parlance among art students. G. H. Fleming, *Rossetti and the Pre-Raphaelite Brotherhood* (London, 1967), p. 49, points out that such advice was current even before it was advanced by Hunt and Ruskin. What Hunt certainly did contribute was single-mindedness and fervor. It *is* significant that Rossetti used the term within a month of taking up with Hunt (see *Letters*, I, 39). Rossetti continued to promote the precept now and again throughout his career, but with an offhandedness or jauntiness that betrays his lack of deep interest or dedication: "I am prevented from working on it [a woodblock illustrating Allingham's *The Maids of Elfin Mere*] from nature except by flying visits to London on Sundays, and I am loth to finish it without nature" (Letter of November 1854, in *Letters*, I, 230). "I heard him once remark that it was 'astonishing how much the least bit of nature helped if you put it in . . . . ' " (Thomas Hall Caine, *Recollections of Dante Gabriel Rossetti*, 1st ed. [Boston, 1883], p. 38). Rossetti's "discordant phases of profession" (Hunt, I, 169–170) did much to destroy Hunt's "orthodox" Pre-Raphaelitism. Without Rossetti Pre-Raphaelitism would have been easier to define, but perhaps it would not have been worth the definition.

7. William Rossetti's diary for Oct. 16, 1868, as printed in *Rossetti Papers: 1862 to 1870*, ed. William M. Rossetti (London, 1903), p. 331, reports Michael Halliday's telling him this in conversation as being Millais' "doctrine."

8. See, for instance, Robin Ironside, *Pre-Raphaelite Painters: With a Descriptive Catalogue by John Gere* (London, 1948), p. 13:

As we read such a picture as Holman Hunt's *Hireling Shepherd*, in which the interest is ostensibly centered on the scene of seduction engaging the principal figures, our attention is repeatedly arrested, amid the general glare, by the vividly given intricacies of such minutiae as the foreground weeds or the moth that spreads its wings across the shepherd's half-closed palm.

9. Hunt, I, 341. We also know of Rossetti's conciliatory attempts from his own words: in a letter of July 2, 1863 to Miss Ellen Heaton, quoted in Rosalie

Mander, "Rossetti's Models," *Apollo*, LXXVIII (July 1963), 22, he writes,

Do you know I am in somewhat of a dilemma with your picture [eventually called *The Beloved;* see Marillier, opp. p. 140]? . . . it is certainly one of my best things but the model does not turn out to make a perfect Beatrice, and at the same time I do not like to risk spoiling the colour by altering it from any other model. I have got my model's bright complexion, which was irresistible & Beatrice was pale, we are told, nor is the face altogether just what it ought to be.

Two days later he wrote, "The present *Beatrice*, must, I now find, be turned without remedy into Solomon's Bride . . . . "

10. "Dante Rossetti and Elizabeth Siddal," *The Burlington Magazine*, I, no. 3 (May 1903), 274.

11. William M. Rossetti, ed. *Praeraphaelite Diaries and Letters* (London, 1900), p. 263.

12. Entry for March 10, 1855, in Ford Madox Brown's diary, printed in *Ruskin: Rossetti: Preraphaelitism: Papers 1854 to 1862*, ed. William M. Rossetti (London, 1899), p. 33.

13. In an 1854 letter to Dr. Acland, quoted in Doughty, p. 174.

14. *Memorials of Edward Burne-Jones*, ed. Georgiana Burne-Jones, 2nd ed. (London, 1909), I, 231.

15. *Family Letters*, I, 173.

16. A few general descriptions of Elizabeth Siddal are the following: William Rossetti in *Family Letters*, I, 171; Georgiana Burne-Jones, I, 207–208; Frederic George Stephens, *Dante Gabriel Rossetti* (London and New York, 1894), pp. 35–36; and Holman Hunt, *Pre-Raphaelitism*, I, 198–199. Swinburne described her as Lady Cheyne in his novel *A Year's Letters* (the pertinent passage is given in Doughty, p. 274).

17. Stephens, p. 36.

18. See Doughty, p. 119.

19. *Ford Madox Brown: A Record of his Life and Work*, ed. Ford Madox Hueffer (London, New York, and Bombay, 1896), p. 165.

20. Some of the more important works are *Beatrice at a Marriage Feast* (1851); *Giotto Painting Dante's Portrait* (1852); *The Meeting of Dante and Beatrice in Paradise* (1852), a new version in water-colors of half of the 1849 diptych; *Dante Drawing the Angel* (1853), another new version in water-colors of an old theme. Here she appears as Gemma Donati, a lady of pity whom Dante married. *The Annunciation* (1855), a different composition from *Ecce; Dante's Vision of Rachel and Leah* (1855), in which Lizzie appears as Rachel; *The Passover in the Holy Family* (1855–1856); possibly *Dante's Dream* (1856), the smaller, water-color version of this subject; *St. Cecelia* (1856); *The Damsel of the Sanc Grael* (1857?); *Regina Cordium* (1861); and *Beata Beatrix* (1863).

21. Hunt painted her in *Valentine Rescuing Sylvia from Proteus*, her head in *Christians Pursued by Druids*, and her hair in *Light of the World*. Millais painted her as his Ophelia. Walter Deverell painted her as Viola in *Twelfth Night*, and again as Viola in the frontispiece of the April *Germ*.

22. "Introduction to Part I" of *Dante and his Circle*, in *Works*, p. 305.

23. Doughty, p. 195.

24. Quoted from *Some Reminiscences*, I, 198.

25. To his mother, April 13, 1860, as printed in *Letters*, I, 363.

26. To William Rossetti, April 17, 1860, as printed in *Letters*, I, 363.

27. To William Rossetti, June 9, 1860, as printed in *Letters*, I, 367.

28. *Letters*, I, 108–109.

29. "Dante Rossetti and Elizabeth Siddal," 277. The reader may take this remark for what it is worth. William went to great lengths to avoid or deny implicitly the accusations of extramarital sexual relations brought against his brother. He deceived the reader in this matter wherever possible, but his scruples did not permit him explicit, boldfaced denials. Therefore his remark here may probably be taken as truth, especially in the light of the other evidence presented in the text.

30. Doughty, p. 131. In this paragraph I express what is also Professor Doughty's opinion, and refer to the same works of Rossetti that Professor Doughty uses on p. 131 to support his opinion.

31. William M. Rossetti, *Dante Gabriel Rossetti as Designer and Writer* (London, 1889), p. 215.

32. *Family Letters*, I, 167.

33. Quoted from William Sharp, *Dante Gabriel Rossetti: A Record and a Study* (London, 1882), p. 344.

34. This entertaining phrase was uttered by Dr. Gordon Hake in his *Memoirs of Eighty Years* (London, 1892), p. 218. I give it here in its context to show that yet another of Rossetti's friends did not understand his equation of body and soul: Hake speaks of *The Blessed Damozel* as "simple in diction and emotional, and a merit not often found in Rossetti's love poetry is its spiritual character, the lover not being near to incite the girl to passion of the naked kind which pervades his sonnets."

35. See, for example, Doughty,. p 219: Rossetti "fell, as he said, into 'the state of sleepy worry,' which was his habitual reaction to this permanent dilemma of his life."

FOUR: *The Sinful Woman*

1. The poem was retitled *World's Worth* and reworked for the 1881 edition. The final form is a recantation of the first; Father Hilary returns from the steeple's giddy reaches to confess, "O God, my world in Thee!" whereas in 1849 he had cried, "There is the world outside."

2. There are, however, several drawings of Elizabeth Siddal in these years.

3. *Family Letters*, I, 160.

4. *Autobiographical Notes of the Life of William Bell Scott: And Notices of his Artistic and Poetic Circle of Friends 1830 to 1882*, ed. William Minto (London, 1892), I, 290.

5. W. B. Scott, I, 316.

6. W. B. Scott, I, 293.

7. *Letters*, I, 150.

8. See *The Honeysuckle*.

9. Doughty, p. 122.

10. See Patricia Thomson, *The Victorian Heroine: A Changing Ideal* (London, 1956), pp. 131–157.

11. In addition to the Pre-Raphaelite paintings mentioned above, there is also J. L. Tupper's remark, "Why to draw a sword we do not wear to aid an oppressed damsel, and not a purse which we do wear to rescue an erring one?" The remark appears in his article, "The Subject in Art," in the third number of *The Germ*. The most convenient reference is probably the volume pub. Portland, Maine, 1898, p. 134.

12. *Family Letters*, I, 184.

13. Jenny's "eyes . . . as blue skies" suggest her basic purity, but do not assert any holiness or superhumanity. She is a lily of the field, not an angel.

In a pen-and-ink sketch (1853) for *Found*, there is a sky, but it is heavily beclouded, and darkened, and it is still night.

14. Doughty, p. 194. In 1859 the engagement was broken. William claimed that his brother was "properly, though I will not say very deeply censurable" (*Family Letters*, I, 201). But the betrayed Hunt, according to Edward Clodd, felt that "Rossetti, whose principles were exceedingly lax, beguiled the girl away from him" (Edward Clodd, *Memories* [New York, 1916], p. 200). "In real life," remarks Professor Doughty, "Annie was obviously no apt example of the moral she had illustrated in . . . *The Awakened Conscience*" (p. 259).

15. W. B. Scott, I, 314–315.

16. There are two stories and two dates (that of 1859 being demonstrably false) given for the meeting of Gabriel and Fanny. I follow the account told by Fanny to Mr. Samuel Bancroft, Jr., and supported in all essential respects by Professor Paull F. Baum in *Rossetti's Letters to Fanny Cornforth*, ed. Baum (Baltimore, 1940), pp. 1–8. Fanny's given name, by the way, was Sarah Cox, and her married names were, first, Hughes and then Schott.

17. *Letters to Fanny*, p. 4.

18. *Family Letters*, I, 203.

19. *Family Letters*, I, 203.

20. In a letter of Dec. 4, 1895 to W. M. Rossetti. Printed in *The Swinburne Letters*, ed. Cecil Y. Lang, VI (New Haven, 1962), 92.

21. *Letters*, III, 1368. The probable date of the letter is November 3, 1875.

22. "Called on Stanhope. He was painting on his picture of a gay woman in her room by the side of Thames at her toilet. 'Fanny' was sitting to him." Entry for Dec. 16, 1858 from diary of George Price Boyce; "Extracts from Boyce's Diaries: 1851–1875," ed. Arthur E. Street, *The Old Water-Colour Society's Club*, XIX (1941), 32.

Fanny appears as a prostitute in several studies for *Found*, and in the unfinished oil itself; in *The Farmer's Daughter* (1861?); and probably was one of a number of models for the figure of Mary Magdalene in *The Magdalene at the Door of Simon the Pharisee* (1858; see Doughty, p. 682). As I mention, she also seems to have "sat" to his revision of *Jenny*.

23. See entry for Jan. 17, 1859, "Boyce's Diaries," 33. Professor Doughty presents evidence for believing Fanny a prostitute on p. 251, and in a note on p. 681.

24. If no other evidence were available the following series of facts would suffice: Fanny married a Timothy Hughes in 1860, yet served as Rossetti's "housekeeper" from 1862. Hughes died in November 1872. In telling the story of her life to Mr. Bancroft, the simple Fanny put the time of her husband's death "within a year or two after their marriage." In trying to cover her tracks she showed all too plainly where they led. For this information the reader may see *Letters to Fanny*, pp. 9–10.

25. *Letters to Fanny*, p. 18. As we shall see, this remark is not entirely true.

26. See *Letters to Fanny* for some of them.

27. See Henry Treffry Dunn, *Recollections of Dante Gabriel Rossetti . . .*, ed. Gale Pedrick (New York and London, 1904), pp. 38–42.

28. See Doughty, p. 253.

29. *Letters*, III, 1057, 1186, 1202, 1215–1216, 1216, 1241, and 1374.

30. *Athenaeum*, no. 1982 (Oct. 21, 1865), p. 546. The reviewer, probably Frederic G. Stephens, is praising *The Blue Bower*.

31. See Thomas Hall Caine, *Recollections of Rossetti*, 2nd ed. (London, 1928), p. 125.

32. In a letter of Dec. 4, 1895 to W. M. Rossetti. Printed in *The Swinburne Letters*, VI, 92.

33. *Works*, p. 420. On p. 490n, he says that it was "not perhaps surpassed by any poem of its class in existence."

34. The relevant expressions are from stanza two, "Thy soul is the shade that clings round [my heart] to love it," and stanza four, "What is it keeps me afar from thy bower,— / My spirit, my body, so fain to be there?"

FIVE: *Dreamland Diversion*

1. *Memorials of Edward Burne-Jones*, ed. Georgiana Burne-Jones, 2nd ed. (London, 1899), I, 151.

2. Doughty, pp. 210 and 226.

3. Burne-Jones, II, 191–192.

4. William M. Rossetti, *Some Reminiscences* (New York, 1906), I, 213. I do not think that the possibility of an extramarital affair some thirteen years after Burne-Jones met Rossetti (see *Letters*, III, 685) is cause to modify this account of the young man.

5. Val C. Prinsep, "A Chapter from a Painter's Reminiscence: The Oxford Circle: Rossetti, Burne-Jones, and William Morris," *The Magazine of Art*, n.s. II (Feb. 1904), 170.

6. *Letters*, I, 293. The date of the letter is March 6, 1856.

7. Entry for May 22, 1858, "Extracts from Boyce's Diaries: 1851–1875," ed. Arthur E. Street, *The Old Water-Colour Society's Club*, XIX (1941), 30.

8. Thomas Hall Caine, *Recollections of Dante Gabriel Rossetti*, 1st ed. (Boston, 1883), p. 197.

9. In a letter of July 1856, quoted in J. W. Mackail, *The Life of William Morris* (London and New York, 1922), p. 109.

10. *Letters*, I, 336.

11. *Letters*, II, 433.

12. William Sharp, *Dante Gabriel Rossetti: A Record and a Study* (London, 1882), p. 155.

13. Edward Shanks, "Dante Gabriel Rossetti," *The London Mercury*, XVIII, no. 103 (May 1928), 71, attributes an attitude to Rossetti that is more fittingly applied to Burne-Jones and Morris: he says that escape " . . . was really the essence of the movement of which, in England, Rossetti was the leader. The main thing was to get away from an unpleasant world and the best way of doing so was to invent another." And Professor Doughty (pp. 232–233) believes that Rossetti pointed Burne-Jones and Morris the way to the love of "a beauty remote from that of life and action, saddened with unreal sorrows, swept by passions existing for themselves alone, decorative agonies and ecstasies of the soul, yet real for them beyond any mundane reality."

14. *Letters of James Smetham*, eds. Sarah Smetham and William Davies (London and New York, 1892), p. 103. The letter is dated September 25, 1860.

15. Ford M. Hueffer ("Ford") in *Ford Madox Brown: A Record of his Life and Work* (London, New York, and Bombay, 1896), pp. 34–35, speaks of the typical "preoccupied, rapt expression peculiar to the listener of sounds inaudible to others" that we find in Rossetti's paintings.

16. See Burne-Jones, I, 116; and Ford Madox Brown's diary for March 17, 1855, with William Rossetti's footnote, in *Ruskin: Rossetti: Preraphaelitism: Papers 1854 to 1862*, ed. William M. Rossetti (London, 1899), p. 34. Dante Rossetti's *Arthur's Tomb* is dated 1854, although Doughty (p. 187) dates a *Launcelot and Guenevere* 1855.

17. Occasional attempts have been made to restore them.

18. *Letters*, I, 337.

19. *Letters to Fanny*, p. 14.

20. Miss Siddal uses the same setting to dramatize her own situation, in what can be seen as a retort to Rossetti's employment of her here: "And thou art like the poisonous tree / That stole my life away." From "Love and Hate," quoted in *Some Reminiscences*, I, 198.

21. *Letters*, I, 340.

SIX: *The Victimized Woman*

1. He wrote to his mother on April 13, 1860, "I have hardly deserved that Lizzie should still consent to it, but she has done so, and I trust I may still have time to prove my thankfulness to her" (*Letters*, I, 363). Four days later he wrote William, "The ordinary license we already have, and I still trust to God we may be enabled to use it. If not, I should have so much to grieve for, and what is worse so much to reproach myself with, that I do not know how it might end for me" (*Letters*, I, 364).

2. "Extracts from Boyce's Diaries: 1851–1875," ed. Arthur E. Street, *The Old Water-Colour Society's Club*, XIX (1941), 37.

3. Her close friend Swinburne wrote to his mother, at Lizzie's death, "happily there was no difficulty in proving that illness had quite deranged her mind . . ." (*The Swinburne Letters*, ed. Cecil Y. Lang, I [New Haven, 1962], 50). That the inquest attempted to establish no such thing does not affect the trustworthiness of his view concerning her sanity—a view based on extensive and sympathetic personal observation.

4. Vincent O'Sullivan in his *Aspects of Wilde* (New York, 1936), p. 193n., says that the account given by Violet Hunt of Lizzie's death is "substantially the same as that [given] by Wilde . . . . " She asserts (*The Wife of Rossetti: Her Life and Death* [New York, 1932], p. 304) in her highly colored and often incorrect account, that Gabriel visited Fanny in Wapping (considered a center of prostitution) upon leaving Lizzie at home on the evening in question. Of course neither of these sources is very authoritative or reliable, and I am inclined to believe that Rossetti's whereabouts on the evening in question were not so melodramatically significant.

5. See Helen Rossetti Angeli, *Dante Gabriel Rossetti: His Friends and Enemies* (London, 1949), pp. 196–198 and pp. 269–273. See also Doughty, pp. 293–304.

6. *My Story* (New York, 1909), p. 196. The reader will approach Caine with caution. Although not dishonest he was highly suggestible and sometimes inaccurate. It may be that he was merely seeking attention here by pretending to give substance to rumors already extant. But the passage does agree with what we know about the marriage, and I give it here as a good summary rather than good evidence.

7. In a letter of March 2, 1862 (a month after his wife's death) to Mrs. Herbert Gilchrist, Rossetti remarked "I already begin to find the inactive moments the most unbearable, and must hope for the power, as I most surely feel the necessity, of working steadily without delay" (*Letters*, II, 444).

8. *Memorials of Edward Burne-Jones*, ed. Georgiana Burne-Jones, 2nd ed. (London, 1909), I, 229.

9. *Family Letters*, I, 265.

10. *Letters*, II, 584.

11. See *Autobiographical Notes of the Life of William Bell Scott . . .* , ed. William Minto (London, 1892), II, 113–114; and *Family Letters*, I, 339.

12.   See W. B. Scott, II, 112. Although Scott was notoriously unkind to his old friend in his evaluation of him, and very bad on dates, his recounting of simple incidents, for a spiteful and disappointed old man, was remarkably fair. He often reported incidents and conversations that told against himself and for Rossetti, without seeming to recognize their implications.

13.   See *Family Letters*, I, 307–316.

14.   At the time of the near attempt reported by Scott, negotiations were in progress for the exhumation of Gabriel's poems in MS from Elizabeth's grave. This violation was extremely disturbing to him, and in 1876, apparently out of fear of supernatural consequences, he forbade his burial in the family plot at Highgate Cemetery, her resting place. Even after this date Caine reports (*My Story*, p. 195) that Rossetti " . . . had never forgiven himself for the weakness of yielding to the importunity of friends and the impulse of literary ambition which had led him to violate the sanctity of his wife's grave in recovering the manuscripts he had buried in it." For an account of Lizzie's part in Rossetti's attempted suicide in 1872, see Chapter Ten.

15.   *Praeraphaelite Diaries and Letters*, ed. William M. Rossetti (London, 1900), p. 231. His verse translation of Dante's passage may have been made at about the same time.

16.   Marillier, pp. 66, 81, 116, and 237, calls the work both a triptych and a diptych. If he is correct in calling the work reproduced opp. p. 66 a "replica," then the work must have been a triptych.

17.   "Dante Rossetti and Elizabeth Siddal," *The Burlington Magazine*, I, no. 3 (May 1903), 295.

18.   In a letter of Nov. 27, 1886 to William Rossetti printed in *The Swinburne Letters*, V, 177, Swinburne says that he suggested an ending for *The Bride's Prelude* to Rossetti: "D. G. R. told me that what had hindered him from continuing the poem was that he could not think of a satisfactory close to the story . . . . "

19.   In Chapter Four, while discussing the reasons for Rossetti's interest in the sinful woman, I mentioned a number of works (*A Last Confession*, and the several works of Faust's Margaret) more properly associated with the theme of the victimized woman. In fact the two fantasies grew out of the same concerns, the only difference between them being, really, whether or not the despoiled yet pure lady is to be saved. The new heroine may be seen as a fallen (or falling) woman *without* a savior.

20.   William Morris's *Defense of Guenevere* furnishes an interesting point of general comparison with this poem, for both try to defend the lady from her illicit sexual behavior.

21.   Quoted in Doughty, p. 233.

22.   See "P. R. B. Journal" in *Praeraphaelite Diaries and Letters*, p. 277.

23.   See John Guille Millais, *The Life and Letters of Sir John Everett Millais* (London, 1899), I, 146. Hughes's work is reproduced in color in *Time Magazine*, LXXXIII, no. 7 (Feb. 14, 1964), 74.

24.   Not only Millais, but also Lady Burne-Jones (I, 222) and Violet

Hunt (p. 301) associate Lizzie with Ophelia. Apparently the identification was a commonplace among the friends of the couple. According to Helen M. Madox Rossetti (*Art-Journal Easter Annual*, 1902, p. 16) Lizzie was indeed the model for Rossetti's Ophelia.

25. *Letters*, I, 214.

26. In a letter to Edmund Bates, dated Sept. 24, 1879. *Letters*, IV, 1668.

27. See I Chron. XIII.

28. Quoted in Helen M. Madox Rossetti, *Art-Journal Easter Annual*, p. 16.

29. There is also a pen-and-ink sketch for this work, done in 1865. It has been suggested that the work depicts, not Act III, Scene 1, but rather the following passage, Act II, Scene 1:

He took me by the wrist and held me hard;
Then goes he to the length of all his arm,
And, with his other hand thus o'er his brow,
He falls to such perusal of my face
As he would draw it. Long stay'd he so.
At last, a little shaking of mine arm,
And thrice his head thus waving up and down,
He rais'd a sigh so piteous and profound
As it did seem to shatter all his bulk
And end his being.

The passage might well have inspired Rossetti's disposition of characters, but finally he meant his painting to represent Act III, Scene 1. The epigraph, the jewel-box, and the book on which Ophelia's hand rests (in the earlier scene she was sewing) all point to the later passage.

30. Marillier, p. 136, says Laertes, but Laertes' encounter with his sister later in the scene does not end with his leading her away, as does Horatio's encounter (see 11. 73–74). Helen M. Madox Rossetti (p. 17) makes the correction, but without explanation.

31. I can find no reproduction of the earlier work; the identity is based upon the word of Messrs. H. C. Marillier and C. Fairfax Murray. See Marillier, pp. 69–70, and 136–137.

32. "While this kind of devotion [i.e., pilgrimages] was in favor," comments Warburton on these lines from *Hamlet*, "love intrigues were carried on under this mask." Quoted from *Hamlet*, I, ed. Horace Howard Furness, *A New Variorum Edition of Shakespeare*, III (London, 1877), 330n.

33. See Doughty, p. 417, which also calls attention to the sonnet, "Life in Love" (*HL* XXXVI), written shortly after the exhumation:

Even so much life hath the poor tress of hair
Which stored apart, is all love hath to show
For heart-beats and for fire-heats long ago:
Even so much life endures unknown, even where,
'Mid change the changeless night environeth,
Lies all that golden hair undimmed in death.

34. William M. Rossetti, *Dante Gabriel Rossetti as Designer and Writer* (London and New York, 1889), p. 257.

35. From Doughty, p. 300. See Doughty pp. 300–301 and 385 for further confirmation that the sonnet refers specifically to Lizzie. See also Paull F. Baum, ed. *The House of Life: A Sonnet Sequence* (Cambridge, Mass., 1928), pp. 216–217.

36. Watts-Dunton, "Rossettiana: A Glimpse of Rossetti and Morris at Kelmscott," *English Review*, I (Jan. 1909), 329.

37. See Marillier, pp. 144–145.

38. Rossetti finally abandoned the projected poem because it was discovered that James Hogg's *Mary Burnett* had a similar plot.

39. W. B. Scott, II, 157. The date of the letter is Sept. 15, 1871.

40. See *Rossetti as Designer and Writer*, p. 155: "Its first part was completed by 10th September, and the remainder proceeded rapidly, being finished by the 23d of the same month." Buchanan's article appeared in the October issue of the *Contemporary Review*.

41. From "The Monochord," *HL* LXXIX (1870?).

SEVEN: *The Femme Fatale*

1. I quote from the version of each poem that offers the closest parallel.

2. The idea for the poem came from the *Gesta Romanorum*, which Rossetti looked at in 1849. A prose version of *Staff and Scrip* was written at the time (see William M. Rossetti, *Dante Gabriel Rossetti as Designer and Writer* [London and New York, 1889], p. 127). This fact does not negate the possibility of Lizzie's later influence upon the work.

3. *Family Letters*, I, 103.

4. See, for example, *Family Letters*, I, 82, 100, 101, and 108.

5. The description holds also for *Jan Van Hunks*, composed mostly in 1847, a serio-comic poem in which Jan loses a smoking contest to the devil (see Chapter Eleven).

6. Diary for Dec. 13, 1854, in *Ruskin: Rossetti: Preraphaelitism: Papers 1854 to 1862*, ed. William M. Rossetti (London, 1899), p. 23.

7. In a letter to William Rossetti. *Rossetti Papers: 1862 to 1870*, ed. William M. Rossetti (London, 1903), p. 373.

8. *Letters*, I, 42.

9. On this matter there is a plethora of second- and third-hand insinuation. For example, Hall Caine reports "faint glimpses [in Rossetti's conversation] of almost fatal flirtations on that borderland of a rather boisterous Bohemia . . . " (*My Story*, [New York, 1909], p. 181). John Henry Middleton, Cambridge Professor and Director of the South Kensington Museum, said that Rossetti "was addicted to loves of the most material kind both before and after his marriage, with women, generally models, without other soul than their beauty" (the remark is attributed to him by Wilfred Scawen Blunt in *My Diaries* [London, 1919], pp. 86, 88). G. C. Williamson mentions in *Murray*

Marks and his Friends (London and New York, 1919, p. 133) that Rosa Corder was "declared to have been on intimate terms with Rossetti . . . ." See also Doughty, pp. 203 and 243.

10. Marillier, p. 106. See p. 105 and opp. p. 106 for the earlier and later versions of this painting.

11. A tamer, sweeter version is the small water-color of the same year, illustrated in Marillier, opp. p. 34, but the animal qualities under discussion show to better advantage in the oil (reproduced here; the major work and first conception of the theme). A drawing of 1867, printed in T. Martin Wood, ed. *The Drawings of D. G. Rossetti* (London, n.d.), Plate XXXI, portrays the grossest Venus of all. Rossetti, troubled by his original conception, found that the revisions made in the water-color version affected "the character of figure, action and expression, which please me much better as to charm and delicacy" (*Rossetti as Designer and Writer*, p. 49).

12. William Allingham, *A Diary*, ed. H. Allingham and D. Radford (London, 1907), p. 100. The entry is for June 26, 1864.

13. That Rossetti was drawn to these lines because they treat of feminine hair, a fetish of his, is likewise probable.

14. Written 1864–1868 according to Paull F. Baum, ed. *The House of Life: A Sonnet Sequence* (Cambridge, Mass., 1928), p. 184. Frederic George Stephens, *Dante Gabriel Rossetti* (London and New York, 1894), p. 68, gives "net" as a variant for "web."

15. See Henry Treffry Dunn, *Recollections of Dante Gabriel Rossetti and His Circle (Cheyne Walk Life)*, ed. Gale Pedrick (New York and London, 1904), p. 80. Apparently Rossetti had told Dunn the Talmudic legend of Lilith, including perhaps this detail. Dunn's editor continues, "The legend had a peculiar fascination for Rossetti."

16. Marillier, p. 133.

17. *Rossetti's Letters to Fanny Cornforth*, ed. Paull F. Baum (Baltimore, 1940), p. 23.

18. See *Family Letters*, I, 241–242.

19. Quoted in *Rossetti as Designer and Writer*, p. 69.

20. In a letter of Jan. 23, 1855 to Allingham. *Letters*, I, 239. The remark refers to Rossetti's choice of Tennyson's poems for illustration in the Moxon edition of 1857.

21. About 1873, when he reworked *Lady Lilith*, he also had his oil *Venus Verticordia* of 1864 returned for a repainting that was, according to William, "not far from disastrous" (*Rossetti as Designer and Writer*, p. 45).

22. The works are *The Madness of Ophelia* (1864), *An Old Song Ended* (1869), "A Superscription" (1869), and the prose outline, *Michael Scott's Wooing* (1870).

23. See *Hamlet and Ophelia* (1866), *Beata Beatrix* (Marillier, opp. p. 126), and *The Madness of Ophelia*.

24. A replica of *Venus Verticordia* and the illustrative poem; "A Superscription"; *Eden Bower; A Sea Spell; For "The Wine of Circe"*; the poem, *Cas-*

sandra; the poem, *Troy Town,* and a design for an illustration of the ballad; prose "cartoons" called *The Orchard Pit, The Doom of the Sirens, The Philtre,* and *The Cup of Water;* a verse fragment (only tenuously related to the prose "cartoon"), *Michael Scott's Wooing. Pandora* was begun and an illustrative sonnet written.

EIGHT: *Jane Morris and the Conflict of Fantasies*

1. William Holman Hunt, *Pre-Raphaelitism and the Pre-Raphaelite Brotherhood* (London and New York, 1905), 1, 169–170. Although Hunt is generally a clumsy judge of Rossetti, this remark is an excellent observation.

2. Doughty, p. 8. Additional evidence come to light since Professor Doughty's 2nd ed. (1960) reinforces his "design," although it does not remove the design from the realm of conjecture. Both R. Glynn Grylls (Lady Rosalie Mander) in "The Reserved Rossetti Letters" (*TLS*, no. 3231 [Jan. 30, 1964], p. 96) and R. C. H. Briggs in "Letters to Janey" (*The Journal of the William Morris Society*, I, no. 4 [Summer 1964], 2–22), having examined the letters of Rossetti to Mrs. Morris, which she ordered withheld from public perusal till fifty years after her death, report that they reveal Rossetti to be deeply in love with her, although (to quote Lady Mander) "there is nothing to show that she reciprocated his feelings nor that he expected her to do so." Of course judicious editing by Mrs. Morris may have fostered this impression.

Also apropos is R. C. Ellison, "An Unpublished Poem by William Morris," *English*, XV (1964), 100–102. The poem of suppressed sorrow (written ca. 1872), as Professor Ellison points out, seems to refer to Morris' trips to Iceland, and his wife's great willingness to have him out of the way.

A word is also in order on Miss Grylls' later *Portrait of Rossetti* (London, 1964), for it opposes an assumption basic to my own study. In her highly readable and otherwise sound study, she attacks Doughty's "design," believing that there was no scandal connected with the relationship between Rossetti and Jane Morris. Except in marginal ways, her argument is unsuccessful. Although she is in the privileged position of having seen what survives of the correspondence between Rossetti and Mrs. Morris, her argument is not founded upon or even strengthened by it. In fact she ignores unwelcome implications within the very correspondence on which her argument is supposed to turn:

> Janey showed appreciation of his pictures with girlish enthusiasm, telling him how she had insisted on unpacking for herself the box in which he had sent her some drawings and decided to hang them over her bed "so that I may always have the pleasure of feeling them near me in bed and seeing them when dressing and undressing . . . . " (p. 181)

There is more here than artistic appreciation, or "girlish enthusiasm," which is all that Miss Grylls makes of the passage. What is almost certainly being indirectly expressed is Janey's desire for Rossetti. It is Miss Grylls' overlooking of such evidence as this, on the grounds that it is not proof positive and that it does not support her own well-meaning impulse to be "kind" to Rossetti that renders her speculations doubtful.

As spokesman for the defense of Rossetti's personal reputation, Miss Grylls does persuade me that there does exist, within the realms of possibility, the unlikely possibility that there was no illicit love-relationship between him and Jane Morris. But she carries the analogy of the courtroom into the grave—bad practice for a biographer, which accounts for her special pleading and the distortions that grow out of it. If Rossetti stood to lose from posterity's conclusion in this matter—if the analogy of a courtroom were indeed applicable—one might well go along with Miss Grylls and, on the principle that a man is to be considered innocent until proved guilty, give him (in her words) "the benefit of the doubt." But Rossetti has been dead eighty-eight years, and all those close to him are dead. It does not really matter, especially in this day and age, whether or not he professed the Thirty-Nine Articles or slept with William Morris' wife—except in so far as these concerns contribute to an understanding of his imaginative sensibility, which lives on. Under these circumstances, if the evidence points to a strong likelihood that some may consider unflattering, I see no reason to reject that likelihood, even though conclusive proof has not been established.

Finally, I ought to say that my own argument is not invalidated if one does not believe that certain sexual acts took place. What is really at issue for me is what went on in Rossetti's *mind*, and the poems and paintings are evidence enough for that.

3. See Thomas Hall Caine, *Recollections of Rossetti*, 2nd ed. (London, 1928), pp. 200–201, where it is reported that Rossetti admitted to falling in love with an unnamed rival to Lizzie. See also Doughty, pp. 237–238, 369, and 649–650. See also Rossetti's prose fragment, *The Cup of Water* (1870; *Works*, p. 615), in which a King and a Forester's daughter fall in love, but because of the King's previous engagment to a Princess they forego their mutual happiness. The King persuades her to marry his friend, the Knight (William Morris?), who also loves her, in his stead. See also *The Stream's Secret* (1869–1870), which describes a secret love long frustrated:

> For then at last we spoke
> What eyes so oft had told to eyes
> Through that long-lingering silence whose half-sighs
> Alone the buried secret broke,
> Which with snatched hands and lips reverberate stroke
> Then from the heart did rise.

I find it hard to believe that Rossetti was capable of the uncharacteristic self-sacrifice and self-discipline that these passages assert, but certainly something happened between him and Janey in 1857 which Rossetti, in retrospect, believed to have been love.

4. Marillier, opp. p. 86 and bet. pp. 74 and 75, respectively.

5. Thomas Hall Caine, *My Story* (New York, 1909), p. 157.

6. Well might there be a similarity here, for "our illustrated Tennyson"

is the volume published by Moxon in 1857, to which several of the early Pre-Raphaelites, including Rossetti, contributed illustrations. That of Oriana was done by Holman Hunt.

    7. *Letters of Henry James*, ed. Percy Lubbock (New York, 1920), I, 16–18.

    8. *Family Letters*, I, 199.

    9. The skeptical are referred to photographs of her: see Doughty, opp. p. 480; Violet Hunt, *The Wife of Rossetti: Her Life and Death* (New York, 1932), opp. p. 216 and opp. p. 230; and Helen Rossetti Angeli, *Dante Gabriel Rossetti: His Friends and Enemies* (London, 1949), opp. p. 120 and opp. p. 210.

    10. *Family Letters*, I, 244.

    11. *Family Letters*, I, 244.

    12. *Old Familiar Faces* (London, 1916), p. 9.

    13. Graham Robertson, *Time Was* (London, 1931), p. 94.

    14. Quoted in Doughty, p. 373.

    15. E. P. Thompson, *William Morris: Romantic to Revolutionary* (London, 1955), pp. 197–199. Incidentally, Jane Morris' "unexplained ailments" of "nervous origin" lead to a suggestive parallel. R. C. H. Briggs ("Letters to Janey," 5) notes that "the dominant theme [in Rossetti's letters to her] is Rossetti's obsessive concern for Mrs. Morris' health"; and we have seen Rossetti earlier demonstrate a similar "obsessive concern" for the health of Lizzie. Perhaps—to range far in psychological speculation—guilty feelings lie behind his solicitude toward both.

    16. "Wherever I can be at peace there I shall assuredly work; but all, I now find by experience, depends primarily on my not being deprived of the prospect of the society of the one necessary person" (*Letters*, III, 1062).

    17. Rossetti described the state of love very aptly as a "tumultuous trance" ("Venus Victrix," *HL* XXXIII).

    18. Such states may be found as well in *HL* II, IV, VIa, VII, XIII, XVI, XXVII, XXX, and the "Willowwood" sequence. Rossetti almost always describes "still-lifes." Even the frankly sexual sonnets, VIa and VII ("Nuptial Sleep" and "Supreme Surrender"), describe moments of rest rather than exertion. Perhaps they would be the healthier for a little exercise.

    19. The finally completed oil of 1881 is illustrated in Marillier, opp. p. 202, and in color in W. D. Paden, "*La Pia de' Tolomei* by Dante Gabriel Rossetti," *Register of the Museum of Art, The University of Kansas*, II, no. 1 (Nov. 1958), 24–25. I find this provocative and painstaking study of *La Pia* and its relationship to Rossetti's life to be most congenial to my own views on Rossetti.

    20. Cf. the passage from Eliot's *The Waste Land:* "Highbury bore me. Richmond and Kew / Undid me . . . "

    21. Rossetti made the association explicitly in remarking upon another painting of Janey: "Proserpine looks yearningly towards the momentary light which strikes into her shadowy palace, and the clinging ivy which strays over the wall (in the picture) further suggests the feeling of memory, which indeed might equally be given as a name to the picture." Rossetti in a letter to

Leyland, dated Oct. 4, 1873. Quoted in Val Prinsep, "A Collector's Correspondence," *Art Journal*, LIV (Aug. 1892), 252.

22. A somewhat reversed image, similar in purport, occurs in the sonnet of 1871, "Severed Selves" (*HL* XL): "Two souls, the shores wave-mocked of sundering seas."

23. See Marillier, pp. 158–159, for a history of its production. The mercenary considerations that influenced its development weigh against my discussion of it as personally relevant.

24. See *Family Letters*, I, 250, and *Rossetti Papers: 1862 to 1870*, ed. William M. Rossetti (London, 1903), p. 339.

25. Professor Doughty (p. 384) calls them "a belated but mutual admission of long suppressed passion." Rossetti himself described the first sonnet as "divided love momentarily reunited by the longing fancy" ("The Stealthy School of Criticism," *Works*, p. 619). Certainly the moment described could have been merely fanciful, but this sonnet could also be a highly figurative account of an actual kiss and meeting. Rossetti's apparently misleading protestations against the autobiographical inspiration for his later poems (see Doughty, pp. 378–380) call his remark on "Willowwood" into question as well.

Cf. Rossetti's two suppressed Italian sonnets (printed in Doughty, p. 688), written in early June 1869, and his "The Kiss" (*HL* VI), of uncertain date, but written by 1870.

26. In an interesting note, Doughty, pp. 688–689, indicates passages from the poetry that suggest Janey's appearance.

27. See above, Chapters Two and Three.

28. See "Willowwood-2" (*HL* L), where Love's song is likened to the song of a dead soul waiting for its "new birthday."

29. See "Willowwood-3" (*HL* LI):

Alas! if ever such a pillow could
Steep deep the soul in sleep till she were dead,—
Better all life forget her than this thing,
That Willowwood should hold her wandering!

30. Reproduced in T. Martin Wood, ed. *The Drawings of D. G. Rossetti* (London, n.d.), Plate XXVII. In this time of his own poetic rebirth, Rossetti resumed the portrayal of poets (see *The Return of Tibullus to Delia*—probably relevant to Gabriel's renewed friendship with Janey—and the several works of this time taken from Dante). Orpheus is probably yet another poetic personality assumed by Rossetti's imagination as his own.

31. Rossetti's association of the first kiss to the story of Orpheus was extended to his contemporary sonnet, "The Kiss" (*HL* VI):

For lo! even now my lady's lips did play
With these my lips such consonant interlude
As laureled Orpheus longed for when he wooed
The half-drawn hungering face with that last lay.

Note two adjustments on the original story. First, there is a reversal of sexes; it is the lady who is the Orpheus, the savior. Her playing has a progressively exalting effect upon the poet, whom she "raises":

I was a child beneath her touch,—a man
When breast to breast we clung . . .
A spirit when her spirit looked through me,—
A god when all our life-breath met . . .

And second, the lady's kiss is an improvement upon the music of Orpheus, possessing what Orpheus "longed for": presumably a permanent elevation of the lover.

32. Frederic George Stephens, *Dante Gabriel Rossetti* (London and New York, 1894), p. 178, said of *Pandora*, picture and poem, "they both illustrate his power of projecting himself into a subject which, in itself, seemed to have been made on purpose for him."

33. Doughty, p. 390. The basic similarity between the myth of *Proserpine* and *La Pia, Aurea Catena, Mariana,* and *Orpheus and Eurydice* is obvious. Rossetti's *Proserpine* was one of his most successful designs. Several copies exist, the first a crayon of 1871 (see Marillier, opp. p. 174). Professor Doughty's comment, quoted in the text, is sufficient indication of its relationship to Rossetti's friendship with Janey. "The subject was originally intended for Eve holding the apple: it was converted by afterthought into Proserpine holding the Pomegranate" (William M. Rossetti, *Dante Gabriel Rossetti as Designer and Writer* [London and New York, 1889], p. 80). Frederic Stephens says of *Proserpine*, "as to [the] subject, every friend of the painter knew that he was prouder of having invented it than of his share in devising, or rather applying to art any other theme in which he excelled" (p. 187).

34. The titles, *Dark-lily* and *Perlascura,* may refer to the color of Janey's hair, of course, but one would be poetically shortsighted to see no more than that.

NINE: *Jane Morris and the Heavenly Lady*

1. In "Subjects for Pictures," *Works,* p. 615.

2. *Letters,* IV, 1760. A more extensive account of the work is given in Helen Rossetti Angeli, *Dante Gabriel Rossetti: His Friends and Enemies* (London, 1949), pp. 215–216.

3. Rossetti's translation, *Works,* p. 341.

4. *Works,* p. 343.

5. *Memorials of Edward Burne-Jones,* ed. Georgiana Burne-Jones, 2nd ed. (London, 1909), I, 231.

6. In 1869 there was an entirely different study of the theme, drawn from the daughter of William Graham, one of Rossetti's patrons.

7. I mention in passing another Dantesque lady whom Rossetti depicted. About 1875 he made a nude study called *Madonna Pietra,* taken from a sestina of Dante's that he had translated (see *Works,* pp. 355–356). In a footnote Rossetti is careful to say that the lady was not Beatrice. Madonna is

conventionally hard-hearted, and Rossetti draws her holding a crystal ball, which reflects a rocky landscape signifying the lady's own heart (her name, of course, means "stone"). I have not seen any illustration of the study, nor have I been able to determine whether Janey was its model. Since it is a nude, I doubt it, for none of Rossetti's few other nudes are drawn from her or any other of his regular models.

8. Perhaps the clearest indication that Janey inspired the poems written at this time is a remark of that discreet friend of both, Theodore Watts-Dunton: "when [Rossetti] loved a woman it was because he must, not because he would; and there is not one love-sonnet in his book which is a merely literary production" ("The Truth about Rossetti," *Nineteenth Century*, XIII [1883], 417).

9. From a letter of June 19, 1870 to Miss Isa Blagden. Printed in *Critical Comments on Algernon Charles Swinburne and D. G. Rossetti: With an Anecdote Relating to W. M. Thackeray*, [ed. Thomas J. Wise] (London, 1919), p. 11.

10. In this context see "The Monochord," *HL* LXXIX (1870): "Oh! what is this that knows the road I came, / The flame turned cloud, the cloud returned to flame . . . ?"

11. See "Love Enthroned," *HL* I (1871).

12. See "Her Gifts," *HL* XXXI (ca. 1871); "The Lamp's Shrine," *HL* XXXV (ca. 1871); and "Secret Parting," *HL* XLV (ca. 1868–1869).

13. See "Supreme Surrender," *HL* VII (1870); "Soul Light," *HL* XXVIII (ca. 1871); and "Through Death to Love," *HL* XLI (1871). The concept of a soul-harvest appears also in *HL* XXVII, XLIV, LXVIII, LXXIII, LXXXI, LXXXV, LXXXVI, and XCIV.

14. These two lines, which end the first and second quatrains of "The Portrait," *HL* X, were used in conjunction by Rossetti as an epigraph to a portrait of Janey, painted in 1869.

15. See *HL* V, VI, LIV, XCII, XCIII.

16. See *HL* XX, XXVII, XXIX, XXXVII, XLV, LIII, LVII, LXII.

17. William Sharp, *Dante Gabriel Rossetti: A Record and a Study* (London, 1882), p. 408, observed of *The House of Life*, "the impression . . . remains that the series is, in the main, a record of individual emotions, suggested by the presence and absence of embodied love and what such presence and absence individually entail, a record of such and of little further . . . . " The remark correctly indicates the immediate cause of the various emotions, although it could be more specific about the religious and metaphysical nature of what the presences and absences entail.

18. The order was followed in the earlier, 1870 volume as well. "Death in Love" (XXIII) was preceded by "Parted Love" (XXI). The other sonnets were not included in the earlier volume, and probably not written till 1871.

19. A similar sequence is observed in the volume of 1870, even though many (I presume) occasionally inspired "optimistic" sonnets were written thereafter.

20. See, for example, "Secret Parting," *HL* XLV (?1868–1869):

> Because our talk was of the cloud-control
> And moon-track of the journeying face of Fate,
> Her tremulous kisses faltered at love's gate . . .

And also "The Soul's Sphere," *HL* LXII (?1871):

> Some prisoned moon in steep cloud-fastnesses,—
> Throned queen and thralled . . .

21. See *Family Letters*, I, 245.

22. Two sonnets are excepted as irrelevant to my argument. "Body's Beauty" (*HL* LXXVIII), which describes Lilith, has been examined already in discussing Fanny Cornforth; and "A Superscription" (*HL* XCVII), in discussing Lizzie as a vengeful victimized woman. Both Lilith and Might-have-been are perfect femmes fatales, but they were not inspired by Janey, and therefore they have no place in this chapter.

23. This little "moment" is clearly related to two others in Rossetti's works, namely, *The Cup of Water* (a prose tale that Rossetti wrote in 1870, approximately a year later than the sonnet) and "Willowwood-1" (*HL* XLIX), where the poet stoops to kiss the absent love's face reflected in the well. All three possess, as their basic element, a beloved woman who bears a welcome death partly in the shape of a refreshing drink of water, and partly in the form of a kiss.

24. Professor Baum's paraphrase, "O my soul, are songs of Death no temptation to thee?" Baum, ed. *The House of Life: A Sonnet Sequence* [Cambridge, Mass., 1928], p. 200, puts the emphasis where it belongs, upon Rossetti's thoughts of his own death, but it shies away from taking "heaven" in any religious or metaphysical sense. Professor Baum does observe appropriately that "the whole sonnet is an echo of Rossetti's contemplation of suicide in 1868–1869," and "there is an obvious reminiscence of I Cor. xv, 55" ("O Death, where is thy sting, O grave, where is thy victory . . . But thanks be to God, who giveth us the victory over death").

TEN: *Jane Morris and the Femme Fatale*

1. See the last note to Chapter Seven for a list of such works from 1868 through 1870. Thereafter came two reproductions of *Lucretia Borgia* in water-color (1871); *Ligeia Siren*, a crayon study of 1873 for *The Sea Spell* (1877); the sonnet "Hero's Lamp" (*HL* LXXXVIII, 1875); *Mnemosyne* (1876), which was first undertaken as a depiction of Hero; and *Madonna Pietra*, a crayon study of ca. 1875.

2. A crayon drawing, *Ligeia Siren* (1873), is said to have served as a preliminary study for *The Sea Spell*, but I do not know whether the sea-bird was depicted in the earlier work.

3. William Sharp, *Dante Gabriel Rossetti: A Record and a Study* (London, 1882), p. 247.

4. It was a medieval convention to contrast the tree of man's damnation

with the cross, the tree of his redemption. It was characteristic of Rossetti to confound them.

5. The kiss-in-the-apple recalls the kiss-in-the-water of "Willowwood-1" and *The Cup of Water*.

6. Other works more or less related to this fantasy are *The Sea Spell*, just discussed, in which the siren plays her lute under an apple tree; and the various paintings of *Proserpine*, in which the heroine is portrayed regarding the pomegranate that she has tasted, thus dooming herself to spend half of each year in the Underworld. "The subject was orginally intended for Eve holding the apple" (William M. Rossetti, *Dante Gabriel Rossetti as Designer and Writer* [London and New York, 1889], p. 80). Finally there is the ballad *Troy Town* (1869), in which the fantasy is extended to the story of Helen by means of the association of the apple of evil with the prize which Paris granted to Venus. In her prayer to Venus for the heart of Paris, Helen reminds her,

> Once an apple stirred the beat
> Of thy heart with the heart's desire:—
> Say who brought it then to thy feet?

And Helen describes her own breasts as apples:

> Each twin breast is an apple sweet . . . .
> Mine are apples grown to the south,
> Grown to taste in the days of drouth,
> Taste and waste to the heart's desire:
> Mine are apples meet for his mouth.

As Paris once gave Venus an apple, so now should she give him the breasts of Helen. The refrain, "O Troy's down, / Tall Troy's on fire," reminds us that the fruit of sexuality will again be disaster.

7. There is yet another probably unconscious sinister implication here. The forgotten book and blossom recall the book and blossoms of his *Paolo and Francesca* (see above, p. 87), where the falling objects symbolize the downfall of the lovers themselves.

8. See Paull F. Baum, ed. *The House of Life: A Sonnet Sequence* (Cambridge, Mass., 1928), p. 105.

9. See above, Chapter Five.

10. Marillier, p. 172.

11. *Rossetti Papers: 1862 to 1870*, ed. William M. Rossetti (London, 1903), p. 417.

12. Letter of March 9, 1870 to Swinburne (*Letters*, II, 812).

13. *Autobiographical Notes of the Life of William Bell Scott . . .* , ed. William Minto (London, 1892), II, 169. Rosalie Glynn Grylls, *Portrait of Rossetti* (London, 1964), p. 114, offers the very likely suggestion that Scott, in his characteristic way, was confusing the article with the later pamphlet. Her supposition would bring his account into better agreement with William's and Gabriel's accounts. Her suggestion makes all the more persuasive my view that what principally damaged Rossetti were specific statements to be found in the pamphlet alone.

14. W. B. Scott, II, 172.

15. *Family Letters*, I, 307.

16. *Family Letters*, I, 305.

17. See Doughty, p. 501: "reputation, brilliance, wit, sarcasm, all were at the service of Buchanan's enemies."

18. Before the appearance of Buchanan's article Rossetti had had to face surprisingly little moral criticism of his work, largely because he had published and exhibited so little. The unfavorable articles that had appeared dealt almost solely with aesthetic considerations. A few of the infrequent germane remarks prior to Buchanan are the following:

> "The Blessed Damozel," which is aglow with what has been pronounced
> mystical, imaginative love, but which, as it seems to us, expresses in a
> sufficiently carnal manner the author's belief that earthly passion and
> affections, in no wise elevated or clarified, so far as we observe, is to last
> on into eternity and be the stuff of heaven . . . .

The article appeared in *The Nation*, XI (July 14, 1870), New York, 29–30, and its author was James Russell Lowell. Lowell was an editor of the *North American Review*, which published an unfavorable review of Rossetti a few months later (CXI [Oct. 1870], 471–480):

> And the love to which he confines himself will be found to be at bottom a
> sensuous and sexual love, refined to some extent by that sort of worship of
> one's mistress as saint and divinity which the early Italians made a
> fashion, certainly, whether or not it was ever a faith by which they lived.

A small notice anticipating Buchanan's attack appeared in *The Contemporary Review*, XIV (1870), 480–481. These are the strongest and most detailed criticisms that I find. Rossetti would have been quite unused to Buchanan's line of argument.

19. *The Fleshly School of Poetry and Other Phenomena of the Day* (London, 1872), p. 69.

20. *Fleshly School*, p. 11.

21. *Fleshly School*, p. 68.

22. *Fleshly School*, p. 68.

23. *Fleshly School*, pp. 86–87.

24. See William M. Rossetti, *Family Letters*, I, 305.

25. Browning habitually composed with some real incident or personality in mind. William Bell Scott (II, 180) implies that he believed the relationship between Rossetti's situation and the poem to be intentional. For a full discussion of this matter see William Clyde DeVane, "The Harlot and the Thoughtful Young Man: A Study of the Relation between Rossetti's *Jenny* and Browning's *Fifine at the Fair*," *Stud. Phil.*, XXIX (July 1932), 463–484.

26. Quoted in Doughty, p. 516.

27. *Family Letters*, I, 308.

28. *Family Letters*, I, 307.

29. *Family Letters*, I, 308.

30. To ask some unanswerable questions: is it possible that Rossetti

associated these gypsies, preparing for the holiday fair, with Fifine and the fair of that poem? Is it possible that Fanny, whom he met first at some celebration at the Royal Surrey Gardens, "a notable place of public entertainment" (Paull F. Baum, ed. *Rossetti's Letters to Fanny Cornforth* [Baltimore, 1940], p. 5), is also to be included in this complex of associations?

31. Gordon Hake, *Memoirs of Eighty Years* (London, 1892), p. 221. Professor Doughty (p. 519) suggests that it was the matter of Lizzie's death that was discussed.

32. *Family Letters*, I, 313.

ELEVEN: *The Attenuation of Fantasy*

1. It is probably no coincidence that the word "peace" is also prominent in Dante's presentations of Beatrice, "the enemy of all disquiet." We think of his *pace d'amore*, and of the description of Beatrice in the *Vita Nuova* that Rossetti translated,

And with her was such very humbleness
That she appeared to say, "I am at peace."

2. On the basis of her reading the Rossetti-Jane Morris correspondence, Rosalie Glynn Grylls takes issue with the more commonly held view that they grew apart in Rossetti's later years. See *Portrait of Rossetti* (London, 1964), p. 212, and pp. 235–240.

3. The term is used by Graham Robertson, *Time Was* (London, 1931), p. 95, to describe Marie Spartali Stillman, but it is equally applicable to Alexa Wilding. "It is wrong to suppose that he employed no other models" than Fanny and Janey, "but the fact remains that all the voluptuous figures do bear a most confusing resemblance to Mrs. Schott, and all the pensive ones—even those that are designedly portraits of quite other people—to Mrs. Morris" (Evelyn Waugh, *Rossetti: His Life and Works* [London, 1928], p. 134).

4. *Family Letters*, I, 339.

5. Quoted in Doughty, p. 583.

6. See *Autobiographical Notes of the Life of William Bell Scott . . .*, ed. William Minto (London, 1892), II, 113–114. Rossetti associated bird's notes with voices from the dead frequently and from his youth. In 1880 Rossetti wrote the following fragment (*Works*, p. 246):

This little day—a bird that flew to me—
Has swiftly flown out of my hand again.
Ah have I listened to its fugitive strain
For what its tidings of the sky may be?

Thirty years earlier, in the 1850 version of *The Blessed Damozel*, the lover yearning for his dead lady exclaims,

Ah sweet! even now, in that bird's song,
Strove not her accents there
Fain to be hearkened . . . ?

And we recall Rossetti's claim that Poe's *Raven* was the inspiration for *The Blessed Damozel*.

7.   In Thomas Hall Caine, *My Story* (New York, 1909), p. 224.

8.   *Recollections of Rossetti*, 2nd ed. (London, 1928), p. 202.

9.   In W. B. Scott, II, 308. For the complete incident see 306–308.

10.   *My Story*, p. 203.

11.   *Family Letters*, I, 378.

12.   *Recollections*, 1st ed. (Boston, 1883), pp. 150–151.

13.   First quotation: *Recollections*, 1st ed., pp. 103–104. Second quotation: *My Story*, pp. 57–58.

14.   *Letters*, IV, 1655. The letter is dated July 29, 1879.

15.   *Letters*, IV, 1511.

16.   *Rossetti's Letters to Fanny Cornforth*, ed. Paull F. Baum (Baltimore, 1940), p. 76.

17.   John Skelton, *The Table-Talk of Shirley*, First Series (Edinburgh and London, 1895), p. 92.

18.   See Doughty, p. 608.

19.   *My Story*, p. 115.

20.   Quoted in Doughty, p. 575.

21.   Frederic George Stephens, *Dante Gabriel Rossetti* (London and New York, 1894), p. 203.

22.   W. B. Scott, II, 140.

23.   *Family Letters*, I, 381–382.

24.   In practice he had always dissociated them to some extent. As we have seen, the whole movement of *The House of Life* is away from personal experience and toward universal speculation. In this respect he left self behind. And from the beginning of his career, whatever the passionate source of an inspiration, the execution of a work was always a slow, considerate, laborious process of distillation and revision. Nevertheless, his theory, expressed from *Hand and Soul* through *The House of Life*, had always been that poetry was a reflection of "soul"—of the heart's affections. It is primarily a change in profession rather than practice that I am noting.

25.   *My Story*, p. 114.

26.   *My Story*, p. 137.

27.   *Recollections*, 1st ed., p. 171.

28.   Quoted in Doughty, p. 379. Here, apparently, Rossetti is hiding a fact under a truth. Ultimately, of course, the life involved is life representative, but we have good reason to believe that the lives involved were originally his and Janey's. See Doughty, pp. 378–381, for a fuller discussion of this topic. Most persuasive on this score is the letter of Rossetti apparently to Janey, quoted by Rosalie Glynn Grylls, *Portrait of Rossetti*, p. 185. See also her note, p. 213.

29.   See Doughty, p. 400n.

30.   *Family Letters*, I, 283–284.

31. William M. Rossetti, *Dante Gabriel Rossetti as Designer and Writer* (London and New York, 1889), p. 67.

32. See *Recollections*, 1st ed., p. 171.

33. Doughty (pp. 612–613) remarks that the commemorative sonnets are not entirely impersonal either; Rossetti drew from the careers of the poets what seemed appropriate to himself. Analogues were not hard to find; he described London as

A city of sweet speech scorned—on whose chill stone
Keats withered, Coleridge pined, and Chatterton
Breadless, with poison froze the God-fired breath.

Tiber, Nile, and Thames (1881)

But London was also the city of his own miseries. He wrote of Coleridge dreaming of "heaven lost" (*Samuel Taylor Coleridge*, 1880), and of Keats, "Weary with labour spurned and love found vain" (*John Keats*, 1880). He selected from the lives of the poets exactly those woes that had a counterpart in his own life.

34. I except Berold's account, discussed below, of his dreams when down in the sea.

35. In *A Last Confession* the narrator's love for the murdered ward is described as a "father's, brother's love," and in *Jenny* the young adventurer likens the prostitute to his innocent "cousin Nell."

36. See Herbert H. Gilchrist, "Recollections of Rossetti," *Lippincott's Monthly Magazine*, LXVIII (November 1901), 573.

37. *Family Letters*, I, 108. The source for the story was "Henkerwyssel's Challenge," a short story by John Rutter Chorley. It was found by Gabriel in *Tales of Chivalry*, and it appeared first in *The Winter's Wreath for 1830*, London, 1829. See *Jan Van Hunks*, ed. John Robert Wahl, New York, 1952. Rossetti pared away an obtrusive narrator and much else that was incidental. The torment described in the last stanza was Rossetti's own touch.

38. A letter quoted in *The Ashley Library: A Catalogue . . .* , [ed. Thomas J. Wise], IV (London, 1923), 152–153 as well as *The English Review*, I (1909), 323ff.

39. *My Story*, p. 222.

40. In the previous chapter I discuss the extent to which he did associate fire with love.

TWELVE: *An Assessment*

1. *Ruskin: Rossetti: Preraphaelitism: Papers 1854 to 1862*, ed. William M. Rossetti (London, 1899), p. 234. The letter was probably written in 1859.

2. On this matter see Doughty, p. 385, and esp. pp. 475–476.

3. Doughty, p. 532.

4. Again and again one meets with misleading statements like the following:

In a certain sense Rossetti . . . was never wholly awake, had never gone
outside that house of dreams . . .

>   (Arthur Symons, *Studies in Strange Souls* [London, 1929], p. 46)

. . . to the painter life had been a dream into which nothing entered that
was not as impalpable as itself.

>   (Thomas Hall Caine, *Recollections of Dante Gabriel Rossetti*,
>   1st ed. [Boston, 1883], p. 282)

Rossetti . . . did not bother . . . about the "actuality" of his subject.

>   (Nicolette Gray, *Rossetti, Dante, and Ourselves* [London, 1947], p. 14)

Gabriel, who cared nothing for truth of any material kind

>   (William Gaunt, *The Pre-Raphaelite Tragedy* [London, 1942], p. 23)

5.   *Praeraphaelite Diaries and Letters*, ed. William M. Rossetti (London,
1900), p. 1.

6.   Frederick Shields records in his diary for Aug. 17, 1881, "To Rossetti's;
an evening wasted in Joe Miller'isms, of which he is too fond." *The Life and
Letters of Frederick Shields*, ed. Ernestine Mills (London and New York, 1912),
p. 267.

7.   *Memorials of Edward Burne-Jones*, ed. Georgiana Burne-Jones, 2nd ed.
(London, 1909), I, 116.

8.   In Caine, *My Story* (New York, 1909), p. 137.

9.   Doughty, *A Victorian Romantic: Dante Gabriel Rossetti*, and T. Earle
Welby, *The Victorian Romantics: 1850–70*, London, 1929.

10.   *The Pre-Raphaelite Imagination: 1848–1900* (Lincoln, Nebraska, [1969]),
p. 195. Mr. Hunt's fresh and thoroughly intelligent study has come to hand
too late for my own work to benefit fully from it. Except for my remarks here
on Burne-Jones, the occasional similarities of observation and quotation between his book and mine are entirely coincidental (as reference to my doctoral
dissertation, Harvard, 1965, will show) and—I like to think—largely corrobo-
ratory.

11.   Walter Pater, *The Renaissance: Studies in Art and Poetry* (London,
1910), p. 235.

12.   *The Portable Oscar Wilde*, sel. and ed. Richard Aldington. Viking
Portable Library (New York, 1946), p. 255.

13.   From "Preface" to *Vagabunduli Libellus* (London, 1884), p. x.

14.   The *Autobiography of William Butler Yeats* (New York, 1938), p. 257.

15.   I do not do Yeats full justice here (let alone the importance of the
concept of the woman in the literature of the nineteenth century as a whole),
but what I say is essentially true. In *Romantic Image* (London, 1957), Frank
Kermode treats the dancer in some detail as "one of Yeats's great reconciling
images, containing life in death, death in life, movement and stillness, action
and contemplation, body and soul . . . " (p. 48). I would say that Yeats and
Rossetti are alike in turning to woman to charm away the distinction between

matter and spirit. But poetic or artistic activity is not crucial to Rossetti's holism, as it is to Yeats's. For Yeats (and, according to Kermode, for the Romantic Movement in general, as it extends through and beyond Yeats), feminine subject and artistic activity symbolize one another, or, better, become one, to the point that nobody can "know the dancer from the dance." In effect, the dancer's biography, biology, and personality are secondary to and become submerged within the spirit of her own artistic activity; as a person she is, finally, danced away. The less dancer and the more dance the better. Rossetti, on the other hand, does not try to make subject and medium symbolize each other or become one. For him, the holy powers of reconciliation preside within the woman herself, not within poetry or the Romantic Image (to use Kermode's term) into which she can be transformed. The activity of the poetic imagination remains medium, subordinate to subject, which fully retains its truth to life. Rossetti would not have had a moment's trouble in telling "the dancer from the dance," nor would he have hesitated in his preference.

Bibliography

A secondary but sizable service performed by William E. Frede-man's *Pre-Raphaelitism: A Bibliocritical Study* (Cambridge, Mass., 1965) is the elimination of the need, in works on Pre-Raphael-itism that come after it, for an extensive bibliography. I therefore limit my list to (A) works cited; (B) works consulted pertaining to the concerns of my study but peripheral to the general area of Pre-Raphaelitism; and (C) a selection of works related to Rossetti published since Professor Fredeman's book went to press. Works falling under more than one of these three headings are listed only under (A).

A. *Works Cited*

Allingham, William. *A Diary*, ed. H. Allingham and D. Radford. London, 1907.

Angeli, Helen Rossetti. *Dante Gabriel Rossetti: His Friends and Enemies*. London, 1949.

The Ashley Library: A Catalogue of Printed Books, Manuscripts and Autograph Letters Collected by Thomas James Wise [ed. Thomas James Wise]. 11 vols. London: privately printed by the Dunedin Press Ltd., 1922–1936.

Baum, Paull F., ed. *Dante Gabriel Rossetti: An Analytical List of Manuscripts in the Duke University Library: With Hitherto Unpublished Verse and Prose*. Durham, N.C., 1931.

Blunt, Wilfred Scawen. *My Diaries*. London, 1919.

Boyce, George Price. "Extracts from Boyce's Diaries: 1851–1875," ed.

Arthur E. Street, *The Old Water-Colour Society's Club*, XIX (1941), 9–71.

Briggs, R. C. H. "Letters to Janey," *The Journal of the William Morris Society*, I, no. 4 (Summer 1964), 2–22.

Browning, Robert. *Critical Comments on Algernon Charles Swinburne and D. G. Rossetti: With an Anecdote Relating to W. M. Thackeray* [ed. T. J. Wise]. London: privately printed by Richard Clay and Sons, Ltd., 1919.

———. *Fifine at the Fair*. London, 1872.

Buchanan, Robert. *The Fleshly School of Poetry and Other Phenomena of the Day*. London, 1872.

Burne-Jones, Georgiana. *Memorials of Edward Burne-Jones*. 2nd ed., 2 vols. London, 1909.

Caine, Thomas Hall. *My Story*. New York, 1909.

———. *Recollections of Dante Gabriel Rossetti*. Boston, 1883.

———. *Recollections of Rossetti*. 2nd ed. London, 1928.

Cary, Elisabeth Luther. *William Morris: Poet, Craftsman, Socialist*. New York and London, 1902.

Clodd, Edward. *Memories*. New York, 1916.

Dante (Alighieri). *Paradiso*, Italian text with English trans. by John D. Sinclair. Galaxy Book. New York, 1961.

DeVane, William Clyde. "The Harlot and the Thoughtful Young Man: A Study of the Relation Between Rossetti's *Jenny* and Browning's *Fifine at the Fair*," *Stud. Phil.*, XXIX (July 1932), 463–484.

Doughty, Oswald. *A Victorian Romantic: Dante Gabriel Rossetti*. 2nd ed. London, 1960.

Dunn, Henry Treffry. *Recollections of Dante Gabriel Rossetti and his Circle (Cheyne Walk Life)*, ed. Gale Pedrick. New York and London, 1904.

Ellison, R. C. "An Unpublished Poem by William Morris," *English*, XV (1964), 100–102.

Fleming, G. H. *Rossetti and the Pre-Raphaelite Brotherhood*. London, 1967.

Fredeman, William E. *Pre-Raphaelitism: A Bibliocritical Study*. Cambridge, Mass., 1965.

———. "Rossetti's 'In Memoriam': An Elegaic Reading of *The House of Life*." *Bull. of John Rylands Libr.*, XLVII (1965), 298–341.

Gaunt, William. *The Pre-Raphaelite Tragedy*. London, 1942.

The Germ: Thoughts Towards Nature in Poetry, Literature, and Art: MDCCCL. Portland, Maine: Thomas B. Mosher, 1898.

Gilchrist, Herbert Harlakenden. "Recollections of Rossetti," *Lippincott's Monthly Magazine*, LXVIII (November 1901), 571–576.

Gray, Nicolette. *Rossetti, Dante, and Ourselves*. London, 1947.

(Grylls: see Mander)

Hake, Gordon. *Memoirs of Eighty Years*. London, 1892.

Harris, Adelaide Evans. "The Heroine of the Middle English Romances," *Western Reserve University Bulletin: Literary Section Supplement*. n.s. XXXI. Pub. as *Western Reserve Studies*, II, no. 3 (Aug. 1928).

Haselmayer, Lewis A., Jr. "Chaucer and Medieval Verse Portraiture." Doctoral dissertation, Yale University, 1937.

Hueffer, Ford Madox. *Ford Madox Brown: A Record of his Life and Work*. London and New York, 1896.

Hunt, John Dixon. *The Pre-Raphaelite Imagination: 1848–1900*. Lincoln, Nebraska, [1969].

Hunt, Violet. *The Wife of Rossetti: Her Life and Death*. New York, [1932].

Hunt, William Holman. "Memories of Rossetti," *Musical World and Dramatic Observer*, LXX, no. 27 (July 5, 1890), 526–528.

———. *Pre-Raphaelitism and the Pre-Raphaelite Brotherhood*. 2 vols. New York, 1905–1906. A 2nd ed., revised by M. E. Holman Hunt, was pub. 1913.

Ironside, Robin. *Pre-Raphaelite Painters: With a Descriptive Catalogue by John Gere*. London, 1948.

James, Henry. *Letters*, ed. Percy Lubbock. 2 vols. New York, 1920.

Johnson, Wendell Stacy. "D. G. Rossetti as Painter and Poet," *Victorian Poetry*, III (Winter 1965), 9–18.

Kermode, Frank. *Romantic Image*. London, 1957.

Larg, David. *Trial by Virgins: Fragment of a Biography*. London, 1933.

Lees, Francis Noel. "The Keys are at the Palace: A Note on Criticism and Biography," *College English*, XXVIII (1966), 101–108; reprinted in *English Institute Essays*, 1967, pp. 135–149.

Lowell, James Russell. "Dante Gabriel Rossetti's Poems." Rev. in *The Nation*, XI (July 14, 1870) 29–30.

Mackail, John William. *The Life of William Morris*. London and New York, 1899.

Mander, Lady Rosalie (pseud. Rosalie Glynn Grylls). *Portrait of Rossetti*. London, 1964.

———. "The Reserved Rossetti Letters," *TLS*, no. 3231 (Jan. 30, 1964), p. 96.

Marillier, H. C. *Dante Gabriel Rossetti: An Illustrated Memorial of his Art and Life*. London, 1899.

McGann, Jerome J. "Rossetti's Significant Details," *Victorian Poetry*, VII (1969), 41–54.

Millais, John Guille. *The Life and Letters of Sir John Everett Millais*. 2 vols. London, 1899.

Mills, Ernestine. *The Life and Letters of Frederick Shields*. London and New York, 1912.

"Mr. Rossetti's Pictures." Anon. rev. in *Athenaeum*, no. 1982 (Oct. 21, 1865), pp. 545–546.

Myers, F. W. H. "Rossetti and the Religion of Beauty," *Cornhill Magazine*, XLVII (1883), 213–224. Repub. in *Essays: Modern*. London, 1883.

O'Shaughnessy, Arthur William Edgar. *Poems*, sel. and ed. W. A. Percy. New Haven, 1923.

O'Sullivan, Vincent. *Aspects of Wilde*. New York, 1936.

Paden, W[illiam] D. "*La Pia de' Tolomei* by Dante Gabriel Rossetti," *Register of the Museum of Art, The University of Kansas*, II, no. 1 (Nov. 1958), 1–48.

Pater, Walter Horatio. "Dante Gabriel Rossetti," in *Appreciations: With an Essay on Style*. 5th ed. London, 1910, pp. 205–218. First pub. 1889.

————. *Miscellaneous Studies: A Series of Essays*. London, 1913.

————. *The Renaissance: Studies in Art and Poetry*. London, 1910.

"*Poems*. by Dante Gabriel Rossetti." Anon. rev. in *North American Review*, CXI (Oct. 1870), 471–480.

Praz, Mario. *The Romantic Agony*, trans. Angus Davidson. 2nd ed. London and New York, 1951.

Prinsep, Val C. "A Chapter from a Painter's Reminiscence: The Oxford Circle: Rossetti, Burne-Jones, and William Morris," *The Magazine of Art*, n. s. II (Feb. 1904), 167–172.

————. "A Collector's Correspondence," *Art Journal*, LIV (Aug. 1892), 249–252.

————. "Rossetti and his Friend [Mr. Frederick Leyland]," *Art Journal*, LIV (May 1892), 129–134.

Robertson, W. Graham. *Time Was*. London, 1931.

Rossetti, Dante Gabriel. *The Blessed Damozel: The Unpublished Manuscript, Texts, and Collation*, ed. Paull F. Baum. Chapel Hill, N.C., 1937.

————. *Dante Gabriel Rossetti's Letters to Fanny Cornforth*, ed. Paull F. Baum. Baltimore, 1940.

———. *His Family Letters*, ed. w. memoir by William Michael Rossetti. 2 vols. London and Boston, 1895.

———. *The House of Life: A Sonnet Sequence*, ed. Paull F. Baum. Cambridge, Mass., 1928.

———. *Jan Van Hunks*, ed. John Robert Wahl. New York, 1952.

———. *John Keats: Criticism and Comment* [ed. Thomas J. Wise]. London, 1919. Privately printed.

———. *Letters of Dante Gabriel Rossetti*, ed. Oswald Doughty and John Robert Wahl. 4 vols. Oxford, 1965–1967.

———. *Rossetti Papers: 1862–1870*, comp. William Michael Rossetti. London, 1903.

———. *Works*, ed. William Michael Rossetti. London, 1911. The most extensive ed., and the only one with William's not always reliable dates.

Rossetti, Helen M. Madox. "Dante Gabriel Rossetti," *Art Journal Easter Annual*, 1902.

Rossetti, William Michael. "Dante Rossetti and Elizabeth Siddal," *Burlington Magazine*, I (May 1903), 273–295.

———. *Dante Gabriel Rossetti as Designer and Writer*. London and New York, 1889.

———, ed. *Praeraphaelite Diaries and Letters*. London, 1900.

———, ed. *Ruskin: Rossetti: Preraphaelitism: Papers 1854 to 1862*. London, 1899.

———. *Some Reminiscences*. 2 vols. New York, 1906.

Scott, William Bell. *Autobiographical Notes of the Life of William Bell Scott: And Notices of his Artistic and Poetic Circle of Friends: 1830 to 1882*, ed. William Minto. 2 vols. London, 1892.

Shakespeare, William. *The Complete Works of Shakespeare*, ed. George Lyman Kittredge. Boston, 1936.

———. *Hamlet*, I, ed. Horace Howard Furness. *A New Variorum Edition of Shakespeare*, III. London, 1877.

Shanks, Edward. "Dante Gabriel Rossetti," *The London Mercury*, XVIII (May 1928), 67–78.

Sharp, William. *Dante Gabriel Rossetti: A Record and a Study*. London, 1882.

Shields, Frederick. "Some Notes on Dante Gabriel Rossetti," *Century Guild Hobby Horse*, n.s. I (1886), 140–154.

Skelton, John. *The Table-Talk of Shirley*. First Series. Edinburgh and London, 1895.

Smetham, James. *Letters*, ed. Sarah Smetham and William Davies. London and New York, 1892.

Sonstroem, David. Review of *Letters of Dante Gabriel Rossetti*, ed. Doughty and Wahl, vols. I and II. In *Victorian Studies*, X (1966), 220–222.

Stephens, Frederic George. *Dante Gabriel Rossetti*. London and New York, 1894. 2nd ed., 1908.

Swinburne, Algernon Charles. *The Swinburne Letters*, ed. Cecil Y. Lang. 6 vols. New Haven, 1959–1962.

Symonds, John Addington. *Vagabunduli Libellus*. London, 1884.

Symons, Arthur. *The Fool of the World and Other Poems*. London, 1906.

———. *Poems*. 2 vols. New York, 1927.

———. *Studies in Strange Souls*. London, 1929.

Thompson, E. P. *William Morris: Romantic to Revolutionary*. London, 1955. 2nd ed., 1961.

Thomson, Patricia. *The Victorian Heroine: A Changing Ideal*. London, 1956.

Valency, Maurice. *In Praise of Love: An Introduction to the Love-Poetry of the Renaissance*. New York, 1958.

Waller, R. D. *The Rossetti Family: 1824–1854*. Manchester, 1932.

Watts-Dunton, Walter Theodore. *Old Familiar Faces*. London, 1916.

———. "Rossettiana: A Glimpse of Rossetti and Morris at Kelmscott," *English Review*, I (Jan. 1909), 323–332.

———. "The Truth about Rossetti," *Nineteenth Century*, XIII (March 1883), 404–423.

Waugh, Evelyn. *Rossetti: His Life and Works*. London, 1928.

Welby, T. Earle. *The Victorian Romantics: 1850–70*. London, 1929.

Wilde, Oscar. *The Portable Oscar Wilde*, sel. and ed. Richard Aldington. Viking Portable Library. New York, 1946.

Williamson, G. C. *Murray Marks and his Friends: A Tribute of Regard*. London and New York, 1919.

Wood, Esther. *Dante Rossetti and the Pre-Raphaelite Movement*. London and New York, 1894.

Wood, T. Martin. *Drawings of Rossetti*. Modern Master Draughtsmen Series. London, n. d.

Yeats, William Butler. *The Autobiography of William Butler Yeats*. New York, 1938.

B. *Works Peripheral to Pre-Raphaelitism*

Aldington, Richard, ed. *The Religion of Beauty: Selections from the Aesthetes*. London, 1950.

Beerbohm, Sir Max. *And Even Now*. New York, 1921.

————. *Mainly on the Air*. 2nd ed. New York, 1958.

Brophy, John. *The Face in Western Art*. London, 1963.

Calverton, V. F. *Sex Expression in Literature*. New York, 1926.

Finck, Henry T. *Romantic Love and Personal Beauty: Their Development, Causal Relations, Historic and National Peculiarities*. London, 1887. An outrageous book.

Fletcher, Jefferson B. *The Religion of Beauty in Women: And Other Essays on Platonic Love in Poetry and Society*. New York, 1911.

Gregorovius, Ferdinand. *Lucretia Borgia: According to Original Documents and Correspondence of her Day*, trans. John Leslie Garner. New York, 1903.

Piper, David. *The English Face*. Aylesbury, G. B., 1957.

Pound, Ezra. *The Spirit of Romance*. London, 1910.

Symonds, John Addington. *An Introduction to the Study of Dante*. London, 1872.

Taylor, Sir Henry. *Philip van Artevelde: A Dramatic Romance*. 2nd ed. 2 vols. London, 1834.

Utley, Francis Lee. *The Crooked Rib: An Analytical Index to the Argument About Women in English and Scots Literature to the End of the Year 1568*. Columbus, Ohio, 1944.

C. *Recent Works on Rossetti*

Buckley, Jerome Hamilton, ed. with introd. *The Pre-Raphaelites*. Modern Library. New York, 1968.

Coates, Robert M. "Boom or Bust," *The New Yorker*, June 13, 1964, pp. 102, 104–109.

Evans, [Benjamin] Ifor. *English Poetry in the Later Nineteenth Century*. 2nd ed. New York, 1966.

Fredeman, William E. Review of *Letters of Dante Gabriel Rossetti*, ed. Doughty and Wahl, vols. III and IV. In *Victorian Studies*, XII (1968), 104–108.

————. "The Pre-Raphaelites." In *The Victorian Poets: A Guide to Research*, ed. Frederick E. Faverty. 2nd ed. Cambridge, Mass., 1968, pp. 251–316.

Kendall, J. L. "The Concept of the Infinite Moment in *The House of Life*," *Victorian Newsletter*, no. 28 (Fall 1965), pp. 4–8.

Lang, Cecil Y., ed. with introd. *The Pre-Raphaelites and Their Circle: With "The Rubáiyát of Omar Khayyam."* Riverside Ed. Boston, 1968.

Merritt, James D., ed. with introd. *The Pre-Raphaelite Poem*. Dutton Paperback. New York, 1966.

Index

THE index is divided as follows: (A) General; (B) Rossetti's Artistic Works; (C) Rossetti's Literary Works; and (D) Cast of Rossetti's Characters. The last division is included because so many of Rossetti's characters are present in several works, often crossing from one medium to the other. It is included also to dramatize the breadth of his narrative interest as well as the extent to which he relied on traditional narratives as the basis for his imaginative creations. I have omitted most of his nebulous and unnamed ladies and lovers.